WORSE THAN NOTHING

WORSE THAN NOTHING

The Dangerous Fallacy of Originalism

Erwin Chemerinsky

Yale

UNIVERSITY PRESS

NEW HAVEN AND LONDON

Published with assistance from the foundation established in memory of
Philip Hamilton McMillan of the Class of 1894, Yale College.

Yale University Press books may be purchased in quantity
for educational, business, or promotional use. For information, please e-mail
sales.press@yale.edu (U.S. office) or sales@yaleup.co.uk (U.K. office).

Set in Yale and Gothic type by IDS Infotech, Ltd.
Printed in the United States of America.

Library of Congress Control Number: 2022932068
ISBN 978-0-300-25990-2 (hardcover : alk. paper)

A catalogue record for this book is available from the British Library.

This paper meets the requirements of ANSI/NISO Z39.48-1992
(Permanence of Paper).

10 9 8 7 6 5 4 3 2

For my teachers, and especially Earl Bell and David Zarefsky

CONTENTS

CONTENTS

PREFACE

I first taught constitutional law in the fall of 1980. Few people at that point had heard the word "originalism." About a decade earlier, Robert Bork had written an article urging courts to adhere strictly to the text and the Framers' original intent in interpreting the Constitution.[1] The article drew relatively little attention at the time it was published. But Bork's theory took on significance after the Supreme Court's decision in *Roe v. Wade* in 1973, as conservatives looked for a way to criticize that ruling and, more generally, the liberal decisions of the Warren Court.[2]

By the early 1980s, there was a flurry of scholarship on constitutional interpretation. Some of the biggest names in constitutional law – Paul Brest, Ronald Dworkin, John Hart Ely, Larry Tribe – advanced devastating critiques of limiting constitutional interpretation to the text and the Framers' intent.[3]

But these criticisms did not stem the growth of originalism. The conservative Reagan administration and especially Attorney General Edwin Meese championed it. In a speech to the American Bar Association in 1985, Meese said that it would be the Reagan administration's policy to advance a "jurisprudence of original intention" in all of its actions, including in the briefs that it filed and the judges it appointed.[4] The Federalist Society began and grew enormously, and its members became advocates for it. When Antonin Scalia joined the Supreme Court, in 1986, originalism gained a forceful champion who gave the theory legitimacy and a platform on and off the bench. He acknowledged, in part because of his joining the Court, that "the debate between the majority and dissenting opinions were carried on in originalist terms. . . . In the law schools as well, originalism . . . gained a foothold."[5]

In response to the intellectual attacks, originalism evolved from its initial emphasis on the Framers' intent and focused instead on discovering the "original meaning" for constitutional provisions. It was embraced by many conservative law professors. Even some liberal law professors developed what they called originalist theories, though theirs were much different from the originalism of Bork, Meese, or Scalia.[6]

Today, three of the nine Supreme Court justices — Clarence Thomas, Neil Gorsuch, and Amy Coney Barrett — are self-described originalists. Three others — John Roberts, Samuel Alito, and Brett Kavanaugh — are quite conservative and often couch their opinions in originalist terms. Donald Trump appointed more than a quarter of all federal court judges now on the bench, including over 30 percent of all the federal court of appeals judges, a great many of whom are Federalist Society members and embrace originalism.

Over the four decades that I have been a law professor, I have watched originalism take hold and become not only a reputable approach to constitutional interpretation but one with a strong following among conservative justices, judges, law professors, lawyers, and law students. There have been powerful, even seemingly devastating critiques of originalism, but they have had little impact.[7]

But I have never found originalism convincing as a viable theory of interpretation. For most constitutional provisions, there is no "original meaning" to be discovered. Instead, there is a range of possibilities that allows for exactly the judicial discretion that originalism seeks to eliminate. In many areas where an original meaning can be discovered, it would lead to abhorrent results. Partly for this reason, originalist justices frequently abandon the theory when it does not yield the outcomes they want. All of this matters enormously because originalism is a dangerous approach to constitutional law that would jeopardize many basic rights and advances in equality.

Originalism's adherents do not provide an explanation of why it is desirable to follow the views and understandings from centuries ago. The primary purported benefit of originalism is in constraining judges and preventing them from deciding cases according to their personal moral preferences. Does it achieve that goal? I will show that no theory of constitutional interpretation, including originalism, can actually limit judicial discretion. But even assuming for the sake of argument that originalism does this, the question then must be: Do the benefits thus gained outweigh the costs of limiting constitutional meaning to that from 1787, when the document was adopted, or 1791, when the Bill of Rights was added, or 1868, when the Fourteenth Amendment was ratified? This is the crucial inquiry that originalists fail to address. I seek to show that, when evaluated in this light, originalism should be resoundingly rejected as a way of interpreting the Constitution.

My goal in this book is to explain as clearly as I can why originalism is an emperor with no clothes. Most constitutional law decisions inescapably come down to value choices by the justices or judges deciding the cases. Originalism does not avoid that at all. It only allows conservative justices and judges to pretend that they are following a neutral theory when in reality they are imposing their own values.

——

PREFACE

In this book I describe the rise of originalism, show how its meanings have shifted and how its advocates have defended it over the past few decades, and attempt to explain its allure. I show that originalism fails on its own terms to constrain judging or provide a coherent theory of constitutional interpretation. I then turn to the reasons for this incoherence: the epistemological problem of determining the "original meaning" or "original public understanding" of any constitutional provision and why following originalism's premises leads to a rejection of originalism.

Then there is the question of whether originalism is a desirable way of approaching the Constitution. In many areas of constitutional law, it gives us repugnant answers. Being governed by the views and values that prevailed in 1787 or 1791 or 1868 leads to results that rightly would be deemed unacceptable in our very different world. Moreover, there are many constitutional issues on which originalism is utterly unable to provide guidance adequate for our complex technological time. We live in a world that was unimaginable when the Constitution was written and with a government that is necessarily vastly larger than anyone could have foreseen in 1787.

Despite all of this, originalists claim that they have a neutral methodology that they follow to its conclusions. The proof that this is nonsense is that originalists often ignore originalism when it does not lead to their desired conservative results.

What is the alternative? I argue that the approach to constitutional interpretation that has been followed throughout American history has always relied on the wisdom and lived experience of individual judges. In construing a constitutional provision, they inevitably must consult many sources: the text, the Framers' intent, the structure of the Constitution, tradition, precedent, and modern social needs. These do not lead to determinate results in constitutional cases. But no theory of constitutional interpretation can do that. There is no way to avoid judicial discretion in constitutional decision-making, or even substantially lessen it. A strict reliance on formalism is impossible in any area, and especially in constitutional law.

Given the current composition of the Supreme Court, originalism will be enormously important in the years ahead. We should be very afraid of where originalism will lead the Court, and afraid for the future of constitutional rights and equality. The Court is now very conservative and likely to remain so for a long time. We are on the verge of major changes in constitutional law, all in a right-wing direction.

At the very least, it is important to unmask what has happened. Originalism is not an interpretive theory at all. It is just the rhetoric conservative justices use to make it seem that they are not imposing their own values, when they are doing exactly that. My goal in this book is to help expose originalism as a dangerous fallacy.

WORSE THAN NOTHING

Chapter 1

THE RISE OF ORIGINALISM

Beginning on September 15, 1987, and continuing for an amazing twelve days, the hearings over the confirmation of Judge Robert Bork for the United States Supreme Court mesmerized the nation. Presiding over them was a telegenic young senator from Delaware who was chair of the Senate Judiciary Committee: Joe Biden. Bork, then sixty years old and heavy-set with a scraggly beard, was as qualified to serve on the Court as any nominee in American history. He had been a professor at Yale Law School, focusing on antitrust law. He had also been the solicitor general of the United States, the lawyer in the Department of Justice responsible for representing the federal government before the Supreme Court. At the time of his nomination, Bork was a judge on the United States Court of Appeals for the District of Columbia Circuit. No one, not even the fiercest opponents of his confirmation, questioned his golden resume or his stunning intellect. Throughout the hearings, he demonstrated thorough knowledge of every aspect of constitutional and statutory law and spoke enthusiastically of his desire to be a justice, describing it as an "intellectual feast."

Yet despite Bork's impeccable credentials and careful, well-informed answers to every question thrown at him, the United States Senate rejected his nomination by a vote of forty-two in favor and fifty-eight against. It was one of the most resounding defeats for a Supreme Court nominee in American history.

What happened? It was not just that Bork was politically conservative; no one was surprised that President Ronald Reagan would appoint a conservative to the Supreme Court to replace retiring Justice Lewis Powell. The year before, the Senate had confirmed William Rehnquist to be the new chief justice and Antonin Scalia to take his place as associate justice. Both were known to be conservative. Liberal groups at the time, feeling they had a chance to defeat only one of them, went after Rehnquist. They believed that they could make a better case against him because of his very conservative record in sixteen years as an associate justice. Moreover, they had a devastating weapon: Rehnquist had lied at his earlier confirmation hearings about a memo he wrote as a law clerk for Justice Robert Jackson, urging the reaffirmation of *Plessy v. Ferguson* and the constitutionality of segregation.[1] Rehnquist nonetheless was confirmed to be chief justice by a vote of sixty-five to thirty-three, receiving what was to that point the largest number of no votes against a confirmed justice in U.S. history. (Later, there would be forty-eight votes against the confirmations of Clarence Thomas, Brett Kavanaugh, and Amy Coney Barrett.) Scalia, because liberals had made a strategic choice to target only one of that year's nominees, was confirmed unanimously.

Part of the reason for Bork's rejection is that Powell had been seen as a swing justice on the Court, and liberals worried that his replacement could tip the ideological balance, especially on constitutional protection of abortion rights. Overall Powell was quite conservative. He had been nominated by President Richard Nixon, who had promised to end the Warren Court's liberalism and fill the bench with "strict constructionists." Powell appealed to Nixon as a nominee for many reasons. As a lawyer in Virginia, he had opposed school desegregation and loudly condemned college student protests. He had written a memorandum describing environmental and workplace regulations as an "attack on free enterprise." As a justice, Powell had been a consistent vote against the rights of criminal defendants and authored key conservative opinions, including one rejecting a constitutional right to education.[2] But he had been in the majority in *Roe v. Wade,* and there was fear that his replacement could be a fifth vote to overrule that landmark decision.[3]

Protecting abortion rights was only one part of the story of Bork's defeat. Much of the opposition to Bork could be tied to his judicial philosophy of originalism, then relatively new and little mentioned outside of law review articles by constitutional law professors.

In 1971, Bork had published an article in the *Indiana Law Journal* about what speech should be protected by the First Amendment.[4] He urged a restrictive view, contending that only political expression deserves constitutional protection. The article set out the philosophy that came to be called originalism, though that label would not develop for another decade. At the time, the theory was known as "interpretivism."[5] Robert J. Delahunty and John Yoo have written that "if contemporary originalism can be assigned a definite starting point, that point must be the publication of Robert Bork's" article.[6]

In the article, Bork argued that the Supreme Court should protect only those rights that are explicitly stated in the Constitution or were clearly intended by its drafters. "When the constitutional materials do not clearly specify the value to be preferred," he wrote, "there is no principled way to prefer any claimed human value to any other. The judge must stick close to the text and the history, and their fair implications, and not construct new rights."[7] He added that under this judicial philosophy, the Supreme Court was wrong to protect a right to privacy — including a right to purchase and use contraceptives — because these rights are not mentioned in the Constitution and were not intended by the Framers.[8]

Although Bork's article was written two years before the Supreme Court decided *Roe v. Wade*, opponents of abortion rights quickly latched on to his theory in explaining why that decision was wrong: the Constitution is silent about abortion rights and the Framers obviously did not intend to protect it.[9]

Soon after President Reagan nominated Bork for the Supreme Court, Senator Edward Kennedy set the terms of the debate over the confirmation. "Robert Bork's America," said Kennedy, "is a land in which women would be forced into back-alley abortions, blacks would sit at segregated lunch counters, rogue police could break down citizens' doors in midnight raids, schoolchildren could not be taught about evolution, writers and artists could be censored at the whim of the Government, and the doors of the Federal courts would be shut on the fingers of millions of citizens for whom the judiciary is — and is often the only — protector of the individual rights that are the heart of our democracy."[10]

This put Bork in a difficult situation for his confirmation hearings. He could embrace originalism, but his opponents would focus on the implications: no protection of privacy rights under the Constitution, no protection for women under equal protection because the Fourteenth Amendment was not meant to apply to them, no First Amendment protection for any speech other than political expression. These all were positions Bork had himself espoused as implications of originalism. Or he could try to soften these positions, but then he would be seen as insincere and accused of a "confirmation conversion."

In the hearings, Bork tried to have it both ways. He expressed his originalist views but tried to reassure the senators that as a Supreme Court justice he would follow precedent. He admitted, for example, that under his originalist approach, the Court was wrong to order the desegregation of the District of Columbia public schools because no constitutional provision says that the requirement of equal protection applies to the federal government.[11] He also thought the Court was wrong to hold that malapportionment, in which legislative districts within a state had enormous differences in population, was a denial of equal protection. Under Bork's philosophy, the Court's ruling that the principle of "one person, one vote" required all votes to have approximately equal weight was incorrect and overreaching.[12] He acknowledged that under his originalist view, the guarantee of equal protection cannot be used to limit sex discrimination; the Framers of the Fourteenth Amendment were focused solely on race discrimination. And he admitted that under his approach, there is no constitutional protection of privacy.

Bork was simply being honest about the implications of originalism, but he tried to reassure the Judiciary Committee that he would not overrule precedents even when they went against his philosophy. The senators were not convinced. Hearing Bork describe the implications of originalism confirmed the fears that Senator Kennedy expressed.

Later conservatives would say that Bork was treated unjustly. They even turned his name into a verb. The *Merriam-Webster Dictionary* defines to "bork" as "to attack or defeat (a nominee or candidate for public office) unfairly through an organized campaign of harsh public criticism or vilification."[13]

This revisionist history completely misapprehends what occurred. More than any Supreme Court nominee in history, Bork answered questions about his judicial philosophy in a thorough and honest manner. Subsequent nominees learned to say as little as possible about their views on specific constitutional issues. But that option was not available to Bork because in his 1971 law review article, he had told the world that "it follows . . . that broad areas of constitutional law ought to be reformulated."[14]

Bork's only chance at his confirmation hearings was to convince the senators that he would not radically change constitutional law. He failed because his views indeed would dramatically change the law, and the senators knew it. He was rejected by the Senate not because his positions were mischaracterized but precisely because he had set them out so clearly. The senators saw his originalist views as too dangerous for constitutional rights.

On September 18, 2020, Justice Ruth Bader Ginsburg died at age eighty-seven. Ginsburg had served on the Supreme Court since 1993 and was a hero to the left. She had become an iconic public figure unlike any other justice in American history. Shy and soft-spoken, Ginsburg had been a law professor and the head of the ACLU Women's Rights Project. In 1980, President Jimmy Carter named her to be a judge on the United States Court of Appeals for the District of Columbia Circuit. (Bork would become her colleague there in 1982.) As a justice she was unabashedly liberal, and in pop culture she became "Notorious RBG." Her picture appeared on T-shirts and mugs; several movies were made about her.

With a presidential election just weeks away, President Trump wasted no time in naming a replacement. On September 26, he nominated federal court of appeals judge Amy Coney Barrett to take Ginsburg's place. A month later, on October 26, Barrett was confirmed by a vote of fifty-two to forty-eight. Every Democratic senator voted against her confirmation. Every Republican senator but one, Susan Collins from Maine, voted in favor.

The Republicans' hypocrisy in rushing through the Barrett confirmation was stunning. Just four years earlier, they had refused even to hold hearings on President Barack Obama's nomination of Chief Judge Merrick Garland to replace Justice Antonin Scalia, who died in February 2016. Garland was nominated in March, almost seven months before the presidential election. No one questioned Garland's professional credentials, which were as impressive as Bork's and included twenty-three years as a judge on the United States Court of Appeals for the District of Columbia Circuit. There was nothing the least bit controversial about Garland. He was perceived as a moderate Democrat, left of center but not very liberal. Some progressives complained because Obama had not picked someone further to the left.

But starting on the day Justice Scalia died, Senate Republicans, who held the majority, made clear that they would not consider Garland's nomination. Majority Leader Mitch McConnell said, "The American people should have a voice in the selection of their next Supreme Court Justice. Therefore, this vacancy should not be filled until we have a new president."[15] Many other Republicans, including some on the Judiciary Committee, said the same thing.

Undaunted by their earlier position, the same senators pushed through Barrett's confirmation at lightning speed. Barrett, a graduate of Notre Dame Law School, had clerked for Justice Scalia, and

---

after a time in private practice, she had become a law professor at her alma mater. She was unabashed about her right-wing views and a frequent speaker at Federalist Society events. In 2017, President Trump named her to the United States Court of Appeals for the Seventh Circuit, where she compiled a very conservative record.

When Justice Anthony Kennedy retired in 2018, conservatives pushed Trump to nominate Barrett to the Court rather than Brett Kavanaugh.[16] As political commentator Ruth Marcus noted, Barrett had "a compelling personal and legal story that proved irresistible to social conservatives."[17] Barrett is the mother of seven children, including one with Down syndrome and two adopted from Haiti. She is a deeply committed Catholic and part of a very conservative group called the People of Praise. Her writings as a law professor and her opinions as a judge left no doubt as to her ideology. Conservatives who feared that Kavanaugh might not be far enough to the right championed Barrett.

With Kavanaugh already on the Court in 2020, Barrett was the immediate favorite to take Ginsburg's seat. This allowed Trump to replace Ginsburg with a woman, while Barrett's deep conservativism pleased the Trump political base in the weeks before the election. Barrett had already been vetted two years earlier, which would facilitate a quick confirmation. Trump and the Republicans had no time to spare.

Like Bork more than a quarter century earlier, Barrett is a self-proclaimed originalist. She has repeatedly said that her approach to the Constitution follows that of Antonin Scalia, another originalist, and she reaffirmed this position during her September 26 nomination ceremony at the White House, where she said of Scalia, "His judicial philosophy is mine too."[18] At her confirmation hearings, she explicitly described herself as an originalist, explaining: "So in

English, that means that I interpret the Constitution as a law, that I interpret its text as text and I understand it to have the meaning it had at the time people ratified it. So that meaning doesn't change over time. And it's not up to me to update it or infuse my own policy views into it."[19] This is the classic definition of an originalist.

As a law professor, Barrett focused on the role of precedent. She emphasized that she believed a justice should follow the original meaning of the Constitution and not prior rulings. She wrote that justices should follow the original understanding of the original meaning of the Constitution, not Supreme Court precedents that are in conflict with it.[20] In fact, she argued, following precedent is unconstitutional: "rigid application" of stare decisis "unconstitutionally deprives a litigant of the right to a hearing on the merits of her claim."[21] Trump and conservatives could not do much better: they had found a law professor who had said explicitly that *Roe v. Wade* was wrongly decided and who believed in overruling precedents that conflicted with the Constitution's original meaning.

Although there was strong opposition to Barrett's confirmation and forty-eight Senators voted against her, neither the media nor the Senate Judiciary Committee paid much attention to her judicial philosophy. The very views that caused Bork to be rejected in 1987 did not draw nearly as much controversy in 2020. Why not?

To be sure, the context was different. In 1987, there was a Republican president, but Democrats controlled the Senate. In 2020, both the president and the Senate majority were Republican. Everyone knew that Barrett was going to be confirmed, almost no matter what she said at the confirmation hearings. Senator Lindsey Graham, then the chair of the Judiciary Committee, remarked at the beginning of the hearings that it was a foregone conclusion that almost every

Republican senator was going to vote in favor of her confirmation and every Democratic senator was going to vote against. That is exactly what happened. The hearings were a mere formality.

Bork had to persuade a Democratic Senate not to reject him. He had no choice but to answer the senators' questions or face certain defeat. Barrett only had to be sure she said nothing that would give Republicans a reason to think twice. She did a masterful job of refusing to answer questions. She wouldn't even say that the president cannot change the date of the election. She was polite in saying nothing, but she took the art of the confirmation hearing to a new level of nonresponsiveness. And who can blame her? She knew she had the votes for confirmation and the key was to say nothing that could cause a problem. Saying nothing at all was the solution, and it worked.

But something else had changed, too. Originalism, which seemed radical in 1987, was mainstream by 2020. In addition to Justice Scalia, Justices Clarence Thomas and Neil Gorsuch describe themselves as originalists.[22] Gorsuch declared: "Judges should instead strive (if humanly and so imperfectly) to apply the law as it is, focusing backward, not forward, and looking to text, structure, and history to decide what a reasonable reader at the time of the events in question would have understood the law to be."[23] For decades, the Federalist Society had championed originalism as the only appropriate method of constitutional interpretation. A flock of conservative law professors defended it, and some developed variations on it to try to increase its legitimacy.

But originalism is as radical and as undesirable today as it was when Robert Bork proposed it in 1971. A Court truly committed to originalism would reject a panoply of rights that are considered constitutionally protected even though they appear nowhere in the document's text: the right to marry, the right to custody of one's children, the right to keep one's family together, the right to control the upbringing of one's children, the right to procreate, the right to purchase and use contraceptives, the right to abortion, the right to engage in consensual sexual activity, and the right to refuse medical care. An originalist view of equal protection would provide no constitutional protection against discrimination based on sex or sexual orientation, or any limit on the ability of the federal government to discriminate.

Moreover, it is simply wrong to assume that any constitutional provision has an "original meaning" that can be discerned. Consensus as to the original meaning rarely exists, especially as that meaning applies to the constitutional issues that arise today. Originalist justices pretend to be doing something different, but they are just as likely to impose their values and views as non-originalist ones.

The primary defense of originalism, by Robert Bork and every subsequent supporter, is that it provides a constraint on judges so that constitutional law is not simply a reflection of the preferences of those who are on the Court. But this raises a paradox: originalism can be defined in a way that provides significant constraints on justices, but only at the price of unacceptable results. The only way to rescue originalism from unacceptable results is to define it in a way that eschews constraints. The meaning of constitutional provisions has to be stated so abstractly that originalism becomes indistinguishable from non-originalism. There is no middle ground: either originalism constrains at the price of unacceptable outcomes, or it offers no constraints and so is not really originalism at all.

This was true in 1987 and is no less true in 2022. But now originalism is ascendant and has made its way into popular discourse. Professor Jamal Greene notes that discussions of originalism are found "in newspaper editorials, on blogs, on talk radio" and that "consistently large numbers of Americans report in surveys that they believe that Supreme Court justices should interpret the Constitution solely based on the original intention of its authors."[24] Even Justice Elena Kagan, who is surely not one, has remarked, "We are all originalists."[25]

It easily could have been different. One of the consequences of the 2016 presidential election is that originalism lives on as an important approach to constitutional interpretation. If Hillary Clinton had won the presidency, she would have renominated Merrick Garland — or perhaps someone younger and more liberal — to replace Justice Antonin Scalia. There would have been a majority of Democratic-appointed justices for the first time since 1971. Justice Kennedy's and Justice Ginsburg's successors, too, would have been picked by Clinton. Even if the Senate was controlled by Republicans and Clinton had to select moderates to have them confirmed, these justices surely would have been significantly to the left of Kavanaugh and Barrett. With Clinton's nominations to the Court, a Democratic-appointed majority would have been secure, likely for many years to come.

Originalism would have been relegated to dissents, especially by Justice Thomas, who would have been the sole originalist on the Court. Neither Chief Justice Roberts nor Justice Alito describes himself as an originalist, even though Alito is one of the most conservative justices in American history. No Democratic appointee on the Court embraces originalism. Conservative law professors would continue to champion the idea and would use it to criticize liberal decisions. The academic debate would have continued, but originalism would at best represent a minority view of constitutional interpretation.

Everything, though, is different because Donald Trump won the presidency and put Gorsuch, Kavanaugh, and Barrett on the Court. They are likely to be there a long time. At the time of her confirmation, Barrett was forty-eight years old. If she remains on the Court until she is eighty-seven, the age at which Ginsburg died, Barrett will be a justice until 2059. When she joined the Court, the other conservative justices were fifty-three (Gorsuch), fifty-five (Kavanaugh), sixty-six (Roberts), seventy (Alito), and seventy-two (Thomas). It is easy to imagine at least five of these justices lasting on the Court for another decade or two.

Originalism thus is likely to be more important than ever before and to dominate the Court's interpretation of the Constitution for a long time. This is why it is so important to understand this approach, see its deep flaws, and appreciate why it is so dangerous.

What Is Originalism?

Any understanding of what originalism is must start with the recognition that the intentionally broad language of the Constitution inevitably requires interpretation. What is "speech" or a "search" or "due process" or "cruel and unusual punishment"?

Even seemingly clear language must be interpreted. Article II says that the president must be a "natural born citizen." No one would think that this excludes someone born by Cesarean section or with the use of drugs in childbirth, but in other contexts that would not be thought of as a "natural" childbirth. But what about someone like John McCain or Ted Cruz, who were citizens at birth but were born outside the United States? People have debated whether they qualify as "natural born" citizens.

The First Amendment says that Congress shall make "no law" abridging free exercise of religion or freedom of speech or of the press. But that cannot be taken literally; the Court has never said that any of these rights is absolute. There is no right to kill someone in the name of religion; lying under oath is not an exercise of free speech. We have to interpret what is speech and when it can be restricted. The Second Amendment says, "A well regulated Militia, being necessary to the security of a free State, the right of the people to keep and bear Arms, shall not be infringed." Is this amendment only about a right to have guns for militia service, or does it guarantee a right of individuals to have guns apart from that? The text provides no answer.

The examples are endless. Any text must be interpreted, and that is especially true of a short document like the Constitution that was written to provide a framework for government, not a detailed set of instructions. Long ago, Chief Justice John Marshall observed that the Constitution was not meant to have the "prolixity of a legal code," and that its "nature, therefore, requires, that only its great outlines should be marked."[26]

Originalism is a way of interpreting the Constitution. There are many variations of originalism, but all share a central belief that the meaning of a constitutional provision is fixed when it is adopted and can be changed only by amendment.[27] Professor Eric Segall says that an "originalist judge or scholar is one who believes in the following three propositions: (1) the meaning of the constitutional text is fixed at the time of ratification; (2) judges should give the meaning a primary role in constitutional interpretation; and (3) pragmatic concerns and consequences are not allowed to trump discoverable original meaning."[28] For an originalist, Article I of the Constitution means the same thing today as it did in 1787, when it was adopted; freedom of speech under the First Amendment has the same meaning as when the amendment was ratified in 1791; equal protection under the Fourteenth Amendment has the same meaning as in 1868, when it was added to the Constitution.

Non-originalists believe that the meaning of a constitutional provision can evolve by interpretation as well as by amendment. They, too, of course believe that the text of the Constitution is controlling. But they recognize that rarely does the document's language provide answers to the issues that are litigated before the Supreme Court.

Although non-originalists are interested in the original meaning, if it can be known, they do not feel bound by it. Their interpretation of the text is not confined to the original understanding at the time a provision was adopted. Non-originalists look at many sources in interpreting a constitutional provision: the Constitution's structure, the Framers' intent, original meaning, precedents, traditions, foreign practices, and modern social needs.

Sometimes this gets expressed in a useful and evocative shorthand: non-originalists believe in a "living Constitution" in the sense of a document whose meaning changes over time as it is interpreted in specific cases. Justice Scalia, by contrast, was fond of saying that the Constitution is "dead, dead, dead."[29] Although it is an oversimplification, that really is the question: Is American society better off with a living Constitution or a dead one?

All of this is abstract, but it matters enormously when justices have to consider specific issues. To take a simple example: Does the Eighth Amendment's prohibition of cruel and unusual punishment make the death penalty unconstitutional? For a conservative like Scalia, the only relevant question is whether the Eighth Amendment, when it was adopted, would have been understood as

—

outlawing the death penalty.[30] Since the answer is clearly no, an originalist rejects constitutional challenges to capital punishment. Scalia declared: "Historically, the Eighth Amendment was understood to bar only those punishments that added 'terror, pain, or disgrace' to an otherwise permissible capital sentence."[31]

But for a non-originalist the question is very different. The Supreme Court has said for well over a half century that the Eighth Amendment is to be interpreted based on "evolving standards of decency."[32] Several years ago, Justice Stephen Breyer applied this non-originalist approach to argue that the death penalty is probably unconstitutional. He focused on the lack of evidence that the death penalty deters violent crime, the arbitrariness with which it is imposed, the excessive delays in carrying it out, and the rarity in which it is used.[33]

For an originalist, the issue of whether the Constitution protects a woman's right to abortion is easy: the Constitution says nothing about abortion, and there is no evidence that it was originally meant to protect such a right. But for a non-originalist that is not determinative. The Constitution's text says that "liberty" cannot be deprived without due process. Liberty can be – and has been – interpreted to protect crucial aspects of autonomy even if they are not mentioned in the text of the Constitution. The Supreme Court's majority opinion in *Roe v. Wade* explained that laws prohibiting abortion infringed this fundamental aspect of liberty and that states could not outlaw them before the point at which the fetus is viable.[34]

These are easy examples to illustrate the chasm between originalism and non-originalism. But harder cases require that an originalist confront the question: How is the original meaning of a constitutional provision to be determined? There is disagreement among originalists on this, and their approaches have changed over time.

Early originalists such as Raoul Berger and Robert Bork focused on the Framers' intent as the basis for interpreting the Constitution.[35] The central question was: What did those who drafted the Constitution, or a constitutional amendment, have in mind when they wrote a particular provision? For the seven Articles of the Constitution, determining this entails looking at the records of the Constitutional Convention. Often it meant giving great weight to the Federalist Papers, a series of essays written primarily by Alexander Hamilton and James Madison to persuade New Yorkers to ratify the Constitution.

But critics pointed out the serious problems with this approach. To begin with, there is the difficulty of knowing who counts as a Framer. Is it just those who participated in the Constitutional Convention, or does the term also include the members of Congress who proposed amendments? Does it include members of state ratifying conventions and state legislatures, who approved the Constitution and then its amendments?[36] The larger the group of people involved, the harder it is to identify a common intent.[37] The interpreter must choose whose intent will count — a question that has no determinate, correct answer. Moreover, even if we arbitrarily specify some group as authoritative for purposes of constitutional decision-making, different members of the group undoubtedly had different, perhaps conflicting reasons for adopting any given constitutional provision. In teaching constitutional law, I always point to major issues of constitutional law concerning the scope of executive power and of Congress's spending power on which James Madison and Alexander Hamilton completely disagreed.[38] Each side of a case or a public debate about a constitutional issue can look for statements from Framers that support its position. Given the large number of people involved in drafting and ratifying constitutional provisions, it is a fiction to say that there was a clearly identifiable intent that is waiting to be discovered.

In response to these criticisms, a different version of originalism developed. This one focuses not on how the Framers or ratifiers understood the constitutional language but on the original public meaning of the constitutional language at the time of ratification.[39] Justice Scalia, who directed what he called a "campaign to change the label from the Doctrine of Original Intent to the Doctrine of Original Meaning," explained that originalists now analyze "the original meaning of the text, not what the original draftsmen intended."[40] This was dubbed "New Originalism" or "Originalism 2.0."[41] This philosophy underpinned Scalia's view that the Equal Protection Clause does not safeguard women or gays and lesbians from discrimination because that was not part of the original public meaning of "equal protection." This approach is also how Barrett described her judicial philosophy when testifying before the Senate Judiciary Committee. Although other variations have developed over time, this New Originalism, which seeks to determine original intent based on the "original public meaning" at the time a constitutional provision was adopted, is now the dominant approach. For example, "corpus linguistics" — the use of large, computerized word databases as tools for discovering linguistic meaning — has emerged in recent years as another way to determine the original meaning of a constitutional provision.[42]

All of the different versions of originalism have in common the view that the meaning of a constitutional provision is fixed when it is adopted and can be changed only by amendment. However much they disagree on how to determine that original meaning or the level of abstraction at which to state it, all originalists accept this core idea.

The Myth of Judicial Restraint

One myth should be dispensed with at the outset: that originalism equates with judicial restraint and non-originalism is about judicial activism. This association likely developed because conservatives who attacked the judicial activism of the Warren Court, like Bork, also came to embrace originalism. Originalist constitutional theory developed as a response to the "activist" rulings of the Warren and Burger courts, and during the 1970s and 1980s, the primary commitment of originalists was to "judicial constraint."[43] But a few decades of having originalists on the Court leaves no doubt that they are as activist as non-originalists.

Although the terms "judicial activism" and "judicial restraint" are widely used, they are rarely defined. Conservatives continue to rail against "liberal judicial activism," even though for more than fifty years a majority of the justices on the Supreme Court have been appointed by Republican presidents. I often have the sense that "judicial activism" is just a label for the decisions that people don't like. But we can define judicial activism and restraint in functional terms: a decision is activist if it strikes down laws and restrained if it upholds them; it is activist if it overrules precedent and restrained if it follows precedent; it is activist if it rules broadly and restrained if it rules narrowly.

These criteria are purely descriptive. By this definition, *Brown v. Board of Education* was a very activist decision: it declared unconstitutional laws requiring segregation of the races in education, it overturned a fifty-eight-year-old precedent (*Plessy v. Ferguson*), and it eschewed the narrow approach of finding that the particular schools were separate and unequal.[44] No one, I hope, would question the imperative necessity of the Court's ruling in *Brown*. By contrast, one of the worst Supreme Court decisions in history, *Korematsu v. United States,* was the epitome of judicial restraint.[45] It deferred to the federal government's evacuation of Japanese Americans from the West Coast. As Chief Justice Roberts declared a few years ago: "*Korematsu* was gravely wrong the day it was decided, has been overruled in the court of history, and . . . 'has no place in law under the Constitution.'"[46]

The point is that neither activism nor restraint is inherently good or bad. Moreover, it is simply wrong to equate originalism with judicial restraint. Originalist justices often are very activist in striking down laws, overruling precedent, and ruling broadly. In *District of Columbia v. Heller,* for example, the five conservative justices declared unconstitutional a thirty-five-year-old District of Columbia ordinance prohibiting private ownership or possession of handguns.[47] It was the first time in history that a law regulating firearms was found to violate the Second Amendment. Justice Scalia's majority opinion was very much written from an originalist perspective. In *Citizens United v. Federal Election Commission,* the five conservative justices struck down key provisions of the federal campaign finance law and protected the right of corporations to spend unlimited amounts of money in election campaigns.[48] Each of these decisions declared unconstitutional a law adopted in the legislative process; each overruled precedent; and each was a broad ruling when the Court could have decided the matter more narrowly. Each was five to four, with the five conservative justices, including all who purported to be originalists, in the majority. It was the liberal justices who, in dissent, urged deference to the political process and to precedents.

Even originalists have stopped defending their theory primarily on the grounds of judicial restraint. Now the "primary virtue claimed by the new originalism is one of constitutional fidelity, not of judicial restraint or democratic majoritarianism."[49] We can now firmly reject the notion that originalism is more aligned with judicial restraint than non-originalism. The originalists themselves have abandoned it.

There is a more subtle and important point: both liberals and conservatives at times want activism and at times want restraint. They just disagree as to when. Two cases that came down on consecutive days in 2013 powerfully illustrate this. On Tuesday, June 25, the Court in *Shelby County v. Holder* declared unconstitutional key provisions of the Voting Rights Act of 1965.[50] These provisions required that states with a history of race discrimination in voting obtain prior approval — "preclearance" from the attorney general or a three-judge federal court — before making significant changes in their election laws. The formula for determining which states needed to get preclearance was adopted in 1982. In 2006, Congress voted almost unanimously to extend the act for another twenty-five years, and the extension was signed into law by President George W. Bush. But in a five-to-four decision, with Chief Justice John Roberts writing an opinion that was joined by Justices Antonin Scalia, Anthony Kennedy, Clarence Thomas, and Samuel Alito, the Court held that relying on old data and treating some states differently from others violated the Constitution. Justice Ginsburg, in one of her most famous dissents, vehemently objected and professed the need for judicial deference to Congress: "After exhaustive evidence-gathering and deliberative process, Congress reauthorized the VRA, including the coverage provision, with overwhelming bipartisan support. . . . That determination of the body empowered to enforce the Civil War Amendments 'by appropriate legislation' merits this Court's utmost respect. In my judgment, the Court errs egregiously by overriding Congress' decision."[51]

The next day, Wednesday, June 26, the Supreme Court handed down its decision in *United States v. Windsor* and declared unconstitutional a provision of the federal Defense of Marriage Act which said that for purposes of federal law a marriage had to be between a man and a woman.[52] Justice Kennedy—joined by the four dissenters in *Shelby County*, Ruth Bader Ginsburg, Stephen Breyer, Sonia Sotomayor, and Elena Kagan—found that the denial of marriage equality to gays and lesbians violated the constitutional guarantee of equal protection. The four dissenting justices urged deference to Congress in its decision to not recognize same-sex marriages. Scalia, in an opinion joined by Roberts and Thomas, declared: "This case is about power in several respects. It is about the power of our people to govern themselves, and the power of this Court to pronounce the law. Today's opinion aggrandizes the latter, with the predictable consequence of diminishing the former. We have no power to decide this case. And even if we did, we have no power under the Constitution to invalidate this democratically adopted legislation. The Court's errors on both points spring forth from the same diseased root: an exalted conception of the role of this institution in America."[53] Alito, in a dissent joined by Thomas, likewise urged deference to the political process. The Constitution, he argued, "leaves the choice to the people, acting through their elected representatives at both the federal and state levels."[54]

So on Tuesday, the conservatives declared a law unconstitutional and the liberal justices professed a need for judicial deference. On Wednesday, the liberal justices struck down a federal law and the conservatives decried the lack of deference to the political process.

Only Justice Kennedy was in the majority in both cases. Both liberals and conservatives sometimes preach deference to the political process and sometimes show no deference. They just disagree on the merits and then phrase their objections in terms of judicial activism.

Why More About Originalism?

In the decades since the Bork hearings, originalism has gone from a fringe theory promoted by a few radicals to a mainstream theory espoused by a number of Supreme Court justices. But I want to argue that originalism is no more intellectually defensible, and no less radical, than when Bork was rejected for espousing it in 1987.

For the first hundred or more years of American history, there was a widespread belief in formalism. Although there is no universally accepted definition of formalism, it is generally understood to mean that judges discern the law in an "objective manner" and then apply it to the specific facts as deductively as possible. As the constitutional scholar Fred Schauer explains, "At the heart of the word 'formalism,' in many of its numerous uses, lies the concept of decision making according to *rule*."[55] Justice Scalia often defended his originalist philosophy as a kind of formalism: "Of all the criticisms leveled against textualism, the most mindless is that it is formalist. The answer to that is, *of course it's formalistic!* . . . Long live formalism! It is what makes a government a government of laws and not of men."[56]

In the early twentieth century, Legal Realists attacked formalism with great success.[57] They explained that there are no neutral legal rules; all are value choices to favor some parties or principles over others. Legal rules do not exist apart from the choices of the people who create them. This is what Justice Oliver Wendell Holmes

---

meant when he said, and Justice Felix Frankfurter repeated, that the "law is not a brooding omnipresence in the sky."[58] The content of the law and how it is applied, especially by the Supreme Court, is largely a function of who is on the bench and their values.

Most scholars thought that legal realism had largely vanquished formalism. But now, more than a century after the battle began, the fight between these two visions of law has resurfaced, and formalism, astoundingly, has gained enormously. The arguments against it are as overwhelming today as they were in the early twentieth century. My goal in this book is to show that originalism, like all formalism, is a deeply flawed and dangerous way of approaching constitutional law.

Chapter 2

THE ALLURE OF ORIGINALISM

Scholars have now been debating originalism for half a century. Law reviews are filled with articles defending and criticizing it. Many books have been written about it. In 1971, when it was initially described by Robert Bork, and in 1987 when he went before the Senate Judiciary Committee, it was still a fringe theory used by conservatives to criticize Warren Court decisions. But that has changed. In addition to the (at least) three justices—Thomas, Gorsuch, and Barrett—who describe themselves as originalists, many lower federal court judges, especially those appointed by President Trump, call themselves originalists. Numerous law professors espouse the theory, and the Federalist Society, which has enormous influence in Republican presidential administrations and among conservatives, calls it the only acceptable approach to constitutional interpretation.

Any analysis of originalism must begin by understanding its attractions. What does it promise to do? Why is it still espoused even after decades of powerful criticisms?

Weak Defenses of Originalism

At the outset, it is important to brush aside the weak arguments that are sometimes made for originalism. One is an argument from definition, that interpretation must inherently require giving determinative weight to the original understanding of a constitutional provision. Professor Walter Benn Michaels has written that "any interpretation of the Constitution that really is an interpretation of the Constitution . . . is always and only an interpretation of what the Constitution originally meant."[1] Michaels concluded, based on this definition of interpretation, that "there is no such thing as non-originalist modes of interpretation."[2]

But this is a circular argument: Michaels defines interpretation as requiring originalism and then concludes that only originalism is a legitimate method of interpretation. It is an argument from definition, not an effort to justify the theory. Yet Michaels is not the only scholar to offer this defense of originalism. Professor Edward Melvin wrote that "when a judge takes his oath to uphold the Constitution he promises to carry out the intention of the framers."[3] Taken literally, this statement is incorrect: judges, like all public officials, swear only to uphold the Constitution; they do not take an oath to any particular approach to constitutional interpretation. Melvin, like Michaels, offers a tautology to defend originalism: he defines the oath of office as requiring originalism and then, on the basis of this definition, concludes that non-originalism is impermissible. But arguments from definition aren't arguments at all; they do not defend their conclusion but assume it.

Another weak assertion of originalism is that it is the method of interpretation the Court has used throughout American history, and therefore it is the appropriate way to give meaning to the Constitution. To be sure, statements espousing originalism are not new, even if the label is recent. Although Thomas Jefferson was not involved in drafting the Constitution, being in France at that time (as Alexander Hamilton delighted in pointing out in the musical *Hamilton*), he obviously is an important figure in American history. Jefferson declared: "On every question of construction [we should] carry ourselves back to the time when the Constitution was adopted; recollect the spirit manifested in the debates; and instead of trying [to find] what meaning may be squeezed out of the text, or invented against it, conform to the probable one, in which it passed."[4]

Justice Joseph Story offered a similar endorsement for interpreting the Constitution according to its meaning at adoption in his famous *Commentaries on the United States Constitution:* "The first and fundamental rule in the interpretation of all instruments is to construe them according to the sense of the terms and the intention of the parties."[5] In 1905, in *South Carolina v. United States,* the Supreme Court declared, "The Constitution is a written instrument. As such, its meaning does not alter. That which it meant when it was adopted it means now."[6] All of this led Professor Lawrence Solum to say that for "most of American history, originalism has been the predominate view of constitutional interpretation."[7]

Yet the statements from the Court rejecting originalism are far more common. Countless opinions have explicitly endorsed nonoriginalism. The Court's words in these cases, and the frequency with which it has expressed this view, decisively refute any claim that originalism has been the dominant mode of constitutional interpretation. In *United States v. Classic,* in 1941, the Court said that

in determining whether a provision of the Constitution applies to a new subject matter, it is of little significance that it is one with which the framers were not familiar. For in setting up an enduring framework of government they undertook to carry out for the indefinite future and in all the vicissitudes of the changing affairs of men, those fundamental purposes which the instrument itself discloses. Hence we read its words, not as we read legislative codes which are subject to continuous revision with the changing course of events, but as the revelation of the great purposes which were intended to be achieved by the Constitution as a continuing instrument of government.[8]

Several years earlier, in *Home Building and Loan v. Blaisdell,* the Court explained:

It is no answer to say that this public need was not apprehended a century ago, or to insist that what the provision of the Constitution meant to the vision of that day it must mean to the vision of our time. If by the statement that what the Constitution meant at the time of its adoption it means to-day, it is intended to say that the great clauses of the Constitution must be confined to the interpretation which the framers, with the conditions and outlook of their time, would have placed upon them, the statement carries its own refutation. It was to guard against such a narrow conception that Chief Justice Marshall uttered the memorable warning: "We must never forget, that it is a constitution we are expounding," "a constitution intended to endure for ages to come, and, consequently, to be adapted to the various crises of human affairs."[9]

In *Brown v. Board of Education,* the Court observed: "In approaching this problem, we cannot turn the clock back to 1868 when the Amendment was adopted, or even to 1896, when *Plessy v. Ferguson* was written."[10] Likewise, in declaring poll taxes – the requirement that citizens pay a fee in order to vote—unconstitutional for state and local elections (the Twenty-Fourth Amendment did so for federal elections in 1964), the Court expressly rejected originalism: "The Equal Protection Clause is not shackled to the political theory of a particular era. In determining what lines are unconstitutionally discriminatory, we have never been confined to historic notions of equality any more than we have restricted due process to a fixed catalogue of what was at a given time deemed to be the limit of fundamental rights. Notions of what constitutes equal protection for the purposes of the Equal Protection Clause *do* change."[11]

In *Obergefell v. Hodges,* in 2015, which overturned state laws prohibiting same-sex marriage, the Court could not have rejected originalism more clearly:

> The identification and protection of fundamental rights is an enduring part of the judicial duty to interpret the Constitution. That responsibility, however, has not been reduced to any formula. Rather, it requires courts to exercise reasoned judgment in identifying interests of the person so fundamental that the State must accord them its respect. That process is guided by many of the same considerations relevant to analysis of other constitutional provisions that set forth broad principles rather than specific requirements. History and tradition guide and discipline this inquiry but do not set its outer boundaries. That method respects our history and learns from it without allowing the past alone to rule the present.
>
> The nature of injustice is that we may not always see it in our own times. The generations that wrote and ratified the Bill of Rights and the Fourteenth Amendment did not presume to know

the extent of freedom in all of its dimensions, and so they entrusted to future generations a charter protecting the right of all persons to enjoy liberty as we learn its meaning. When new insight reveals discord between the Constitution's central protections and a received legal stricture, a claim to liberty must be addressed.[12]

Professor Solum is simply wrong in saying that the Court has always been primarily originalist. Very few justices in all of American history have described themselves as originalists or embraced that methodology. As I argue later, a Court that truly embraced originalism would have to overrule countless precedents. But more important, the Court's having used or rejected originalism in the past tells us nothing about whether it is a desirable approach to constitutional interpretation.

The Goals of Originalism

Of the stronger defenses of originalism, the primary one is founded on two interrelated arguments: originalism provides a basis for decisions that is separate from the values or views of those who serve on the Court, and it provides a desirable way of defining the role of an unelected judiciary in a democratic society. Each of these arguments is powerful. It makes intuitive sense that constitutional decisions should rest on something more than the values of whoever is on the Supreme Court at any given moment. At the same time, there is a desire to answer what the late professor Alexander Bickel called the "counter-majoritarian difficulty." How can we make judicial review — unelected judges empowered to strike down democratically enacted laws — consistent with democracy?[13] Bickel described judicial review as a "deviant institution" in American

---

democracy, and originalists think they have the way to make it acceptable.

Robert Bork made both of these arguments in his seminal 1971 article on originalism, and both remain central to defenses of originalism to this day. Bork thought that decisions in a democracy should be made by elected officials except in the narrow range of situations where the Constitution removes matters from popular governance. He wrote:

> The requirement that the Court be principled arises from the resolution of the seeming anomaly of judicial supremacy in a democratic society. If the judiciary really is supreme, able to rule when and as it sees fit, the society is not democratic. . . . For it follows that the Court's power is legitimate only if it has, and can demonstrate in reasoned opinions that it has, a valid theory, derived from the Constitution, of the respective spheres of majority and minority freedom. If it does not have such a theory but merely imposes its own value choices, or worse if it pretends to have a theory but actually follows its own predilections, the Court violates the postulates of the Madisonian model that alone justifies its power. It then necessarily abets the tyranny either of the majority or of the minority.[14]

Professor Randy Barnett, an advocate of originalism, makes this same argument and says, "The intuitive appeal of originalism rests on the proposition that the original public meaning is an objective fact that can be established by reference to historical materials."[15] Professor David Strauss said that the appeal of originalism is the fear that "if judges don't follow the original understandings, they will be free to do whatever they want."[16]

Bork explained that in a democracy, it is not legitimate for justices to make value choices in deciding cases, and it is only when justices follow the original intent of a constitutional provision that they do not usurp democratic rule. "If we have constitutional rights and liberties already," he wrote, "rights and liberties specified by the Constitution, the Court need make no fundamental value choices in order to protect them. . . . No argument that is both coherent and respectable can be made supporting a Supreme Court that 'chooses fundamental values' because a Court that makes rather than implements value choices cannot be squared with the presuppositions of a democratic society."[17] He added that "we are driven to the conclusion that a legitimate Court must be controlled by principles exterior to the will of the Justices. . . . It follows that the choice of 'fundamental values' by the Court cannot be justified."[18]

Six years after Bork wrote this article, Raoul Berger published *Government by Judiciary: The Transformation of the Fourteenth Amendment*.[19] This, too, was a major step in the development of originalism as a constitutional theory. Berger's earlier work had been championed by liberals for its criticism of executive privilege and was used to rebut President Nixon's arguments during the impeachment process.[20] But in *Government by Judiciary*, Berger took an originalist approach to understanding the Equal Protection Clause. He concluded that "the historical records all but incontrovertibly establish that the framers of the Fourteenth Amendment excluded both suffrage and segregation from its reach."[21] Had it been up to him to decide the cases that came before the Warren Court, he would "have felt constrained to hold that the relief sought lay outside the confines of the judicial power."[22]

Berger appeared on William F. Buckley Jr.'s show *Firing Line* to discuss *Government by Judiciary* and especially the perceived shortcomings of several Warren Court decisions.[23] Regarding *Gideon v.*

Wainwright, which held that the Sixth Amendment requires states to provide counsel to all who face possible prison sentences, and *Miranda v. Arizona*, which held that police must administer warnings before questioning a person in custody, the conversation went like this:

MR. BUCKLEY: If your understanding of the limited application of due process under the 14th Amendment is correct, then it would be in a state criminal action entirely up to the state legislature to define the rights of a criminal defendant?

MR. BERGER: That is right.

MR. BUCKLEY: And this right could be exercised even to the point, for instance, of denying him the right to counsel?

MR. BERGER: Rights which we take for granted.[24]

When their conversation turned to *Brown v. Board of Education*, Berger explained that "the big drive" for those who wrote the Fourteenth Amendment was to make the South safe for African Americans and that "the last thing they had in mind was to reconstruct Northern institutions."[25] If it had followed originalist thinking, he said, the Supreme Court would have produced completely different outcomes in cases like *Brown v. Board of Education*. Berger did not personally see this as a selling point for originalism. As he confessed to Buckley, he had to confront the fact that he found himself "in bed with people I detest" in writing *Government by Judiciary*.[26] But as he saw it, those were the consequences of following an originalist approach to the Fourteenth Amendment.

Berger's contribution to the originalist scholarship further cemented the theory as a reaction to the liberal decisions of the Warren and Burger Courts. Like Bork, Berger stressed that originalism was desirable because it avoided decisions that only reflected the views of the individual justices.

In 1985, Edwin Meese III, then attorney general under President Reagan, delivered a speech on "construing the Constitution" before the D.C. Chapter of the Federalist Society Lawyers Division.[27] The Federalist Society had been founded just three years earlier, with Robert Bork and Antonin Scalia speaking at its first symposium.[28] As Meese explained, originalism should be thought of as apathetic to politics: "A jurisprudence that seeks fidelity to the Constitution — a jurisprudence of original intention — is not a jurisprudence of political results. . . . It is a jurisprudence that in our day seeks to depoliticize the law."[29] The central problem with the Supreme Court decisions of "recent decades," Meese asserted, was that the Court's approach was "not constitutional law in any meaningful sense at all."[30] Claims such as these positioned originalism as the sole true theory of constitutional interpretation, delegitimizing any jurisprudential system that used different methods or worked toward different goals. Anything but original intention was, by default, ideological and political — not only wrong but not to be regarded as constitutional law at all.

Meese's speech took originalism from being a theory of law professors in the pages of law reviews to being the stated position of the attorney general of the United States. Soon after the speech, President Reagan nominated Judge Robert Bork to the Supreme Court, and originalism became the subject of extensive public debate. During his confirmation hearings, Bork again expressed the belief that "the only legitimate way" for a judge to find the law is "by attempting to discern what those who made the law intended."[31] He warned, "If a judge abandons intention as his guide, there is no law available to him and he begins to legislate a social agenda for the American people. That goes well beyond his legitimate power."[32] When pressed about his fidelity to the four corners of the Constitution, Bork went so far as to say: "If you had an amendment that says 'Congress shall make no' and then there is an inkblot and you cannot read the rest of it and that is the only copy you have, I do not think the court can make up what might be under the inkblot if you cannot read it."[33] He espoused a strict originalist approach, hemmed in by the edges of the founding document, in stark contrast to the legacy of the Warren Court. Under Bork's framing, any interpretive approach that starts from somewhere other than original intention is legislation from the bench.

What was at stake with Bork's nomination, both sides argued, was the future of the Constitution and ultimately the United States. To those who supported Bork's nomination, the Warren Court signified an illegitimate expansion of judicial power that needed to be reined in. Bork's professed adherence to the intentions of the Framers was a way to accomplish this. To those who opposed the nomination, a return to the bare text meant a loss of liberties and freedoms that had become central to their understanding of American democracy. Anyone with a television set or a newspaper subscription could see the allure — and the threat — of originalism embodied in one man. As commentator Mark Pulliam wrote in 2018, despite being rejected by the Senate, Bork helped originalism "triumph . . . , as demonstrated by the canonization of Scalia and the appointment of Gorsuch and other originalists to the federal bench."[34]

The appeal of originalism, therefore, can be understood by looking at what the theory was meant to reject. Its early proponents believed the Warren Court's decisions overextended the judiciary's power and bent the Constitution to the political whims of the liberal justices then on the bench. Originalism was offered as the antidote, a safeguard against judicial discretion that would prevent judges from imposing their values on the nation. With a fixed intellectual method and a fixed goal, originalism would keep the justices from acting as a "super legislature . . . [a] committee of nine unelected judges [with] the power to reshape our Constitution as they see fit."[35] These early originalists believed that judges must "not construct new rights," precisely what they saw the Warren and even the Burger Courts as doing.[36]

Originalism, as it developed, comes to sound self-evident. Its proponents cast it as the obvious interpretative strategy any rational American would choose, and the option the Founding Fathers chose for their Constitution. As the supreme law of the land, the "Constitution manifests the will of the sovereign citizens of the United States," and the "interpreter's task is to ascertain their will."[37] That will is fixed in the ink on the page. As Lawrence Solum put it in his testimony during Justice Neil Gorsuch's confirmation hearings, "The whole idea of the originalist project is to take politics and ideology out of law. Democrats and Republicans, progressives and conservatives, liberals and libertarians — we should all agree that Supreme Court Justices should be selected for their dedication to the rule of law."[38] Adhering to the words of the Constitution comes to stand for rejecting ideology and politics in judging.

There is tension in this reasoning. Those first originalists said that they alone had a theory that was apolitical and had nothing to do with the values of the justices, but it was also an approach that repudiated the liberal decisions of the Warren Court. How can they argue that their theory is apolitical when it was clearly developed in opposition to liberal decisions and is meant justify conservative results? Originalists reply that there is no contradiction: the decisions they opposed strayed from the original meaning of the Constitution, while the conservative results they prefer flowed directly from their originalist methodology. I have heard conservatives say, more times than I can count, that they are only following their neutral theory to its justified conclusions, whereas liberals are imposing their values and making it all up.

Originalists also defend their approach with another argument: the Constitution's text specifies an amendment process, which provides a mechanism when there is a need for the Constitution to be updated. Changes in the Constitution's meaning, they argue, should come not from interpretation but from the constitutional amendment process set forth in Article V.[39] One originalist remarked: "Since the Constitution provides the formal amendment process, to the extent that it remains unamended, it must be interpreted in the original sense."[40] Admittedly, the process in Article V of the Constitution is notoriously difficult: since the Constitution was ratified in 1787, "more than 11,000 amendments have been proposed, but only 27 have been enacted."[41] Since 1791, when the Bill of Rights was adopted, there have been just seventeen amendments, and two of these instituted and then repealed Prohibition. Originalists would strenuously dispute, however, that the difficulty of amending the Constitution justifies the Court's abandoning interpretation based solely on original meaning.

Originalism is attractive "for ease of explication, for the appearance of value-neutrality, for diverting power from social and political elites, and for divesting our constitutional politics of foreign influence."[42] With centuries between its creation and us, the Constitution may seem to be a neutral statement of enumerated powers and rights. And the Founding Fathers, far removed, may be seen by the American public "as giants or saints who created for us the Constitution that formed the backbone of our nation."[43] Originalism purports to keep judges accountable to the guarantees of the text.[44] There is a sense that our interpretation of any legal document—a contract, a statute, the Constitution — should turn on what it was meant to say.

Originalism also has the appeal of simplicity. Professor Mitchell Berman says that it appeals to a "populist taste for simple answers to complex questions."[45] It is defended as following the usual way in which legal texts are interpreted. As Professor Frank Cross explains: "Originalism simply calls for the legal text to be interpreted according to its contemporary meaning. The process of interpretation arguably calls for nothing else."[46]

Continuing Allure

In the face of a half century of criticisms, originalist theories have been sharpened, and the number of clarifications being considered and debated has grown in the past decade. Today's originalism thus does not necessarily look like yesterday's. "Original intent" has been traded for "original public meaning."[47] Where historical sources run dry or fall short, some self-proclaimed originalists concede that the Constitution may be treated as a framework that "must be filled out over time through constitutional construction."[48] Those who take this position make originalism indistinguishable from non-originalism.

Nonetheless, the principles that lent originalism its initial allure remain. Justice Gorsuch published a book on the subject, *A Republic, If You Can Keep It,* in 2019, with an excerpt appearing in *Time* magazine. As he put it, "When it comes to the social and political questions of the day they care most about, many living constitutionalists would prefer to have philosopher-king judges swoop down from their marble palace to ordain answers rather than allow the people and their representatives to discuss, debate, and resolve them. You could even say the real complaint here is with our democracy."[49] Much like Bork and Meese, Gorsuch captures the allure of originalism by pitting it against other theories of constitutional interpretation. Who would volunteer to empower "philosopher-king judges"? Who would choose the side that opposes democracy? Cast in this light, originalism is the only answer that promises to preserve our way of government.

In times of change and uncertainty and political polarization, originalists tell us that the words of the Constitution do not change. There is stability and simplification in the idea of turning to the text for the answers, regardless of whether this is actually possible. Judges get their authority from the Constitution, and their decisions are legitimate only if they comport with its words. When the nation is bitterly divided, originalism promises to constrain judges on both sides of the aisle to follow the will of We the People.

Variants of Originalism

Over time, many variations of originalism have developed. Their proponents, though they profess to be originalists, are willing to consider original meaning in more abstract, less specific ways than those who first developed the theory. In an influential book titled *Living Originalism*, for instance, Professor Jack Balkin writes that "constitutional interpretation requires fidelity to the original meaning of the Constitution and to the principles that underlie the text. The task of interpretation is to look to original meaning and underlying principle and decide how best to apply them in current circumstances."[50] This method of interpretation "is faithful to the original meaning of the constitutional text . . . [and] is also consistent with a basic law whose reach and application evolve over time, a basic law that leaves to each generation the task of how to make sense of the Constitution's words and principles. Although the constitutional text and principles do not change without subsequent amendment, their application and implementation can."[51] Balkin writes that "in constitutional construction, 'originalist' argument is not a single form of argument; it involves many different kinds of argument, and it often appeals to ethos, tradition, or culture heroes."[52] He states: "The Constitution, and particularly the Fourteenth Amendment, was written with the future in mind. Its drafters deliberately chose broad language embracing broad principles of liberty and equality. Fidelity to the Constitution means applying its text and its principles to our present circumstances."[53]

Balkin labels this theory "living originalism," but it is quite different from the originalism of Scalia, Meese, and Bork. Balkin says, for example, that abortion rights can be justified under his originalist approach.[54] As Professor Eric Segall observes, Balkin constructs a "Fourteenth Amendment doctrine to protect a woman's right to have an abortion, even though we know for certain neither the drafters nor the ratifiers of the Fourteenth Amendment expected that result."[55]

University of Chicago professor William Baude has put forth a variation that he calls "inclusive originalism," which he defines this way: "Under inclusive originalism, the original meaning of the Constitution is the ultimate criterion for constitutional law. . . . This means that judges can look to precedent, policy, or practice, but only to the extent that the original meaning incorporates or permits them."[56] It is perfectly consistent with inclusive originalism, Baude writes, for judges to interpret the open-ended phrases of the Constitution in ways that were "unforeseeable at the time of enactment."[57] This is so "because a word can have a fixed abstract meaning even if the specific facts that meaning points to change over time."[58] He says that any given constitutional interpretation is permissible and consistent with "our law" as long as it is permitted by the "many versions of originalism."[59] Not only are such creative methods of judicial interpretation consistent with inclusive originalism, but "a method like the use of evolving language is likely an example of a sub-method that is *required* by originalism. Giving evolving terms their intended evolving meaning is necessary to be faithful to their original sense."[60]

Baude offers the example of *Obergefell v. Hodges,* which struck down state laws prohibiting same-sex marriage and is, he argues, justified under inclusive originalism.[61] The Court's decision that the "Fourteenth Amendment required states to license same-sex marriages . . . seemed to pick the originalist route."[62] As Segall observed: "That gays and lesbians have a constitutionally protected right to marry under an originalist interpretation of the Fourteenth Amendment is quite extraordinary given that we know for certain that virtually no one alive in 1868, when the Fourteenth Amendment was ratified, would have felt that way."[63]

Baude admits that inclusive originalism is quite different from the version espoused by Bork and Scalia and Meese, and that it "may be frustrating to those who knew originalism in its unruly youth."[64] That is an understatement. If abortion rights can be seen as the product of originalism, as Balkin argues, or if originalism justifies a constitutional right of gays and lesbians to marry, as Baude argues, how is originalism different from non-originalism?

Scholars like Balkin and Baude say they are originalists because they are stressing fidelity to text and original understandings.[65] But like non-originalists, they state those original understandings in a very general way and are willing to let the meaning of the

Constitution change over time. There is no other way that abortion rights or marriage equality can be justified from an originalist perspective. As I will explain in subsequent chapters, any result can be justified if the intent of a constitutional principle is stated at a high enough level of abstraction. The constraint on judging that has animated originalism from the beginning does not exist under the approaches of scholars like Balkin and Baude, and we are left with no way to distinguish originalism from non-originalism.

"I Have a Theory"

One of the most powerful defenses of originalism was Justice Scalia's frequent claim that he had a theory of constitutional interpretation, whereas his critics had nothing to offer but the preferences of whoever was on the Court at the time of a decision.[66] In other words, even if originalism is a flawed theory, it *is* a theory, whereas non-originalists have none. This is a strong rhetorical move because one can admit to originalism's weaknesses yet still claim to win the debate on the grounds that something is better than nothing.

Scalia's position helps explain the continuing allure of originalism. To refute it on its own terms, one would have to show that applying originalist theory is worse than having no theory at all. This would require a careful analysis of whether originalism actually achieves the objectives it purports to achieve. Does it constrain the ideology of the justices who use it, or are they as free to impose their values in deciding cases as non-originalist justices? Is originalism even plausibly less ideological than non-originalism? Is it more consistent with democracy? Overall, would it lead to more desirable results — understanding that "desirable" is an inherently contentious standard — than non-originalism? Are its benefits in constraining justices (assuming that it does this) sufficient to outweigh the costs of limiting the Constitution's meaning to understandings from long ago? These are the questions I will now address.

Chapter 3

THE EPISTEMOLOGICAL PROBLEM

In 1997, I ran for election to a commission to draft a new char-ter for the City of Los Angeles. Los Angeles has fifteen city council districts, and each was to elect one person to a two-year term to draft a proposed charter, which would then be put to the voters for ap-proval in June 1999. Seven people ran in my district and I won. I was then chosen by my fellow commissioners to be the chair of the Elected Los Angeles City Charter Commission.

It was an exercise in constitution drafting. The charter creates the institutions of city government, divides power among them, and prescribes many aspects of how they will operate. The commission faced major issues of separation of powers, both in allocating execu-tive and legislative tasks and in creating the appropriate checks and balances. One of the most important issues was whether to decen-tralize power through a system of neighborhood councils, an issue much like federalism. A heated battle erupted over whether the char-ter should have a bill of rights, since the charter can provide rights beyond those accorded by federal or state law.

The breadth of topics contained in the charter is staggering. In addition to sections about the mayor and the city council, there are provisions concerning such other elected officials as the city attorney and the controller, and appointed officials, including the treasurer, city administrative officer, city purchasing officer, and city engineer. The charter prescribes the timing and manner of elections. It creates numerous city departments, including police, fire, libraries, parks and recreation, ethics, and public works, and it defines how they will be governed. The city also owns three businesses — the airport, the harbor, and the water and power department — each of which is governed by detailed provisions of the charter. The charter describes in detail how two different civil service and pension systems operate: one for police and fire officers, and one for all other city employees.

The goal of the reform process was to design a government for Los Angeles for the next century, draft the document, and then place the proposal before the voters. The existing charter had been written in 1925 for a vastly smaller city and had been amended more than four hundred times. It was several hundred pages long and very unwieldy, filled with conflicting provisions and inexplicable gaps. Everyone thought it needed to be replaced.

But as I quickly learned, that was the only point of consensus. Of the myriad issues involved in the charter reform process, there was agreement about virtually none and intense disagreement about many. Interest groups made strong arguments for competing approaches on almost every topic. Every aspect of the process was extensively reported in the press.

Actually, the process was far more complicated than that. California law creates two vehicles for a city to adopt a new charter. Either a city council can place a proposal before the voters, or the voters can approve an initiative to create an elected commission, which can then present its proposal directly to the voters. Either way, the voters must approve the charter in order for it to go into effect.

In the fall of 1996, Mayor Richard Riordan and members of the Los Angeles City Council had a public struggle over how to conduct charter reform. The city council wanted to control the process, so it preferred to appoint a commission that would report to the council, which then would decide what to propose to the voters. The mayor wanted an independent commission that would take its proposal directly to the voters. Mayor Riordan and the council, whose relationship was often stormy, could not agree on this issue. The council created its appointed commission, but the mayor spearheaded and personally funded an effort to have an elected commission. In April 1997, the voters approved an initiative to create an elected charter reform commission and then elected fifteen members, including me.

The two commissions worked almost entirely separately. Many of their members publicly expressed disdain for the other commission and its work. In November 1998, the appointed commission released its draft charter. The elected commission released its version a month later. March 5, 1999, was the submission deadline for any proposal to be included on the June ballot.

The two commissions disagreed on virtually every important issue. Overall, the appointed commission proposed changes that were much more modest than those favored by the elected commission. For example, the removal of department heads became a very important issue in the last six months of the process. The appointed commission continued the status quo, that the mayor could fire a department head only with the approval of a majority of the city council. The elected commission proposed giving the mayor unilateral authority to fire department heads. This, of course, resembles the issue under the United States Constitution of whether the president can remove cabinet officials.

The elected commission wanted to create an independent commission to draw election district lines for the city council and for Los Angeles's board of education. The appointed commission also proposed a commission, but only to advise the city council, which would retain ultimate control over districting. The elected commission wanted to create a claims board and to strengthen the role of the mayor in managing litigation against city departments. The appointed commission wanted to leave control over litigation in the hands of the city council.

I believed that the differences between the two commissions would be impossible to reconcile. The commissions had seen each other as rivals from their inception. The task of writing a new charter was enormously difficult, even without the complication of a second commission doing the exact same thing at the same time. All efforts at bridging the differences between the two commissions had failed.

In November 1998, I had what turned out to be an important conversation with the chair of the appointed commission, George Kieffer, a partner at a major Los Angeles law firm. He and I had spoken throughout the process, mostly to keep each other up to date about our commissions' activities. In mid-November, we discussed how time was running out on trying to resolve the differences between the two commissions and producing a single charter proposal.

We agreed that having competing proposals on the ballot would make it far less likely that any new charter would be adopted by the voters. The supporters of one proposal would be the constituency to oppose the other.

George and I also agreed that the conference committee created to forge a compromise could not, on its own, resolve the disagreements. The alternative was for the two of us to present to the conference committee a compromise package that could be the basis for a single charter proposal. Each commission would get some of the things it wanted but not others, and the overall package, we agreed, would have to seem fair to both commissions.

We identified the twenty-five most important issues that the two commissions disagreed about and decided that we should prepare a compromise package on these issues, persuade the conference committee to endorse it, and then sell it to the two commissions. We thought that if the commissions could agree on these two dozen issues, the rest could be worked out; but without consensus on these, there was no point in considering the others.

George and I started cautiously with five issues where we thought agreement was most likely. We negotiated a package deal on these. On some issues, we took the elected commission's approach, on some, the appointed commission's approach, and on some, we created a new approach. Our negotiations were lengthy. Each of us knew that we had to sell the proposal to our own commission and that there was no point in proposing something that was sure to be rejected. George had to be mindful, as well, of what ultimately could be sold to the city council.

To make a very long story short, eventually, though with great difficulty and over the mayor's vehement opposition, both commissions adopted a single proposal. We then worked out our huge number of disagreements and put the proposal before the voters, who adopted it in June 1999.

Almost immediately, disputes arose as to what particular provisions meant. Rarely could the commission members offer much

---

clarity. At many points in the drafting process, my commission had reconsidered a decision it had made earlier. With amazing regularity, we would disagree about what we meant by our earlier choice and what we intended to accomplish. The dispute was not over whether the minutes accurately reflected our choices but over what we had intended. These issues immediately became magnified once the charter was adopted, and we found that there never was agreement as to the intended original meaning. If we the drafters disagreed a few weeks after we discussed an issue, how could a court, years later, rely on our intent as authoritative? And that does not even account for the existence of the other commission, whose members surely had their own views about what provisions meant.

Almost immediately after the charter was adopted, an issue arose that none of us had anticipated. Earlier voters had amended the prior charter to impose term limits – a maximum of two terms of four years each – for members of the city council. The charter commissions decided not to change this and included a provision: "No person may serve more than two terms of office as member of City Council. These limitations on the number of terms of office shall apply only to terms of office which begin on or after July 1, 1993."

Michael Woo had served two full terms as an elected member of the Los Angeles City Council, from July 1985 to June 1993. He sought election for a third term, to commence in July 2001, and argued that he was eligible under the language of the new charter.

I am sure that in including this provision in the charter, no one considered the possibility that someone who previously had served two terms in the city council would want to return. Woo and his lawyer wanted members of the charter commissions to support their interpretation. But the best we could say is that we never thought about it.

—

Woo sued and won.[1] The court of appeal focused on the intent of the voters: "We conclude that the voters intended to retain the former term limits law without change and did not intend to make persons who had served two terms of office before July 1993 ineligible to hold office."[2] To speak of the intent of the voters for a single provision in a document of about a hundred pages – a provision that had received no attention in the public debate – is pure fiction.

Disputes about the meaning of charter provisions arose over and over. I often received calls from the city attorney's office or from other lawyers asking about the meaning of particular provisions. Frequently, they were about matters that had never come up in the drafting and deliberation process. Sometimes, I could recall a discussion that was on point to the question. If my position was in accord with what the attorney wanted, I was asked to draft a declaration. If not, the lawyer would keep calling commission members until one was found who would express the desired position. In the early years after the charter was adopted, all of the commission members were still alive. But if you gathered us in a room, we would have found little agreement as to the meaning of particular provisions, and especially how they applied to difficult issues that were arising. If it was impossible to find agreement even among those who had created the document, it was an even greater fiction to say, as the court of appeal did, that the voters who approved the charter had an identifiable intent for specific clauses.

My charter drafting experience made me even more suspicious of looking to contemporaneous practice in deciding the meaning of the Constitution. Why should we assume that the Framers meant to ratify these practices and not change them? In countless areas, our goal in the charter reform process was to alter, not approve, existing arrangements. It would simply be a mistake for a future court to look to the practices that preceded the charter in deciding its meaning.

The Problems with Determining Framers' Intent

My experience as a framer — the charter we drafted still governs the City of Los Angeles — powerfully revealed to me an inherent epistemological problem with originalism. For the vast majority of constitutional issues that arise, there is not a clear original meaning. With so many people involved in drafting and ratifying any given provision, there cannot be.

This epistemological problem has plagued originalism from the outset. Originalists have never found a solution, other than to forgo trying to know the Framers' intent. The first originalists, such as Robert Bork and Raoul Berger, focused on determining the Framers' intent behind whatever constitutional provision was at issue. But critics quickly pointed out the challenges of ascertaining the intention of a multimember body in which each member might have had his own views.[3] The Framers often disagreed during the Constitution's drafting. James Madison and Alexander Hamilton, for instance, disagreed on whether the president has inherent power, a question that has been critical throughout American history. This difference in opinion manifested itself almost right away, on issues such as whether President George Washington could proclaim the United States' neutrality in a war between England and France. Hamilton said yes, noting that while Article I of the Constitution limited Congress to those powers "herein granted," no such restriction existed in the language of Article II as to the president. Madison, though, saw the Constitution as rejecting broad executive prerogatives and thought the president should be limited to the powers enumerated in Article II.

Hamilton and Madison also disagreed over the scope of Congress's taxing and spending power. Madison took the view that Congress could tax and spend only as needed to carry out the other powers specifically granted in Article I of the Constitution. In a 1936 opinion, the Supreme Court explained that "Madison asserted it amounted to no more than a reference to the other powers enumerated in the subsequent clauses of the same section; that, as the United States is a government of limited and enumerated powers, the grant of power to tax and spend for the general national welfare must be confined to the enumerated legislative fields committed to the Congress."[4]

Hamilton took the position that Congress could tax and spend for any purpose that it believed served the general welfare, so long as by doing so it did not violate another constitutional provision. In the same opinion, the Supreme Court noted that "Hamilton . . . maintained that the clause confers a power separate and distinct from those later enumerated, is not restricted in meaning by the grant of them, and Congress consequently has a substantive power to tax and to appropriate, limited only by the requirement that it shall be exercised to provide for the general welfare of the United States."[5]

These disagreements between Hamilton and Madison reflect a larger issue with trying to discern the Framers' intent: a multimember body seldom has a knowable single intent. I repeatedly saw that when we were drafting the Los Angeles City Charter. Different members of the group involved in writing the document had varying and sometimes conflicting reasons for supporting a particular constitutional provision. Some of the purposes might have been articulated, but others might not have been. The drafting of the Constitution was no different. There is not a concrete and knowable "intent of the Framers" waiting to be discovered; inevitably, it is a choice of whose views count and how to characterize them.

In the case of the Constitution, even if we could agree on the relevant group, and even if we discovered a collective intent, the historical materials are too incomplete to support authoritative conclusions. Professor Jeffrey Shaman explains that the "Journal of the Constitutional Convention, which is the primary record of the Framers' intent, is neither complete nor completely accurate. The notes for the Journal were carelessly kept and have been shown to contain several mistakes."[6] As Justice Robert Jackson eloquently remarked, "Just what our forefathers did envision, or would have envisioned had they seen modern circumstances, must be divined from materials almost as enigmatic as the dreams Joseph was called upon to interpret for Pharoah."[7] Virtually the entire record of the Constitutional Convention consists of James Madison's notes. Legal historian William Crosskey makes a persuasive case that there is a "possibility that this testimony may have been, not inadvertently, but deliberately false and misleading as to what the various members had said."[8]

And even if we could surmount all of these problems, on many issues the Constitution is simply silent; the Framers didn't consider the matter. This is exactly what I have seen in the years since the Los Angeles City Charter was adopted. In the vast majority of instances, the issue being litigated is one that we never anticipated or discussed. The United States Constitution is silent on countless crucial constitutional questions. The most significant is whether federal courts have the power to declare laws and executive actions unconstitutional. No provision of the Constitution gives them this power. No court in England had that power, and one would think that if the Framers wanted to change this, they would have said so.

Nor do the records of the Constitutional Convention reveal any discussion of this topic or any desire to create such a power. Edmund Randolph proposed a Council of Revision, which would have consisted of the president and several prominent members of the federal judiciary.[9] The Council of Revision would have had the power to review acts of Congress and exercise a qualified veto over them. Perhaps the rejection of the Council of Revision reflects a desire not to have something like judicial review; or maybe the majority just disagreed with that structure. The crucial point is that judicial review cannot be justified based on the text or on the Framers' intent as expressed at the Constitutional Convention. Alexander Hamilton argued for it in Federalist No. 78, and perhaps it was assumed that it would exist.[10] But this is a thin reed on which to base a power that has been so central to American constitutional law ever since it was created by the Court in 1803, in *Marbury v. Madison*.[11] As I explain in the next chapter, this creates a profound problem for originalists: there is no basis under an originalist approach to Article III to find a power of judicial review.

Examples of constitutional silence are common. Consider, for instance, presidential power. Does the president have the power to remove cabinet officials, or can this authority be limited by Congress? This was the central issue in the impeachment of President Andrew Johnson: Congress had adopted a law, the Tenure in Office Act, to prevent Johnson from firing members of Abraham Lincoln's cabinet. Does the president have the authority to invoke executive privilege and keep secret conversations with or memoranda from advisers? This was the primary question in *United States v. Nixon*, and it ultimately led to the only resignation by a president in United States history.[12] Can the president rescind a treaty?[13] The Constitution says that the president can enter into treaties with approval of two-thirds of the Senate, but it says nothing about their revocation. Originalism provides no way to answer questions where the Constitution is silent and there is no Framers' intent to be found. And these are just a few examples from one area of constitutional law.

The problems I observed with the Los Angeles City Charter are exponentially greater for the Constitution. The Framers could not have anticipated an infinite variety of constitutional issues that have arisen since 1787. To try to resolve these questions by looking for the Framers' intent is to search for something that isn't there, and can't be there.

The problems with knowing the Framers' intent become even more complicated when we shift the focus from those who drafted the document to those who ratified it. Professor John Wofford expressed this well: "If we are really searching for the states of mind of those responsible for the presence in the Constitution of a particular provision, it is hard to understand why we should be particularly concerned only with those who drafted the provision or supported it actively. Responsibility is more widely distributed; in order to become part of the Constitution, the provision had to be accepted by the Philadelphia Convention or by the Congress, and then ratified by the states acting either through legislatures or through special conventions. Yet, to admit the relevance of such a large number of states of mind is to set forth a task virtually impossible to fulfill."[14] Discerning the intentions of multiple conventions with multiple members is even harder than searching for the intent of the drafters of particular provisions. Interpreting the city charter according to this expanded view of original intent requires determining what was meant not only by the members of the two charter commissions that drafted it but also by the voters who ratified it. To speak of some unified intent concerning particular provisions is to indulge a total fiction.

The Problems with "Original Meaning"

In response to these criticisms, originalists moved their focus from identifying the Framers' intent to trying to identify the "original meaning" of a constitutional provision. The original-meaning approach says that a constitutional provision should be interpreted as it would generally have been understood when it was ratified.[15] As Justice Scalia put it, this form of originalism provides for a "rock-solid, unchanging Constitution," and insulates constitutional interpretation from the values and preferences of individual judges.[16] Practically, this approach focuses on the everyday meaning of words as conveyed by contemporaneous dictionaries, public debates, correspondence, treatises, cases, and other written materials.[17] "Corpus linguistics" — the use of large, computerized word databases as tools for discovering linguistic meaning — offers another way to determine the public meaning of how words were used at the time of ratification.[18] With the focus on original public meaning, the statements by Framers and ratifiers are considered, not because they are authoritative, but because they reflect the original meaning of a provision.

But the search for "original meaning" assumes that each constitutional provision had a single, accepted original understanding. The reality is that for most provisions, this single understanding did not exist. Almost always, there were different views as to what the words of the Constitution meant.

The disagreement over the original meaning of the Second Amendment powerfully illustrates this. The Second Amendment states, "A well regulated Militia, being necessary to the security of a free State, the right of the people to keep and bear Arms, shall not be infringed." There are two dominant interpretations of this amendment: that it is solely about preserving a right to have guns for militia service, and that it establishes a right to have guns in circumstances beyond militia service, such as in homes and in public. Either is a reasonable way of construing the text.

From 1791, when the Second Amendment was adopted, until 2008, the Supreme Court took the former approach. Then in *District of Columbia v. Heller*, the Court's five conservative justices shifted to the latter.[19] Dick Anthony Heller, a licensed special police officer who carried a gun in federal office buildings while on duty, was prohibited by a District of Columbia ordinance from possessing a gun in his home. He challenged the law, arguing that the Second Amendment establishes a right to have guns in the home for purposes of security. The government, in turn, argued that the Second Amendment is simply about a right to have guns for militia service. The Court invalidated the ordinance in a five-to-four decision and held, for the first time, that the Second Amendment protects a right to have guns for purposes other than militia service.

In an opinion that has been described as the most originalist opinion in recent Supreme Court history, Justice Scalia looked to grammar, syntax, and usage at the time of framing to conclude that the Second Amendment establishes a right to private possession of a gun.[20] Everything he says is a *plausible* way to interpret the constitutional provision. But there were a number of possible common understandings of the Second Amendment at the time of framing. For instance, as Justice John Paul Stevens demonstrated in his dissent, which also draws upon originalist theories, the phrase "to keep and bear arms" was at the time generally used in military contexts.[21] A reasonably well-informed reader at the time the Second Amendment was adopted could easily conclude that the words describe a "unitary right to possess arms if needed for military purposes and to use them

---

in conjunction with military activities."[22] Scalia ultimately, as all originalists must do, made a judgment call about which of the competing meanings to choose. Originalism provided no constraint at all on the justice's ideology. Depending on how Scalia wanted the decision to come out, he could, with equal validity, have applied the originalist method to reach the opposite result.

The same can be said for Scalia's analysis of the Second Amendment's initial words, "A well regulated Militia, being essential to the security of a free State." He calls this a "prefatory clause" that was understood to be an explanation for the right protected in the "operative clause," "the right of the people to keep and bear arms, shall not be infringed."[23] But a reasonably well-informed reader who looked at the entire Second Amendment could just as easily conclude that the initial language operated as a qualification on the right later protected.[24] Contrary to Scalia's approach, the whole of the Second Amendment could be deemed "operative." Also, the amendment as originally drafted had an exemption from militia service for conscientious objectors, suggesting that the provision was focused on militias and not on a general right to have guns. *Heller* thus demonstrates, not only originalism's failure to reveal a single common understanding, but also its inability to achieve its primary goal of constraining judges. It is hardly coincidence that conservative justices who favor gun rights read the original meaning of the Second Amendment to include a right of individuals to have guns, whereas the liberal justices who favor gun control read the original meaning to include no such right. Both are equally plausible, precisely because there is no clearly correct original meaning to be discovered.

The disagreement over the meaning of the Establishment Clause similarly illustrates that there was not a clear original public understanding for most constitutional provisions. The First Amendment's Establishment Clause reads, "Congress shall make no law respecting an establishment of religion." Originalist justices have argued that courts should mainly rely on history and tradition in applying this clause.[25] They find in its original meaning only a prohibition on government coercion of religious behavior. Justice Scalia, for example, said, "The coercion that was a hallmark of historical establishments of religion was coercion of religious orthodoxy and of financial support *by force of law and threat of penalty*."[26] Justice Thomas has said that "to the extent coercion is relevant to the Establishment Clause analysis, it is actual legal coercion that counts — not the 'subtle coercive pressures.' . . . I would simply add, in light of the foregoing history of the Establishment Clause, that '[p]eer pressure, unpleasant as it may be, is not coercion' either."[27]

But to find this view of the Establishment Clause, originalists have to ignore the extent to which its authors were concerned about creating a secular government.[28] Those who framed the American Constitution insisted that the welfare of the people was best advanced, not by religious establishments and forced conformity to officially endorsed religions, but by the secularization of government authority and the tolerance of diverse religious practices. Unlike the French revolutionaries, who formally rejected religion as a worthwhile feature of civic life and launched a campaign to "dechristianize" France, the American Founders stayed true to the early colonists' views on the importance of religious freedom.[29] But unlike the original colonists, the Founders — having benefitted from greater historical experience and exposure to newer arguments by reformers — concluded that it was vital to separate governing authority from religious authority.

By the time the American Republic was founded, there would be no mention in the founding documents of a Supreme Being (except for a single reference in the Declaration of Independence), no authority given to Congress to legislate on matters of religion, and a prohibition against religious tests for office. At the state level there remained government-authorized "established" religions, but state practices were quickly changing. An establishment of religion (in terms of direct tax aid for a favored church) was the practice in nine of the thirteen British colonies on the eve of the American Revolution, but by 1800 only three U.S. states (New Hampshire, Massachusetts, and Connecticut) still had established churches.[30] Some of the arguments associated with this transformation — especially during Virginia's multiyear debate about assessments in support of particular churches — are among the most important and revered documents in all of American history. Yet originalists ignore this history and focus instead on the practices that support rejecting a separation between church and state.

Consider, for example, the Supreme Court's recent decision in *Trinity Lutheran v. Comer*.[31] The State of Missouri provided cash reimbursements for playground improvements. Trinity Lutheran Church applied for the state grant and was ranked highly but was not given a grant because the Missouri Constitution bans aid to houses of worship.[32] Trinity Lutheran brought suit, arguing that Missouri violated the Free Exercise Clause by refusing to award it the grant, and Missouri defended its position based on the Establishment Clause.

Under an originalist approach that focuses on public meaning, the Court should have focused on public understanding at the time the First Amendment was ratified — or in 1868, when the Fourteenth Amendment was adopted, thereby incorporating the Establishment Clause. A focus on original meaning would have revealed that from early in American history, many states limited aid to religion, and by 1868 most states had laws prohibiting direct or indirect aid to religion.[33] Missouri, like other states, had a long history of barring financial aid to religious institutions. Tennessee, for instance, had a law disqualifying ministers from serving as legislators that dated back to when it first gained statehood in 1796.[34]

The experience in Virginia is especially revealing as to the original meaning of the Establishment Clause with regard to government aid to religion. In 1784, Patrick Henry proposed that a property tax be levied on all citizens, with the money used to support ministers of recognized Christian sects. Each property owner was to specify the denomination to which he wished his payments directed. An amendment was initially passed to drop the word "Christian," so that the tax would support all religious instruction, but Benjamin Harrison, the former governor, had the change reversed.[35] The purpose of the bill was to keep the Christian ministry, particularly the Episcopalian clergy, active and solvent.[36]

The next year, Madison drafted his "Memorial and Remonstrance against Religious Assessments," arguing that the religion "of every man must be left to the conviction and conscience of every man," and therefore "it is the duty of every man to render to the Creator such homage and such only as he believes to be acceptable to him." Importantly, Madison did not merely favor equality or no favoritism among Protestant sects. Rather, he was urging a more general principle of "noncognizance," meaning that the civil authority can take no notice of such matters and should assert no jurisdiction over a person's faith and conscience. His views presage arguments during debates about the First Amendment regarding laws that "respect an Establishment of religion."[37]

Virginia politicians waited until the 1786 state election before finalizing a decision on these debates. The election brought a strong antiassessment contingent into the legislature, and the resulting "Act for Establishing Religious Freedom" (1786), drafted by Jefferson, disestablished the Anglican Church in Virginia.

At the Founding, then, "establishment" likely meant forcing people to financially support a religion not their own.[38] A reasonably well informed person might have understood that being conscripted into financially supporting a religion that was not one's own constituted an impermissible establishment of religion. That is its most plausible original meaning.

Despite this clear indication of an original intent to prohibit government aid to religious institutions, the Court in the *Trinity Lutheran* decision struck down the Missouri law denying government aid to religious institutions. Chief Justice Roberts, in his majority opinion, did not discuss what original understandings would suggest about direct funding to religious institutions, religious schools, or their playgrounds. He merely characterized Missouri's long-held disestablishment principles as "nothing more than [a] policy preference."[39] Quite stunningly, for the first time in American history, the Supreme Court held that the First Amendment *required* the government to give aid to religious institutions. It is impossible to see this as other than the policy preference of the conservative justices, with no relation to anything that can be said to be the original understanding of the First Amendment. This is just one of many instances of conservatives ignoring originalism when it does not yield the result they want—a subject I will return to later. At best, originalists selectively choose from history the evidence that supports their desired conclusion and ignore the evidence that doesn't.

These examples demonstrate the epistemological problem with the search for original meaning: the multiplicity of sources make it a fiction to say that there was one original meaning to any constitutional provision. Justice Scalia said of originalist methodology that

> it often is exceedingly difficult to plumb the original understanding of an ancient text. Properly done, the task requires the consideration of an enormous mass of material — in the case of the Constitution and its Amendments, for example, to mention only one element, the records of the ratifying debates in all the states. Even beyond that, it requires an evaluation of the reliability of the material — many of the reports of the ratifying debates, for example, are thought to be quite unreliable. And further still, it requires immersing oneself in the political and intellectual atmosphere of the time.[40]

The difficulty is that with so much material, it is easy for originalists, or anyone, to pick and choose the sources that support the conclusion they want, and then declare that that is a constitutional provision's original meaning. Conservatives can always justify their results in originalist terms. The problem is that one can make equally plausible originalist arguments for exactly the opposite conclusions. Originalists promise a method of constitutional interpretation that constrains justices and leads to determinate results. But the method they espouse is incapable of doing that.

The Problems in Looking at Contemporaneous Practices

Originalists who focus on original meaning often look to the contemporaneous practices at the time a provision was adopted. This assumes, however, that in writing the Constitution, the Framers

---

sought to codify those particular behaviors. There is no basis for this assumption. Even if a practice was universal at the time a provision was drafted and ratified, that does not establish that the Constitution was meant to enshrine that practice. It certainly is possible that the Framers might have wanted to embody a specific practice in the Constitution, but it also is possible that they wanted the constitutional provision to disapprove the practice – or that, in writing that particular provision, they did not think about the practice one way or another.

Consider, for example, a 1995 case where the Supreme Court's majority opinion focused on original meaning: *Wilson v. Arkansas*, which concerned whether the police must knock and announce before searching dwellings.[41] Justice Thomas wrote the opinion for the Court and expressly followed the philosophy of original meaning, saying that the answer to the constitutional issue is to be found in the practices that existed in 1791. After reviewing this history, Thomas concluded that "knock and announce" is a constitutional requirement because it was the practice in 1791 except when there were exigent circumstances. In many recent Fourth Amendment cases, the justices have engaged in lengthy discussions of the common law as of 1791 in discussing how a constitutional provision should be interpreted today.[42]

It is conceivable that those drafting the Fourth Amendment wanted to codify common-law rules in the Constitution. It also is plausible that they thought the exceptions were too broad, and that by enacting the Fourth Amendment they could discourage or even halt the current practices. And it is possible that the Framers and ratifiers of the Fourth Amendment were not thinking about "knock and announce" or other contemporary issues at all. The existence of a practice tells nothing about its relationship to a constitutional provision.

———

Nor are practices that follow a provision's enactment necessarily useful in determining its meaning. It certainly is possible that subsequent practice reflects the Framers' understanding of what was constitutionally permissible under the new provision. But it also is possible that the Framers wrote the amendment in an effort to outlaw the practice, but faced with the political realities of governing they saw no alternative but to engage in the forbidden behavior. There is a fundamental difference between designing a government and making it work. The choices made in creating a government are not necessarily those made in governing. The Alien and Sedition Acts of 1798 might show that the Framers of the First Amendment, many of whom were still in Congress, meant to allow punishment of seditious libel. But the acts also might mean that once they gained political power, they saw free speech differently.

It seems even more dubious to rely on the absence of a practice in the first Congresses to establish a constitutional limit. In *Printz v. United States*, the Court ruled that the Brady Handgun Violence Prevention Act was unconstitutional in requiring state and local law enforcement to do background checks before issuing gun permits.[43] The Court held that for Congress to commandeer the states and force them to administer a federal mandate was unconstitutional. Justice Scalia's majority opinion stressed that the absence of congressional compulsion of states in the early years of American history was evidence of the meaning of the Tenth Amendment and the scope of congressional power. There are countless reasons why the federal government at that time might have not required states to act, including that they did not think of it, that they thought their goals could best be achieved by direct federal action, that they wanted to establish the federal government's own authority to act, and that political pressures at the time prevented specific mandates. To infer from their inaction that they rejected congressional power to take that action is to assume the truth of one explanation to the exclusion of all others. There may be many reasons why a type of law was not adopted at a given moment. The absence of a specific practice at a specific time does not mean that those then in power thought that the practice was unconstitutional.

Also, the search for original meaning in contemporaneous practices assumes unanimity or near unanimity about what was occurring when the Constitution was ratified. But there was no unanimity on most issues. The result is that the Court simply looks back and finds some practices to support the conclusions it wants to reach. The late constitutional scholar Alfred Kelly complained of what he called "law office" history practiced by the Supreme Court.[44] Practices often varied. The Court chooses its reading of history and selects those practices that confirm the conclusion it wants. It then claims that its ruling is based on history, when history was only an after-the-fact justification for conclusions reached on other grounds.

A powerful example of this is a series of Supreme Court decisions according judges absolute immunity to suits for money damages.[45] The Court has based these decisions largely on its view that judges historically had absolute immunity at common law in 1871, when the Civil Rights Act of 1871 was adopted. Yet a closer look reveals that judges had absolute immunity in only thirteen of the thirty-seven states that existed in 1871.[46]

Nor are dictionaries from the time of the drafting of a constitutional provision a useful way to determine original meaning.[47] The use of dictionaries in Supreme Court opinions has increased enormously as part of the focus on ascertaining original meaning. As Professor Frank Cross explains, "Dictionaries define words in isolation, without context. Typical dictionaries contain multiple meanings for individual words, which occasionally may even be contradictory. . . . Dictionaries may differ in their definitions and there also is the question of which dictionary to use in originalist interpretation. . . . The justices may simply seek out the dictionary that best suits the result they wish to reach."[48]

Focusing on "original meaning" is no more likely to provide definitive answers than the search for Framers' intent. It is every bit as likely to be indeterminate, and there are countless instances where there was no original meaning about constitutional issues that arise.

The Insurmountable Problem of Determining the Level of Abstraction

There is another serious epistemological problem with originalism that is often overlooked. One of the largest difficulties in applying originalism is choosing the level of abstraction at which the original understanding is stated. Whereas some originalists argue that the Court should refer to "the most specific level" at which a right can be identified, others argue that the Constitution's broadly written provisions were meant to be interpreted at the high level of abstraction at which they were written.[49] But if the original understanding is stated at a very general level, then originalism once again becomes indistinguishable from non-originalism.[50] On the other hand, as I will discuss in a later chapter, if we look for the original understanding in very specific terms, it quickly leads to abhorrent results.

The Equal Protection Clause of the Fourteenth Amendment demonstrates how originalism breaks down because of the need to choose among varying levels of abstraction. What was the original understanding of the clause? That it protected former enslaved people?

That it protected those of African descent? All racial minorities? That it stopped all racial discrimination? That it protected all who are part of groups that have been traditionally discriminated against? That it protected everyone from invidious discrimination?

All are reasonable ways of describing the original understanding of the clause. Each can be supported based on Framers' intent or original meaning. But these different levels of abstraction yield very different conclusions. If the amendment is seen as being only about race, then discrimination on the basis of sex or sexual orientation is not a denial of equal protection. Justice Scalia said on many occasions that women were not protected from discrimination by the Fourteenth Amendment because that was not the original understanding.[51] But that stance ignores the language of the Equal Protection Clause — "nor deny to *any person* equal protection of the laws." The text does not limit itself to racial discrimination. Moreover, Scalia's choice of abstraction is an arbitrary selection from many possible ways of stating its purpose.

Many originalist scholars have argued that the Court's decision in *Brown v. Board of Education* is consistent with the Fourteenth Amendment's Equal Protection Clause. They have found, for example, that the clause was intended to enforce a "core idea of black equality against government discrimination" and that "the purpose that brought the Fourteenth Amendment into being was equality before the law, and equality, not separation, was written into the text."[52]

But there is substantial evidence that the ratifiers of the Fourteenth Amendment did not intend to forbid segregated education. For instance, the sponsors of the Civil Rights Act of 1866 expressly said that they did not intend to interfere with segregated education.[53] In 1868, the year the Fourteenth Amendment was enacted, thirteen northern states either permitted school segregation or completely excluded Black children from public education.[54] The United States Senate gallery during the debate on the Fourteenth Amendment was segregated by race.[55] And Congress during Reconstruction maintained the District of Columbia's segregated schools.[56] An originalist approach at "the most specific level" likely leads to the conclusion that *Brown* is inconsistent with any form of original intent, meaning, or understanding. On the other hand, a more general interpretation of the Equal Protection Clause that sees it as ending racial subordination is consistent with *Brown* — but indistinguishable from non-originalism. I will return to this example later to show how originalism, if followed as Bork and Scalia and Thomas define it, would lead to unacceptable results: it would make *Brown v. Board of Education* wrongly decided.

The Impossible Quest for Value-Neutral Judging

Originalists and non-originalists agree that constitutional interpretation must always show fidelity to the document's text. But originalists claim to have an interpretive methodology that is objective and constrained. I have argued that this claim is based on a false premise: what the originalist method requires judges and justices to know is, in fact, impossible to know. But the idea that originalist judges can somehow avoid value choices is nonsense for a more basic reason.

Avoiding these choices is the primary argument put forward in favor of originalism. Conservatives repeatedly emphasize it, and it was Robert Bork's central point in his seminal article advocating originalism, in which he said that "a Court that makes rather than implements value choices cannot be squared with the presuppositions of a democratic society."[57]

In a particularly famous defense of originalism, Attorney General Edwin Meese called on judges to recognize the "text of the document and the original intention of those who framed it . . . [as] the judicial standard in giving effect to the Constitution."[58] Accusing the Supreme Court of "roam[ing] at large in a veritable constitutional forest," he concluded that a "jurisprudence seriously aimed at the explication of original intention would produce defensible principles of government that would not be tainted by ideological predilection."[59]

Antonin Scalia, the justice most associated with originalism, often explained that the only alternative — judges making value choices — was inconsistent with democratic rule. In one opinion, for instance, he defended originalism by declaring: "Although assuredly having the virtue (if it be that) of leaving judges free to decide as they think best when the unanticipated occurs, a rule of law that binds neither by text nor by any particular, identifiable tradition is no rule of law at all."[60]

When John Roberts went before the Senate Judiciary Committee for his confirmation hearings in 2005, he famously said in his opening statement: "Judges are like umpires. Umpires don't make the rules; they apply them. The role of an umpire and a judge is critical. They make sure everybody plays by the rules. But it is a limited role. Nobody ever went to a ball game to see the umpire."[61] Roberts was conveying that he believes the views of justices are irrelevant; they are not to make value choices in interpreting the Constitution, any more than a baseball umpire is expected to make calls based on his views or values.

After the death of Justice Antonin Scalia on February 13, 2016, Republicans repeatedly stressed that Supreme Court justices should just "apply the law" and decide cases without ideology playing any role. Chuck Grassley, the chair of the Senate Judiciary Committee, issued a statement rejecting the idea that a justice's views or life experiences should affect his or her decisions.[62]

This desire for value-neutral judging is an impossible quest. Balancing of competing interests is inescapable, and a justice's ideology and life experiences inevitably determine how he or she – or anyone interpreting the Constitution – strikes that balance. This is a crucial flaw in the claims of originalists and others who claim to have a way to interpret the Constitution that is independent of the justices' values.

No constitutional right is absolute, and constitutional cases constantly involve balancing the government's interest against the claim of a right. To pick an easy example, the Fourth Amendment prohibits "unreasonable" searches and arrests. But what is reasonable or unreasonable often cannot be answered from any original understanding. When the Court considered whether the police can take a DNA sample from a person arrested for a serious crime to see if it matches DNA from an unsolved crime in the police database, the justices explicitly balanced the law enforcement benefits from obtaining the information against the invasion of privacy. They ruled five to four in favor of the government.[63] There obviously was no original understanding regarding the reasonableness of DNA testing.

Over the last half century, the Supreme Court has articulated principles for balancing these interests in most constitutional cases. If the government infringes a fundamental right, such as freedom of speech, or discriminates based on race or national origin, it must meet "strict scrutiny" – its action must be shown to be necessary to achieve a compelling government interest. This is a heavy burden, which the government rarely meets. By contrast, if the government discriminates based on sex or against nonmarital children, its action must

—

meet "intermediate scrutiny" and be shown to be substantially related to an important government interest. All other government actions that discriminate, say, on the basis of age or disability, or that interfere with rights that are not deemed fundamental, need only meet "rational basis review." This means that they will be upheld so long as they are rationally related to a legitimate government purpose. The government almost always prevails under rational basis review.

These tests guide the courts in balancing competing interests. If the government is discriminating based on race or interfering with a fundamental right, the scale is weighted to favor the challenger, and the government must meet a significant burden to justify its action. But if it is a type of discrimination that does not raise suspicion (say a fourteen-year-old challenging not being able to get a driver's license until age sixteen), the scale is weighted to favor the government, and it is the challenger who has to meet a heavy burden.

But deciding what is a "compelling" or "important" or "legitimate" government interest inevitably requires a value choice. It can never be answered by the text of the Constitution or its original understanding. For example, in cases involving whether colleges and universities can engage in affirmative action, the central question is whether diversity in the classroom is a compelling government interest.[64] The justices all agreed that the use of race in admissions must meet strict scrutiny. Their disagreement was entirely over whether achieving diversity is a compelling interest and what a college or university must do to demonstrate that its affirmative action program is necessary.[65] That requires a value choice by the justices. Not surprisingly, the liberal and more moderate justices have found that achieving diversity is a compelling interest, while the most conservative justices reject this as an insufficient basis on which to allow affirmative action programs.

To take another example, laws prohibiting same-sex marriage have to meet at least rational basis review under the Equal Protection Clause. Until 2015, gays and lesbians could not marry, while opposite-sex couples could. None of the justices denied that this was discrimination based on sexual orientation; the issue was whether the discrimination was justified. At the very least, treating gays and lesbian couples differently from opposite-sex couples still had to meet rational basis review, which requires that the government interest has to be rationally related to a legitimate government purpose. Every justice on the Court therefore had to consider whether there is any "legitimate" reason to keep gays and lesbians from marrying. Regardless of whether the original meaning of the Constitution was to provide for marriage equality for gays and lesbians, the originalist justices had to explain why the discrimination was permissible and still needed to find a legitimate reason for denying them the right to marry. Originalism cannot provide this, and it is why the opponents of same-sex marriage had to invent unsupported arguments about such marriages as being harmful to children.

The conclusion is inescapable that anyone interpreting the Constitution — the Supreme Court, lower federal court judges, members of a legislature, you or me — is inevitably engaged in making value choices. Does society's interest in protecting children justify the laws that restrict speech by prohibiting child pornography? Does the need for public safety justify laws keeping ex-felons from having firearms? Does protecting girls from pregnancy justify statutory rape laws that make it a crime to have sex with a girl under age eighteen but not with a boy under eighteen? The examples are endless.

Constitutional law is now, always has been, and always will be largely a product of the views of the justices.[66] The conservative quest for value-neutral judging is a futile one; their claim that they have achieved it through originalism is nonsense.

The ideology and values of each justice on the Court make all the difference. Republicans, of course, know this as much as Democrats. That is why there was such an intense fight over who would replace Justice Scalia, why Merrick Garland never got a hearing from the Republicans, and why President Trump and the Republicans rushed through the confirmation of Amy Coney Barrett. We need to stop pretending that there is such a thing as value-free judging and get rid of silly and untrue slogans like, "Justices apply the law, they don't make the law." Everything the Supreme Court does makes the law.

The core claim of originalists is that they have a methodology that can be applied to lead to determinate results that are not the product of the ideology of the justices on the bench. But that is impossible in any area of law, including constitutional law.

Chapter 4

THE INCOHERENCE PROBLEM

Originalists might respond to the epistemological problem by pointing out that sometimes the original meaning is clear and that when it can be known, it should be followed. That raises a normative question: Assuming the original meaning can be ascertained, is society better off if courts adhere to it?

I will address that question in later chapters. But there is a crucial problem for originalists even where original intent can be known: the Framers likely did not want their views to control constitutional interpretation. There is no indication that the original meaning of the Constitution was to create judicial review or, if it did, that it was meant to create originalist judicial review. In fact, there is evidence, including the Ninth Amendment, to the contrary.

Following the original meaning of the Constitution therefore requires abandoning originalism as a method of constitutional interpretation. This, in short, is the incoherence problem.

75

The Constitution's Silence About Judicial Review

Originalism is primarily about how courts should interpret the Constitution. That leads to an obvious threshold question: How did the Framers intend the courts to do this? Put another way, what was the original meaning of Article III in terms of how judicial review should be performed? There is no reason that this important constitutional question should not be analyzed under the same approach as is used for all constitutional interpretation.

The answer raises significant problems for originalism. Nothing in Article III explicitly authorizes courts to review the constitutionality of laws and executive actions. As Professor Alexander Bickel observed, the "authority to determine the meaning and application of a written constitution is nowhere defined or even mentioned in the document itself."[1]

Article III, section 2, defines the types of "cases" and "controversies" the federal courts may hear, but it says nothing whatsoever about a power to declare laws or executive acts unconstitutional. Nor is this power inherent in the authority granted to courts by Article III. Even if federal courts could not declare laws unconstitutional, they still could exercise their constitutional authority to decide the cases and controversies that come before them. Federal courts could apply federal law, decide diversity cases, and resolve all of the other matters enumerated in Article III, section 2, without being allowed to invalidate a statute or executive action on constitutional grounds. As I mentioned earlier, no such power existed in English courts. One would think that if the Framers meant for the Constitution to deviate from English law and practice in such a fundamental way, they would have been explicit about it.

Nor do the records of the Constitutional Convention reveal discussion of this topic or a desire to give courts the power to strike

76

down laws or executive actions. The crucial point is that judicial review cannot be justified by either the text of the Constitution or the Framers' intent as expressed at the Constitutional Convention. Alexander Hamilton argued for this power in Federalist No. 78, so perhaps it was assumed that judicial review would exist. Some state courts did exercise that power.[2] But this is a flimsy basis for such a consequential authority, which has been central to American constitutional law and government since its creation by *Marbury v. Madison* in 1803.[3] Professor James MacGregor Burns explains that "the Constitution never granted the judiciary a supremacy over the government, nor had the Framers ever conceived it."[4] With no authority for it in the text of the Constitution, and no desire for it recorded at the Constitutional Convention, how can we conclude that the original intent of Article III was to allow courts to decide the constitutionality of laws and executive actions?

There is a compelling argument that a commitment to originalism requires abandoning judicial review altogether. It is incoherent to seek the original meaning for how the courts should exercise a power when there is no indication that the original meaning of the Constitution was ever to give them that power.

There is a more subtle problem with the originalists' embrace of judicial review. As I explained earlier, the premise of Robert Bork's argument for originalism was a response to the role of an unelected judiciary in American democracy—what Alexander Bickel called the "counter-majoritarian difficulty." Other originalists, too, start with the goal of reconciling judicial review with electoral democracy. But Bork's answer is no solution: originalist judicial review is just as incompatible with majority rule as is non-originalism. Under both approaches, unelected judges rule on the constitutionality of actions by popularly elected officials.

Originalists like Bork answer that originalist judicial review is democratic because the people consented to adopt the Constitution, and originalism just follows what was agreed to by ratification. To begin with, it is factually wrong to say that "the people" consented to the Constitution because less than 5 percent of the population participated in ratification.[5] No women and no people of color participated, and only a small fraction of white men did. Moreover, not a single person alive today—not even a living person's grandfather—voted to ratify the Constitution. If originalists consider it undemocratic that our laws are subject to the approval of unelected judges—who at least die or retire someday and whose replacements are appointed by elected officials—how much more undemocratic is it if society is governed by past majorities who cannot be overruled and are *never* replaced? Nor can the failure to amend the Constitution be seen as evidence of majority consent, since amendment requires approval by a supermajority: two-thirds of both houses of Congress and three-fourths of the states.

I very much disagree with the originalist premise that American democracy should be defined as majority rule or that this concept of democracy must be reconciled with judicial review. But originalists like Bork, who start with this definition, must confront the problem that all judicial review, whether originalist or nonoriginalist, is countermajoritarian.

The Original Understanding About Interpretation

Assuming that originalists can surmount this problem and somehow make a convincing case that judicial review is justified under the original meaning of the Constitution, they run right into another problem. Even aside from judicial review, the Constitution must still be interpreted by presidents, members of Congress, state legislators, and government officials at all levels. Originalism requires that all of these people ask: What was the original understanding of how the Constitution should be interpreted?

There is no indication that there was an original intent to interpret the Constitution according to its original meaning. Quite the contrary: there is strong evidence that the Framers of the Constitution never meant their own intent to be controlling. Professor Jeff Powell powerfully expressed this in an article titled "The Original Understanding of Original Intent":

> It is commonly assumed that the "interpretive intention" of the Constitution's framers was that the Constitution would be construed in accordance with what future interpreters could gather of the framers' own purposes, expectations, and intentions. Inquiry shows that assumption to be incorrect. Of the numerous hermeneutical options that were available in the framers' day — among them, the renunciation of construction altogether — none corresponds to the modern notion of intentionalism. Early interpreters usually applied standard techniques of statutory construction to the Constitution.[6]

At the Philadelphia Convention, the Framers explicitly indicated that they did not want their specific intentions to control the Constitution's interpretation. James Madison maintained that the Philadelphia proceedings "can have no authoritative character" and that the document coming out of it "was nothing more than the draft of a plan, nothing but a dead letter, until life and validity were breathed into it by the voice of the people, speaking through [the state] Conventions" that ratified the Constitution in 1788–90.[7]

The delegates also took steps to shield convention records from public view. They met under a rule of secrecy and preserved the records' confidentiality when they adjourned by depositing the documents with George Washington.[8] The records remained in "confidential limbo" until 1818, when John Quincy Adams organized and published them.[9]

Those looking for evidence of original meaning in the Philadelphia debates often use Madison's notes.[10] These are evidently the most comprehensive of several unofficial reports, yet they covered no more than 10 percent of the proceedings.[11] Madison himself treated his notes as private property because he thought that the proceedings "could never be regarded as the oracular guide in expounding the Constitution."[12] Professor Boris Bittker argues that originalists have failed to explain why the Framers' intent should be reconstructed from a private document that Madison intentionally withheld. No delegate to the state ratifying conventions got to see it.[13]

If the Framers anticipated that intent would matter in future interpretations, it was the views of the state ratifying conventions that they thought should be considered. As Professor Powell writes: "To the extent that constitutional interpreters considered historical evidence to have any interpretive value, what they deemed relevant was evidence of the proceedings of the state ratifying conventions, not of the intent of the framers. Only later, during the breakdown of the Republican consensus, did the attention of constitutional interpreters gradually shift from the 'intention' of the sovereign states to the personal intentions of individual historical actors."[14]

As I explained in chapter 3, this poses an impossible task in determining original meaning. So many people, with countless different views, were involved in the state ratifying conventions that it is pure fiction to say there was *an* original understanding. Moreover, the conventions met separately between 1787 and 1790, and though they were open to the public, there were no official reporters.[15] The unofficial reports of the debates "are partisan, inaccurate, garbled, and fragmentary."[16] In 1833, rejecting the possibility of ascertaining a common intent of the Framers from what little is known of the ratification debates, Justice Joseph Story wrote: "Opposite interpretations, and different explanations of different provisions, may well be presumed to have been presented in different bodies, to remove local objections, or to win local favor. And there can be no certainty, either that the different state conventions in ratifying the constitution, gave the same uniform interpretation to its language, or that, even in a single state convention, the same reasoning prevailed with a majority, much less with the whole of the supporters of it."[17] Professor Bittker commented: "If it were true that the ratifiers wanted their intent to control the courts in deciding constitutional issues, they can be justly accused of gross negligence for failing to take even rudimentary steps to preserve their precious thoughts."[18]

Beyond the text of the Constitution, there are scant surviving documents that record the Framers' intent during the drafting and ratification of the Bill of Rights.[19] The principal version of the House debates was written by an author whom Madison described as "a votary of the bottle," whose reports "abound in errors; some of them very gross."[20] No one recorded the debates in the Senate or the state legislatures.[21] Debates leading up to the later amendments are better documented, but there is still much disagreement about the intent of the Fourteenth Amendment.[22]

Strong evidence supports the conclusion that those who wrote the Constitution preferred that their views *not* be controlling. Many scholars have argued persuasively that in choosing to write the Constitution in general language, the Framers desired that it evolve via interpretation and "gather meaning from experience."[23] Judge Gerard Lynch observed that "the framers of particular constitutional provisions consciously intended to leave particular questions of interpretation open for future development by the courts."[24] This is why Chief Justice John Marshall famously declared that "we must never forget, that it is a constitution we are expounding," a constitution "intended to endure for ages to come."[25]

The Framers believed that individuals possess natural rights and that the purpose of government, as John Locke wrote, was to protect these rights.[26] The Framers did not think it necessary to enumerate these natural rights in the Constitution. Professor Robert Clinton explains that "the articulation of concepts of natural law rested principally with the judges. As seen through [the Framers'] eyes, the judges of the day were 'discovering' the natural law."[27] The Framers' view of interpretation was so radically different from that of today as to make it impossible to say that they ever intended the Constitution to be interpreted based on their original understandings.

Originalists might answer that I have ignored how originalism has changed over time. As explained earlier, it initially focused on the Framers' intent, and their rejection of originalism would be relevant under that approach. Now, however, most originalists focus on determining the original meaning of a constitutional provision rather than the specific intent of the Framers. Therefore, they would say, my argument about the drafters' theory of interpretation is misguided and irrelevant.

This, however, does not solve the originalists' incoherence problem. First, there is no evidence that the original meaning of Article III of the Constitution included the understanding that courts should interpret the Constitution based on its original meanings. Originalism would be justified under its own terms only if there was a basis for concluding that the original understanding of Article III was for judicial review to follow the original meaning of the Constitution. There is no support for such an assertion.

Second, even when the focus is on discovering original meaning rather than intent, the Framers' intent is still relevant. There are no words in the text to interpret concerning the power of constitutional judicial review, so original meaning cannot be ascertained based on the Constitution's language or dictionaries defining it. Contemporaneous practices were mixed; some states had judicial review in their state courts, others did not.[28] Nor do contemporaneous understandings support the idea that the original meaning of the Constitution was to be controlling in interpreting the document. People were uncertain not only about what the Constitution meant but about what it actually was.[29] Nearly two years after the Constitution was written, for example, Georgia representative James Jackson took to the floor of the First Congress to draw attention to the amorphous nature of the country's founding document: "Our constitution," he said, "is like a vessel just launched, and lying at the wharf, she is untried, you can hardly discover any one of her properties."[30]

During their early debates, many members of Congress assumed that the Constitution was unfinished and it was their job to help complete it. They embraced Madison's remarks from Federalist No. 37: "All new laws, though penned with the greatest technical skill . . . are considered as more or less obscure and equivocal, until their meaning be liquidated and ascertained by a series of particular discussions and adjudications."[31]

In that essay, Madison reminded his readers that the medium through which human beings communicate is necessarily "cloudy." "No language is so copious as to supply words and phrases for every complex idea." Regardless of how comprehensive the ideas were,

---

"the definition of them may be rendered inaccurate by the inaccuracy of the terms in which it is delivered." This inaccuracy would be amplified "according to the complexity and novelty of the objects defined."[32]

There is thus every reason to believe that the original meaning of the Constitution, if it included judicial review at all, did not embrace originalism as the method for interpreting the document. Originalism then self-destructs; to follow originalism requires abandoning it.

The Text of the Constitution

Everyone, originalists and non-originalists alike, believes that the text of the Constitution is controlling, and the text provides a strong basis for rejecting originalism. An easy example is the Ninth Amendment, which says: "The enumeration in the Constitution, of certain rights, shall not be construed to deny or disparage others retained by the people." The Ninth Amendment addressed an important issue concerning individual rights that was raised at state ratifying conventions. The seven Articles of the Constitution say very little about individual rights. One reason is that the Framers were concerned that they could never enumerate every right held by the people. They feared that delineating some rights while leaving out others would be misinterpreted as denying those other rights' existence. But at the state ratifying conventions, some delegates objected to the absence of a delineation of rights in the Constitution. A Bill of Rights was drafted in the First Congress, and it included the Ninth Amendment to make clear that the Constitution's enumeration of rights is incomplete and that other rights exist and can be protected.

The Ninth Amendment provides explicit textual authority for protecting unenumerated rights. Professor Powell explains that this amendment shows that the Framers "chose to leave a question of constitutional meaning for later interpreters."[33] Indeed, he says, "fidelity to this provision's probable historical meaning requires one not look to history for answers on . . . unenumerated rights."[34] The Ninth Amendment gives courts permission to interpret the Constitution outside of the range of its drafters' original intentions; in other words, it is a constitutional provision that authorizes non-originalism.

Originalists might make two responses to this. First, they might argue that the Ninth Amendment does not say who can protect additional rights and that this role should be left for legislatures and the political process, not for the courts. That may sound reasonable at first. To make this argument, however, an originalist would need to have a basis for concluding that this was the original meaning of the Ninth Amendment. But a generation that believed in natural rights would likely have seen it as the courts' role, assuming judicial review, to define and enforce these rights. There is no evidence that the Ninth Amendment originally meant that only legislatures could safeguard liberties beyond those enumerated in the Constitution.

So an originalist might advance a second argument: the Ninth Amendment allows the protection of additional rights, but it does not say how those rights are to be identified — and originalism is the only appropriate way to determine what they are. Thus the Ninth Amendment must be limited to protecting those rights that can be justified under originalism. The problem with this argument is that it begs the question: Should the Ninth Amendment be seen as allowing non-originalist protection of rights? The only way to argue that it shouldn't would be to show that the original meaning of the Ninth Amendment was limited to those rights that were understood to be protected in 1791, when it was adopted. Originalists will be dismayed to find that not a shred of evidence supports this view.

This point transcends the Ninth Amendment. Much of the Constitution is written in broad, open-ended language. Consider some of the clauses in the Bill of Rights. What constitutes "speech"? What is a "taking" of property? What is "due process" of law? What counts as "cruel and unusual punishment"? There is strong evidence that the original understanding was that these provisions would gain meaning over time. Historian Joseph Ellis persuasively argues that the Framers' humility in knowing they did not have all the answers is what has enabled their Constitution to survive.[35] He says that the Framers aimed to "provide a political platform wide enough to allow for considerable latitude within which future generations could make their own decisions."[36] According to Ellis, Jefferson spoke for the most prominent Framers when he insisted that constitutions ought not to be regarded with "sanctimonious reference" and that law and institutions must develop "hand in hand with the progress of the human mind."[37]

Because the Constitution had to be passed by a supermajority, it had to have broad appeal. To secure the support needed to enact it, Jack Balkin writes, the Framers and ratifiers "use[d] abstract and general language to paper over disagreements that would emerge if more specific language were chosen."[38]

All of this suggests that the original understanding of the Constitution was that constitutional interpretation was never intended to be a quest for original understanding. That is the incoherence problem of originalism.

Text Versus Original Understanding

There is yet another incoherence problem with originalism. What happens when the text and the original understanding are in conflict? Originalism provides no basis for resolving this tension. In fact, originalists often ignore the text when it does not yield the conservative results they seek. Consider two examples: the Fourteenth Amendment's Equal Protection Clause and the Tenth Amendment.

The text of the Fourteenth Amendment mandates that no state may "deny to any person within its jurisdiction the equal protection of the laws."[39] This sweeping language protects all people from discrimination; it says that no person may be denied equal protection of the laws. Yet, as explained in detail in the next chapter, originalists such as Antonin Scalia and Robert Bork emphatically insist that this clause applies only to race discrimination because that was the original understanding of it. They deny that it protects women or gays and lesbians from discrimination. But why should clear text that protects "any person" from discrimination be disregarded? Is there any reason other than their conservative opposition to protecting women and gays and lesbians from discrimination? More generally, why, from an originalist perspective, should there be a search beyond the text when its meaning is clear?

Another example of a conflict between original understanding and text can be found in the Tenth Amendment. It states, "The powers not delegated to the United States by the Constitution, nor prohibited by it to the States, are reserved to the States respectively, or to the people."[40] The text is clear: it says that the United States may exercise powers given to it, states may do anything not prohibited to them, and all other powers are left to the states and to the people, respectively.

The likely original meaning of this provision was to restate a basic postulate of the Constitution: the federal government has limited authority and can act only if the power is granted to it, but states have general authority and can do anything that is not prohibited. Like the Ninth Amendment, it addresses a concern raised in the state ratifying conventions: it clarifies the respective powers of the federal and state governments. This is exactly how the Supreme Court interpreted the Tenth Amendment in *United States v. Darby* in 1941, when it said, "The Amendment states but a truism that all is retained which has not been surrendered."[41]

If Congress has the constitutional authority to adopt a law, by definition that law cannot violate the Tenth Amendment. An originalist confronted with a challenge to a federal law as violating the Tenth Amendment would be required by originalism to dismiss the challenge as without merit so long as the Constitution gave Congress the power to pass the statute. But that is not what originalists have done. For the past three decades, the Supreme Court has said that the Tenth Amendment prevents Congress, even when it is authorized by Article I of the Constitution, from adopting laws that compel state governments to act. Conservative justices in their quest to protect states' rights and limit federal power have interpreted the Tenth Amendment in a way that cannot be justified based on its text or any evident original understanding.

In 1992, in *New York v. United States,* the Court for the first time struck down a federal law for violating the Tenth Amendment for "commandeering" state governments.[42] A federal law, the Low-Level Radioactive Waste Policy Amendments Act of 1985, required states to provide for the safe disposal of radioactive wastes generated within their borders. The act provided monetary incentives for states to comply with the law and allowed them to impose a surcharge on radioactive wastes received from other states. Additionally, and most controversially, to ensure effective action by the states, the law provided that the states would "take title" to any wastes within their borders that were not properly disposed of by January 1, 1996, and afterward would "be liable for all damages directly or indirectly incurred."[43]

The Supreme Court ruled that Congress, pursuant to its authority under the Commerce Clause, could regulate the disposal of radioactive wastes. But by a six-to-three margin, it held that the "take title" provision was unconstitutional because it forced state governments to choose between "either accepting ownership of waste or regulating according to the instructions of Congress."[44] Justice Sandra Day O'Connor, writing for the Court, said that it was impermissible for Congress to impose either option on the states. Forcing them to accept ownership of radioactive wastes would impermissibly "commandeer" state governments. Requiring state compliance with federal regulatory statutes would impermissibly impose on them a requirement to implement federal legislation. The Court concluded that it was "clear" that under the Tenth Amendment and the limits placed on Congress's powers under Article I, "the Federal Government may not compel the States to enact or administer a federal regulatory program."[45] Allowing Congress to commandeer state governments, O'Connor wrote, would undermine government accountability because Congress could make a decision but the states would be held responsible for a policy choice they had not made.[46]

Where can this anticommandeering provision be found in the text of the Tenth Amendment? What is there to suggest that the original understanding of the Tenth Amendment was to prohibit commandeering by the federal government? Nothing said in the Congress that proposed the amendment or in the states that ratified it supports the Court's interpretation.

Having invented the anticommandeering principle out of whole cloth, the Court applied it again in *Printz v. United States* in 1997.[47] The issue was whether the Brady Handgun Violence Prevention Act of 1993 violated the Tenth Amendment by requiring that state and local law enforcement officers conduct background checks on prospective handgun purchasers. In a five-to-four decision, with Justice Scalia writing the majority opinion, the Court found the provision unconstitutional. Scalia's opinion emphasized that Congress was impermissibly commandeering state executive officials to implement a federal mandate. Where did he find the evidence of original intent supporting this holding? He observed that historically, particularly in the early years of the United States, Congress had not exercised such a power.[48]

From an originalist perspective, this is a strange argument. It points only to the absence of action as evidence of original meaning. The text of the Tenth Amendment does not limit commandeering, nor is there any indication that the Tenth Amendment was originally understood to limit commandeering. Only an absence of action by Congress early in American history is seen to support the view that the Tenth Amendment prevents commandeering of state governments. No one, including Justice Scalia, can point to any positive evidence that the Tenth Amendment's original meaning was to stop commandeering.

My point is that originalism provides no coherent way of resolving differences between the text and the original understanding.

Originalists pick and choose the result they prefer, which inevitably corresponds to their ideological views.

Originalists claim that they have a theory of constitutional interpretation and their critics don't. But originalists don't have a theory either, if one of the requirements of a theory is some semblance of internal consistency. Originalism cannot be justified based on an originalist interpretation of the Constitution. The theory itself commands us to abandon it.

Chapter 5

THE ABHORRENCE PROBLEM

Can the federal government blatantly discriminate based on race or sex or disability or sexual orientation? For an originalist, the answer must be yes. No provision in the Constitution says that the federal government cannot deny equal protection of the laws. This is not surprising for a document that was written in the late eighteenth century and protected the institution of slavery. The Fourteenth Amendment is explicit that it is about limiting state governments, and that was its intent and its public meaning in 1868. From an originalist perspective, equal protection simply does not apply to or limit the federal government.[1] It does not matter which originalist theory is used — Framers' intent, original public meaning, "corpus linguistics," or anything else — nothing in the United States Constitution says that the federal government must adhere to a requirement for equal protection.

This is not an isolated absurdity. Following originalism leads one to many unacceptable results. As Justice William Brennan put it: "Anyone defending the narrow historical approach . . . must also be prepared to defend the contemporary use of pillorying, branding, and cropping and nailing of the ears, all of which were practiced in this country during colonial times."[2]

The Constitution was written in the late eighteenth century for a largely agrarian society where slavery existed in many states. The values of that time were in many ways tremendously different from ours. In every aspect — transportation, communication, commerce — the eighteenth-century world was unlike that of the twenty-first century. It makes no sense to say that the Constitution is limited to the understandings at the time of its drafting or of those who adopted the amendments after the Civil War.

Originalists have three choices. One is to state the original meaning for a constitutional provision in a much more abstract way, following not the specific original meaning but the provision's general goal. But once they do this, originalism becomes indistinguishable from non-originalism. If original meaning is stated generally enough, any result can be justified.[3] A second possibility is for originalists to abandon originalism when it does not lead to the results they want. In chapter 7, I will give many examples where they have done exactly this. A final possibility is for originalists to accept that the result would be repugnant and to urge that the Constitution be changed through an amendment.

In this chapter, I will focus on three examples of how following originalism would lead to repugnant results: segregation, as well as racial discrimination generally, is constitutionally permissible under originalism; equal protection provides no protection for anyone other than racial minorities; and the First Amendment allows the government to prohibit blasphemy and seditious libel (false criticism of the government and of government officials). These, of course, are just a few examples. I will conclude by explaining why relying on the constitutional amendment process is not sufficient to solve originalism's abhorrence problem.

Racial Segregation and Discrimination

One of the most powerful and irrefutable arguments against originalism is that it tells us *Brown v. Board of Education* was wrongly decided.[4] Under originalism, segregation is constitutional and all the decisions invalidating it were wrong. The evidence is overwhelming that the original understanding of the Equal Protection Clause accepted the constitutionality of laws mandating racial segregation.

No Supreme Court decision in history is more important than *Brown*. In *Plessy v. Ferguson,* in 1896, the Supreme Court upheld laws that mandated that Blacks and whites use "separate, but equal facilities."[5] A Louisiana law adopted in 1890 required railroad companies to provide separate but equal accommodations for whites and Blacks; the law mandated separate coaches, divided by a partition, for each race.[6] In 1892, Louisiana prosecuted Homer Adolph Plessy, who was seven-eighths Caucasian, for refusing to leave a railroad car assigned to whites.

The Supreme Court concluded that laws requiring "separate, but equal" facilities are constitutional and declared: "We cannot say that a law which authorizes or even requires the separation of the two races in public conveyances is unreasonable, or more obnoxious to the Fourteenth Amendment than the acts of Congress requiring separate schools for colored children in the District of Columbia, the constitutionality of which does not seem to have been questioned, or the corresponding acts of state legislatures."[7]

"Separate but equal" became the law of the land even though separate was anything but equal. The Supreme Court reaffirmed *Plessy v. Ferguson* in several subsequent cases. In *McCabe v. Atchison, Topeka & Santa Fe Railway Co.*, for example, the Court upheld an Oklahoma law requiring separation of the races on railroads but ruled that if there was a dining car for whites, one must also be available for Blacks.[8]

"Separate but equal" was expressly approved in the realm of education. In *Cumming v. Board of Education*, in 1899, the Court upheld the government's operation of a high school open only for white children even though none was available for Black children. The Court emphasized that local authorities were to be given discretion in allocating funds between Blacks and whites and that "any interference on the part of Federal authority with the management of such schools cannot be justified except in the case of a clear and unmistakable disregard of rights secured by the supreme law of the land."[9]

In *Berea College v. Kentucky*, in 1908, the Court affirmed the conviction of a private college that had violated a Kentucky law requiring the separation of the races in education.[10] In *Gong Lum v. Rice*, it concluded that Mississippi could exclude a child of Chinese ancestry from attending schools reserved for whites.[11] The law was settled that racial segregation was permissible, the Court said, and it did not "think that the question is any different, or that any different result can be reached . . . where the issue is as between white pupils and the pupils of the yellow races."[12]

No one thought that state-mandated segregation was inconsistent with the original meaning of the Fourteenth Amendment. But after World War II, the NAACP Legal Defense Fund launched a series of challenges to state-mandated segregation, focusing especially on the argument that laws requiring segregation of schools violated equal protection. In its 1952–53 term, the Supreme Court granted review in five cases that challenged the separate-but-equal doctrine in elementary and high school education.[13] At the time, seventeen states and the District of Columbia had segregated public schools.[14] The five cases before the Supreme Court involved schools that were totally unequal. One case, for example, was a challenge to South Carolina's educational system.[15] The white schools had one teacher for every twenty-eight students; the Black schools had one for every forty-seven students. The white schools were brick and stucco; the Black schools were made of wood that was often rotting. The white schools had indoor plumbing; the Black schools had outhouses.[16]

The five cases were argued together during the 1952–53 term, but because the justices could not agree on a decision, the cases were set for reargument for the following year. The Court asked the parties for briefs on several questions that primarily focused on the intent of the Framers of the Fourteenth Amendment. Although the term "originalism" had not yet been coined, it appeared from their questions that the justices were going to take an originalist approach to deciding these cases. Had the Court actually done so, it portended upholding laws requiring segregation. The evidence shows that the people who proposed, drafted, and ratified the Fourteenth Amendment from 1866 and 1868 did not believe that they were doing away with segregated schools. There is general agreement that the original and central purpose of the Equal Protection Clause was to protect Black people from the Black Codes — laws enacted after the end of slavery to retain Black people as a source of cheap labor and deprive them of basic liberties.[17] Crucially for those who interpret the Constitution according to original meaning, the same Congress that ratified the Fourteenth Amendment also voted to segregate the District of Columbia public schools.[18]

—

In the summer between the two Supreme Court terms, Chief Justice Fred Vinson died of a heart attack and President Dwight Eisenhower appointed California governor Earl Warren to be the new chief justice. The cases were argued on October 13, 1953, and through intense effort, Chief Justice Warren persuaded all of the justices to join a unanimous decision holding that separate but equal was impermissible in the realm of public education.[19]

On May 17, 1954, the Supreme Court released its decision in *Brown v. Board of Education*.[20] *Brown,* one of the five cases decided together, involved a challenge to the segregation of the Topeka, Kansas, public schools. The opinion, written by Chief Justice Warren, began by explaining that the constitutionality of segregation in education could not be determined from the Framers' intent or the original understanding of the Fourteenth Amendment. The historical sources of the Fourteenth Amendment "at best . . . are inconclusive," Warren wrote, and the enormous changes in education made history of little use in resolving the issue.[21] He was explicit in rejecting originalist reasoning: "In approaching this problem, we cannot turn the clock back to 1868 when the Amendment was adopted, or even to 1896 when *Plessy v. Ferguson* was written. We must consider public education in the light of its full development and its present place in American life throughout the Nation. Only in this way can it be determined if segregation in public schools deprives these plaintiffs of the equal protection of the laws."[22]

If the justices in *Brown* had adhered to originalism, they would have said something like this: "We know public schools today are different from public schools in 1868, and we know that people's views about race and equality have changed. But the original meaning of the Fourteenth Amendment allows segregated schools, and we are bound by

---

97

that meaning despite fundamental changes in society. If this is to be changed, it must be by constitutional amendment."[23] This ruling would not have been limited to the constitutionality of segregating public schools. The Jim Crow laws that segregated every aspect of life in southern and some northern states would have been constitutional.

Because originalism is hard to square with *Brown*, originalists often dislike talking about it.[24] When people mentioned the case around Justice Scalia, he would call it "waving the bloody shirt of *Brown*."[25] I once attended an event where he spoke, and a student asked him how he reconciled *Brown* with his originalist theory of constitutional interpretation. Scalia said tersely, "Even a broken clock gets it right twice a day. Next question."

Some originalists understandably have tried to square *Brown* with originalism. One way they have sought to do this is by reconsidering the historical record. Professor Michael W. McConnell, for example, argued that in the years after the Fourteenth Amendment was ratified, the records of the congressional debates surrounding the Civil Rights Act of 1875 showed that majorities in both houses of Congress showed support for compulsory school desegregation.[26] He contends that because these debates constitute the most extensive congressional discussion of school segregation during Reconstruction, they shed light on the original understanding of the Fourteenth Amendment. Yet he conceded that segregation "almost certainly enjoyed the support of a majority of the population even at the height of Reconstruction."[27] The Federalist Society has disseminated McConnell's historical analysis of *Brown*.[28]

From an originalist perspective, there are many problems with McConnell's analysis. First, he focuses not on the Congress that ratified the Fourteenth Amendment on June 13, 1866, but on congressional debates almost a decade later. Second, he cannot explain away

———

the fact that the Congress that ratified the Fourteenth Amendment also voted to segregate District of Columbia public schools. If one is to be true to originalism, that seems decisive in terms of that Congress's original understanding. Third, as we have seen, originalists have stopped looking at Framers' intent in determining original meaning in favor of a focus on the public understanding of the words when adopted. McConnell does exactly that in looking not at the drafters of the Fourteenth Amendment but at a later group of representatives and senators. But he selects quotations from those who support his position, without any evidence that the majority of Congress at the time disapproved of segregated schools. Fourth, as we have also seen, one cannot look only at the understanding of members of Congress in deciding original meaning. The understanding of the states that ratified the Fourteenth Amendment is crucial as well. McConnell admits that strong sentiment at the time approved of segregation, writing that "school desegregation was deeply unpopular among whites, in both North and South, and school segregation was very commonly practiced."[29] That makes it very difficult to say that the original meaning of the Fourteenth Amendment was to eliminate racially segregated schools.

Others have also tried to reconcile *Brown* with originalism, with no more success.[30] Professor Jack Balkin uses the underlying principles of the Equal Protection Clause to conclude that racial segregation of public schools violates the Constitution. He writes that "constitutional construction is inevitably a presentist endeavor, drawing on the resources of the entire constitutional tradition that precedes the interpreter. Interpreting the equal protection clause today means interpreting it after the New Deal, after the civil rights revolution, and after the second wave of American feminism. . . . We must decide in the present which constructions are most faithful to the text."[31]

I agree with every word of that, but Robert Bork, Antonin Scalia, or Clarence Thomas would never call it originalism. Balkin's approach to originalism is indistinguishable from non-originalism. Interpreting the Equal Protection Clause from a "presentist" perspective to achieve its general goal can be used to justify virtually any result.

Under Balkin's approach, *Brown* can be justified; but his conclusion is not based on the original understanding of equal protection at the time the Fourteenth Amendment was ratified. Whenever scholars have tried to justify *Brown* from an originalist perspective, they inevitably end up stating the goal of equal protection more generally and ignoring the specific understandings at the time.[32] Professor David Strauss has observed that many originalists' efforts to claim *Brown* require them to change the level of generality by asserting that the Fourteenth Amendment enshrined a principle of racial equity.[33] He rightly points out that this kind of maneuver allows originalists to justify anything.[34] Professor Michael Dorf writes that "conservatives who are generally sympathetic to originalism cannot openly say that *Brown v. Board of Education* was wrongly decided," and so they "concoct implausible accounts of the Reconstruction Era understanding of segregation."[35]

It is not just that *Brown v. Board of Education* cannot be justified under originalism or that, under that theory, laws mandating segregation are constitutional. Many other, equally abhorrent forms of race discrimination are constitutional and must be upheld under the original meaning of the Equal Protection Clause. If the Court were true to originalism, for example, laws prohibiting interracial marriage would have been upheld. In 1776, seven of the thirteen colonies had laws prohibiting interracial marriage.[36] As the United States expanded, all of the states with slavery prohibited interracial marriage, as did other states, such as Illinois and California. Even as late as 1967, sixteen states had laws prohibiting interracial marriage.[37] There is no indication at all that the Congress that proposed the Fourteenth Amendment, or the states that ratified it, saw the Equal Protection Clause as invalidating these laws. It would not be tenable to claim that there was a desire to eliminate antimiscegenation laws, given their prevalence in so many states. That is why the Supreme Court initially upheld such laws on the ground that they did not discriminate; the Court saw them as treating Blacks and whites equally.

In *Pace v. Alabama,* in 1883, the Court upheld an Alabama law that provided harsher penalties for adultery and fornication if the couple were composed of a white and a Black than if they were of the same race.[38] Tony Pace, a Black man, and Mary Cox, a white woman, were Alabama residents who had been arrested in 1881 because their sexual relationship violated the state's antimiscegenation statute. They were charged with living together "in a state of adultery or fornication," and each was sentenced to two years' imprisonment in the state penitentiary.[39] When they challenged their convictions based on equal protection, the Supreme Court upheld the Alabama law and said that because whites and Blacks both were subject to punishment there was no constitutional violation.

Later, the Court rightly abandoned the original understanding of the Fourteenth Amendment and recognized that racial classifications are impermissible under the Equal Protection Clause because they are based on assumptions of racial superiority and inferiority. In *McLaughlin v. Florida* (1964), the Court overturned a Florida law that prohibited the habitual occupation of a room at night by unmarried interracial couples.[40] In the majority opinion, Justice Byron White wrote that *Pace* "represents a limited view of the Equal Protection Clause which has not withstood analysis in the subsequent decisions of this Court."[41] The state had offered no acceptable justification for why a race-neutral law could not adequately serve the purpose of punishing premarital sexual relations.

In its landmark 1967 decision *Loving v. Virginia*, the Supreme Court declared unconstitutional a state miscegenation statute that made it a crime for a white person to marry outside the Caucasian race.[42] The state had argued that the law was permissible because it burdened both whites and minorities. The Court responded that "we reject the notion that the mere equal application of a statute concerning racial classifications is enough to remove the classifications from the Fourteenth Amendment's proscription of all invidious racial discriminations. . . . There can be no question but that Virginia's miscegenation statutes rest solely upon distinctions drawn according to race. The statutes proscribe generally accepted conduct if engaged in by members of different races. . . . There can be no doubt that restricting the freedom to marry solely because of racial classifications violates the central meaning of the Equal Protection Clause."[43]

No originalist could have written that. Whether the focus is on the Framers' intent, contemporaneous practices in 1868, or original understandings, there simply is no way an originalist can say that laws prohibiting interracial marriage violate equal protection. Nor could an originalist argue that they are unconstitutional because they violate a fundamental right to marry. That right is not mentioned in the Constitution, and there is no evidence of any original understanding to support it.

Other Types of Discrimination

In *United States v. Virginia*, Justice Scalia declared that the Fourteenth Amendment's Equal Protection Clause, as originally understood, does not apply to discrimination based on gender.[44] Its original meaning was limited to addressing race discrimination against people of African descent. Although, as we have seen, the clause says without qualification that "no person" shall be denied equal protection of the laws, there is no doubt that its original understanding was solely about race discrimination. In the *Slaughter-House Cases,* in 1873, five years after the amendment was ratified, the Court declared that the Equal Protection Clause was meant only to protect Blacks, adding, "[W]e doubt very much whether any action of a State not directed by way of discrimination against the negroes as a class, or on account of their race, will ever be held to come within the purview of this provision."[45]

Shortly after the Fourteenth Amendment was ratified, the Court expressly rejected claims that sex discrimination could be challenged as violating the Equal Protection Clause. In 1872, four years after ratification, in *Bradwell v. Illinois,* the Court upheld an Illinois law that prohibited women from being licensed to practice law.[46] The very short majority opinion ruled against Myra Bradwell. Justice Joseph P. Bradley, in a concurring opinion, directly addressed the claim of sex discrimination: "The paramount destiny and mission of women are to fulfill the noble and benign offices of wife and mother. This is the law of the creator. And the rules of civil society must be adapted in the general constitution of things, and cannot be based on exceptional cases."[47] He concluded that "in view of the peculiar characteristics, destiny, and mission of woman, it is within the province of the Legislature to ordain what offices, positions and callings shall be filled and discharged by men."[48]

The Court reaffirmed *Bradwell* in 1894, in *In re Lockwood.*[49] It ruled that Virginia could exclude a woman from practicing law even though she had been admitted to the bars of the Supreme Court and the District of Columbia. In between *Bradwell* and *Lockwood,* the

Supreme Court in *Minor v. Happersett,* in 1874, upheld the constitutionality of excluding women from voting.[50]

All of this confirms exactly what Justice Scalia and Robert Bork argued: the original understanding of equal protection was limited to race discrimination and does not provide a basis for overturning other types of discrimination. They thought the Supreme Court was wrong in finding a denial of equal protection in discrimination against women, gays and lesbians, people with disabilities, noncitizens, and nonmarital children.[51] Eliminating constitutional limits on such discrimination would render wrong dozens and dozens of Supreme Court decisions and thousands of lower court rulings that provided protection for victims of discrimination. It is at odds with very language of the Equal Protection Clause. Most Americans would not want to live in the kind of society Bork's and Scalia's reading would permit.

Understandably, originalist scholars have recoiled from this consequence of their theory. But the only way they can interpret "equal protection" more broadly is by focusing on the clause's general goal rather than its specific original meaning. For example, in an article titled "Originalism and Sex Discrimination," Professors Steven Calabresi and Julia Rickert conclude that the clause was intended to be a prohibition on caste.[52] They explain that even though the Framers and ratifiers in 1868 would not have understood sex discrimination as enforcing a caste, today we properly see it that way.[53] Thus, they claim, modern sex discrimination doctrines are correct even though the Court arrived at them by non-originalist reasoning.

But if a constitutional provision can be interpreted in this way, based on its general purpose, then originalism becomes indistinguishable from non-originalism.[54] If the word "liberty" can be interpreted as protecting basic aspects of freedom and autonomy, then *Roe v. Wade* — a central target of originalists — can be justified under originalism. When original understanding is defined in such an abstract way, it can justify literally any result and does nothing to restrain judges from ruling according to their personal convictions. Originalists avoid the repugnant consequences of their theory only at the cost of giving up the primary reason to follow originalism in the first place.

That is the theory's abhorrence problem: either it leads to results that most Americans would find totally unacceptable, or else it becomes non-originalism. Originalist justices choose whichever alternative yields the results they want. Professor Scott Gerber has said of Justice Thomas, for instance, that he "is a 'liberal originalist' on civil rights and a 'conservative originalist' on civil liberties and federalism."[55] Gerber explains, "Justice Thomas appeals to the *ideal* of equality at the heart of the Declaration of Independence when he decides questions involving race, but to the Framers' *specific* intentions — as manifested in the text and historical context of the Constitution — when he decides questions involving civil liberties and federalism."[56] This allows Thomas to have different stances on issues involving race, such as segregation and affirmative action, where he clearly rejects the original understanding of the Fourteenth Amendment, while relying on a narrow understanding of the Framers to reach politically conservative results in religion and abortion cases.[57]

The original understanding of the Equal Protection Clause was solely about race discrimination. Scalia and Bork admitted this. But it would be far worse for our society if there was no constitutional protection for other kinds of discrimination.

Freedom of Speech

Another area where the originalist approach leads to unacceptable results is freedom of speech under the First Amendment. To begin with, the amendment says, "*Congress* shall make no law." This would mean that there is no constitutional limit on what the president or the courts do to restrict speech. Presidential executive orders limiting expression or judicial awards of damages for speech, such as in defamation cases, could never be challenged under the First Amendment.[58] No one has suggested that under its original understanding the First Amendment applied to any institution other than Congress.

But the problems with an originalist approach to free speech go well beyond that. The government surely could outlaw blasphemous speech such as taking the Lord's name in vain, because this was prohibited when the Constitution was ratified. William Blackstone, and other free speech thinkers such as James Wilson, did not believe that atheism or ridiculing Christianity should be protected under the common law.[59] Blasphemy laws remained prominent in America even into the twentieth century.[60]

Following the Revolution, the English common law crime of blasphemy became part of American common law.[61] The system was reinforced when almost all the states either kept their English colonial statutes criminalizing blasphemy or adopted new ones.[62] Some of these provisions were extremely harsh. In Maryland, the penalties included literally drilling a hole into the blasphemer's tongue and a fine of £20 sterling for the first offense, up to death for a third offense.[63] In Connecticut and New Hampshire in the 1760s, laws against blasphemy and "breach of the sabbath" were consistently enforced.[64] In 1782, Massachusetts adopted a statute whose punishments included up to a year in jail, whipping, hanging, or a large fine.[65] The penalties in Rhode Island's 1798 statute included a fine of $100 and imprisonment for up to two months.[66]

In his famous 1971 article advocating originalism, Robert Bork said that only political speech should be deemed protected by the First Amendment.[67] Under this approach, there would be no constitutional protection for artistic expression, sexual speech, commercial speech, or much else that the courts have safeguarded under the First Amendment.

Following originalism would also allow the government to restrict even political speech. Most notably, seditious libel — false criticism of the government and government officials — was not thought to be protected in the founding era. Charges of seditious libel were often used to bring those who published criticisms of the government to court. Blackstone's view, which was highly influential, was that prior restraints on speech are wrong, but it was acceptable to punish people for their expression after publishing.[68]

Seditious libel laws were created in England in the early 1600s by the Star Chamber, the judicial branch of the king. Constructive treasons were tried in common law courts and required a jury trial to secure a conviction and, moreover, still required an overt act. People could not be accused of treason based on speech alone.[69] Nor were common law crimes under the Star Chamber's jurisdiction. To punish critical speech, the chamber decreed the crime of seditious libel.[70] Truth was no defense: criticism alone was enough for conviction.[71]

Later, after it assumed control of common law, the Star Chamber decreed that seditious libel was to be part of the common law and therefore under jurisdiction of the King's Bench.[72] Many criticized this restriction on speech because it was not naturally absorbed into the common law but had been created by edict in service to the

---

Crown.[73] Despite this resistance, however, seditious libel became enmeshed into the fabric of English common law courts, which is why Blackstone's commentaries presented it as a common law crime.[74] By the end of the 1600s, when the Star Chamber's licensing laws and prior restraint of publishing had lapsed, the law of seditious libel continued.[75]

Originalists often point to contemporaneous events as revealing the understanding of a constitutional provision at the time it was adopted. Congress adopted the Alien and Sedition Acts in 1798 — with many of the Constitution's drafters and ratifiers participating.[76] The law prohibited the publication of "false, scandalous, and malicious writing or writings against the government of the United States, or either house of the Congress of the United States, or the President of the United States, with intent to defame . . . ; or to bring them . . . into contempt or disrepute; or to excite against them . . . hatred of the good people of the United States, or to stir up sedition within the United States, or to excite any unlawful combinations therein, for opposing or resisting any law of the United States, or any act of the President of the United States."[77] The law did allow truth as a defense, and it required proof of malicious intent.

The Federalists under President John Adams aggressively used the law against their rivals, especially Democratic-Republican newspapers. The Alien and Sedition Acts were a major political issue in the election of 1800, and after he was elected president, Thomas Jefferson pardoned those who had been convicted under the law. The acts were repealed, and the Supreme Court never ruled on their constitutionality. But in *New York Times Co. v. Sullivan*, in 1964, the Court declared: "Although the Sedition Act was never tested in this Court, the attack upon its validity has carried the day in the court of history."[78]

—

Under originalism, *New York Times Co. v. Sullivan* was wrongly decided, a position recently taken by Justice Thomas, whose view would seemingly mean that the government can adopt laws like the Alien and Sedition Acts that make falsely criticizing the government a crime.[79] Adhering to originalism leaves little space for freedom of speech under the First Amendment. Adhering to the public understanding of freedom of speech from the late eighteenth century would give the government broad latitude to punish speech critical of the government and its officials. The chilling of speech that we take for granted would be enormous.

Why Not Just Rely on Amendments?

These few examples of how following originalism would lead to repugnant results are only the beginning; there are many more. As Justice Brennan pointed out, "pillorying, branding, and cropping and nailing of the ears" would be allowed under the Eighth Amendment because they were practiced in this country at the time it was ratified.[80] As Justice Scalia argued, there would be no constitutional limits on the length of sentences, no matter how draconian, and no matter how minor the crime.[81]

From an originalist perspective, the federal government could discriminate without constitutional limits. As mentioned earlier, the Constitution imposes no equal protection requirement on the federal government. The Fourteenth Amendment, by its text and original meaning, says that states cannot deny equal protection, and no one has suggested that it was meant to apply to the federal government. In *Bolling v. Sharpe*, a companion case to *Brown v. Board of Education* that concerned the segregation of the District of Columbia public schools, the Warren Court held that equal protection applies

---

to the federal government through the Due Process Clause of the Fifth Amendment.[82] Feeling that it would be unacceptable to allow the federal government to discriminate in a manner prohibited to the states by the Fourteenth Amendment, the Court avoided this embarrassment by interpreting the Fifth Amendment to include an implicit requirement of equal protection.[83] It simply declared that "discrimination may be so unjustifiable as to be violative of due process."[84]

It is now well settled that the requirements of equal protection are the same, whether the challenge is to the federal government under the Fifth Amendment or to state and local governments under the Fourteenth. The Supreme Court has expressly declared that "equal protection analysis in the Fifth Amendment area is the same as that under the Fourteenth Amendment."[85] But there is no plausible argument that this reflects the original meaning of the Fifth Amendment's Due Process Clause.

Under originalism, there is a strong argument that *none* of the Bill of Rights should be applied to state and local governments. Charles Fairman, in an exhaustive study of the Framers' intent on this issue, concluded: "[The theory that the] privileges or immunities clause incorporated Amendments I to VIII found no recognition in the practice of Congress, or the action of state legislatures, constitutional conventions, or courts. . . . Congress would not have attempted such a thing, the country would not have stood for it, the legislatures would not have ratified."[86]

Justice Thomas has repeatedly made an originalist argument that the Establishment Clause of the First Amendment, which prohibits laws "respecting an establishment of religion," does not apply to state and local governments at all. He has explained that the clause "states that 'Congress shall make no law respecting an establishment of religion.' On its face, this provision places no limit on the States with regard to religion. The Establishment Clause originally protected States, and by extension their citizens, from the imposition of an established religion by the Federal Government."[87] Elsewhere, Thomas has said that the "Establishment Clause is a federalism provision, which, for this reason, resists incorporation."[88] By this view, the clause was meant solely as a limit on the federal government, to keep it from establishing a church that would rival state churches. It follows from Thomas's view that a state may have an official religion and even coerce religious participation; the Establishment Clause imposes no limits on state and local governments.

Was it unconstitutional to elect Kamala Harris as vice president? Article II of the Constitution refers to the president and vice president with the pronoun "he." There is no doubt that the original meaning of the Constitution was that these offices be held by men.[89] Women were not even given the right to vote until 1920, with the adoption of the Nineteenth Amendment. Under originalism, it is unconstitutional to elect a woman as president or vice president until the Constitution is amended.

The examples are endless of how originalism, if truly followed, would lead to repugnant results. Originalists have an answer to this: amend the Constitution. A central tenet of originalism is that the only appropriate way to change the meaning of the Constitution is through the amendment process delineated in Article V. Professors John McGinnis and Michael Rappaport, in their defense of originalism, argue that we should use the Article V amendment process whenever the Constitution has undesirable provisions that we as a society want to change.[90] The benefit of the amendment process is that it requires strong supermajoritarian support from many legislative bodies rather than the decisions of a small number of relatively homogenous judges.[91] Moreover, McGinnis and Rappaport argue that judicial updating and the use of the amendment process are mutually exclusive.[92] Once the Supreme Court updates a provision the justices see as undesirable, the momentum to form a consensus to amend the Constitution will likely be gone.[93] Moreover, they contend, the supermajoritarian amendment process leads to superior results.[94] Even when it yields the same result as judicial updating, the supermajoritarian process is better, in their view, because it cannot be overturned as easily.[95]

But in the real world, amendments are unlikely and rare. The Constitution has been amended only twenty-seven times since 1787, and only seventeen times since the Bill of Rights was adopted in 1791. Professor Stephen Carter, who has espoused an originalist view of at least some parts of the Constitution, remarked that "Article V is very nearly a dead letter."[96] Likewise, Professor Sanford Levinson observed that "as a practical matter . . . Article V makes it next to impossible to amend the Constitution with regard to genuinely controversial issues, even if substantial — and intense — majorities advocate amendment."[97] It is highly unlikely that the amendment process would cure the repugnant results inherent to an originalist approach to the Constitution.

But the problem with relying solely on the amendment process is more profound than an inconveniently slow and difficult process. Protecting minorities and the rights of individuals would require approval of the supermajority of Congress and the states. To use an example I raised earlier, it is unimaginable that the Constitution would have been amended to declare segregation of schools unconstitutional or to eliminate the Jim Crow laws. Neither Congress nor the requisite number of states would have ratified such amendments. In 1956, ninety-six southern congressmen issued a declaration denouncing

Brown v. Board of Education and calling on states to "resist forced integration by any lawful means."[98]

Moreover, it is highly unlikely that enough states would have ratified such an amendment even if Congress had managed to pass it. Because more than a quarter of the states had laws segregating their schools, it is almost unimaginable that three-quarters of the states would have ratified an amendment ending segregation. As jurist Edmund Cahn observed, "As a practical matter it would have been impossible to secure adoption of a constitutional amendment to abolish 'separate but equal.' "[99]

Nor would a constitutional amendment to protect women or other groups from discrimination have been likely to pass. The Equal Rights Amendment was approved overwhelmingly by Congress in 1972 yet still has not been deemed ratified. I doubt that anyone believes Congress and the states would enact an amendment to protect gays and lesbians from discrimination.

These are not isolated examples. Surely, no one thinks there could have been a constitutional amendment to abolish prayer in public schools, to expand the rights of criminal defendants, or to do many other things the Court has done to expand individual liberties.

The underlying point also is a normative one: the rights of individuals and the protection of minorities from discrimination should not require the action of a supermajority. That is what relying solely on the amendment process would mean.

A theory must be judged by its real-world consequences. Any theory that would make *Brown v. Board of Education* incorrectly decided, not allow equal protection to apply to sex discrimination, or permit the government to punish blasphemy should be flatly rejected as unacceptable. Faithfully and consistently following originalism would

---

lead to repugnant results. It would yield a society that makes life poorer, harder, and more insecure for all but a few. Even if it were not unacceptable for other reasons — if the original understanding of all provisions were never in doubt, if the theory truly prevented judges from following their ideological and personal convictions, and if the Framers intended their descendants to rigorously follow the precise original understanding of each provision, none of which is true — the abhorrence of originalism's results would be enough to merit its rejection.

Chapter 6

THE MODERNITY PROBLEM

In 2010, the Supreme Court heard oral arguments in a case where the plaintiffs were challenging the constitutionality of a California law that prohibited the sale or rental of violent video games to minors without parental consent.[1] Many states had adopted similar statutes. Legislators were shocked by the games' graphic violence and were distressed by studies that showed a correlation between playing such games and violent behavior. The concern was that the participatory aspect of video games makes them different from comic books, television programs, or movies, all of which also can have violent content.

As was his practice, Justice Scalia was very active in the oral argument, and he pressed the attorney defending California's law about whether the law could be reconciled with the original understanding of the First Amendment. Finally, Justice Alito interjected: "I think what Justice Scalia wants to know is what James Madison thought about video games."[2] Putting it that way shows the absurdity of trying to answer today's constitutional questions by looking at the world of 1787, when the Constitution was drafted, or 1791, when the First Amendment was ratified, or 1868, when the Fourteenth Amendment was approved.

The Court, in a seven-to-two decision, found that video games are a form of speech and that the California law was unconstitutional. Justice Scalia wrote the majority opinion. I do not disagree with the decision, but I question whether it can be squared with Scalia's view that the meaning of a constitutional provision is fixed at the time it was adopted and can be changed only by constitutional amendment. The premises of the decision—that the First Amendment protects the rights of children and that content-based restrictions of speech must meet strict scrutiny—cannot be found in the original understanding of the First Amendment. That is before we even get to the issue of whether video games were intended to be protected as speech.

To state the obvious, our world is vastly different from that which existed at the nation's beginning. There are thus countless constitutional questions for which originalism can provide no answer. In this chapter, I want to focus on three constitutional issues on which no original understanding can have existed: whether the Fourth Amendment applies to surveillance technology; how the country's enormous growth in size and complexity changes the way it must be governed; and how free speech applies to the media of the twentieth and twenty-first centuries. It is absurd to try and decide such matters based on the original meaning of a document that was written when all of these were unimaginable. If originalists want to adhere to their methodology for questions like these, they will only create more examples of the abhorrence problem we saw in the previous chapter. Or perhaps, originalists will deal with such cases by stating the original meaning of the constitutional provision in a very abstract way. But if they do, then originalism becomes indistinguishable from non-originalism, and anything can be justified.

———

The Fourth Amendment and Modern Technology

The Fourth Amendment says, "The right of the people to be secure in their persons, houses, papers, and effects, against unreasonable searches and seizures, shall not be violated, and no Warrants shall issue, but upon probable cause, supported by Oath or affirmation, and particularly describing the place to be searched, and the persons or things to be seized." The consensus is that the Fourth Amendment was meant to require that there be individualized suspicion — reason to believe that the individual had committed a crime or had evidence of a crime — before the police engaged in a search or an arrest.

The seminal Supreme Court case involving the Fourth Amendment is *Boyd v. United States*, in 1886.[3] Boyd, an importer, argued that the seizure of his property for alleged customs violations infringed on his Fourth Amendment rights. In his majority opinion, Justice Joseph P. Bradley wrote that the meaning of the Fourth Amendment could be understood by looking at English history. Even though the amendment was almost a century old, there were no Supreme Court precedents about it, so the Court instead looked to earlier decisions. In England, Bradley explained, courts were able to give "general warrants" to search people's houses and papers when the police were looking for evidence of a crime. English law required no individualized suspicion that the person being searched had committed a crime or had evidence of a crime. Bradley described the strong reaction against general warrants and pointed to the 1765 English decision in *Entick v. Carrington* as a pivotal moment changing this law.[4] That case was an action for trespass against police who had entered a person's home in November 1762, broken open his desks and boxes, and searched and examined his papers.

The court found this to be an impermissible trespass, and Bradley's opinion in *Boyd* described it as one of "the landmarks of English liberty" that "was welcomed and applauded by the lovers of liberty in the colonies as well as in the mother country."[5]

This case, Bradley continued, is the key to understanding the Fourth Amendment. "Every American statesman, during our revolutionary and formative period as a nation, was undoubtedly familiar with this monument of English freedom, and considered it as the true and ultimate expression of constitutional law."[6] It was "in the minds" of those who drafted the Fourth Amendment and should be understood as the explanation "of what was meant by unreasonable searches and seizures."[7] Under this explanation, the Fourth Amendment, above all, imposed a requirement for individualized suspicion.

It was also clear, however, that the Fourth Amendment assumed that the police had to make a physical trespass in order to conduct a search. This made sense in 1791, when the Fourth Amendment was adopted, and it still made sense in 1886. But advancing technology now allows police to engage in surveillance and gather evidence against persons without needing to trespass on their property. As soon as telephones were adopted, police could wiretap them and listen to conversations without needing to engage in a physical trespass. Today, they can monitor people's movements and conversations through cellular location information, satellite technology, and much more.

Initially, the Supreme Court's answer was that the Fourth Amendment does not apply to these new technologies at all and therefore imposes no limits on the police when there is not a physical trespass. This is a perfect illustration of the modernity problem: the original understanding of the Fourth Amendment provides no guidance for dealing with technology that could not have been anticipated. The originalist answer, finding no constitutional protection at all, leads to abhorrent results such as those I discussed in chapter 5.

When the Supreme Court first dealt with wiretapping under the Fourth Amendment, in 1928, it held that the Constitution imposed no limits so long as installing the device did not entail a physical trespass. This crucial case was *Olmstead v. United States,* which defined the scope of the Fourth Amendment for four decades.[8] The case arose out of a prosecution for violating the National Prohibition Act of 1919. The key evidence was gained by wiretapping telephones. Without getting a warrant, the police put taps on telephone wires outside the houses of four individuals and on those leading to their main office.[9] The Court stressed that "the insertions were made without trespass upon any property of the defendants. They were made in the basement of the large office building. The taps from house lines were made in the streets near the houses."[10] The police listened to conversations through these wiretaps for many months and obtained the crucial evidence by which Olmstead and the other defendants were convicted.

The question presented to the Court was whether this police wiretapping was a warrantless search and thus a violation of the Fourth Amendment. In a five-to-four decision, the Court ruled that it was not a search, and no warrant was needed, because the wiretapping had not involved a physical trespass on the property.

Chief Justice William Howard Taft wrote the opinion for the Court. Taft, who is the only person to have been both president and a Supreme Court justice, wrote that "the amendment does not forbid what was done here. There was no searching. There was no seizure. The evidence was secured by the use of the sense of hearing and that only. There was no entry of the houses or offices of the defendants."[11] The Fourth Amendment, Taft explained, did not apply since the police did the eavesdropping by tapping into wires outside the home, and "the intervening wires are not part of his house or office, any more than are the highways along which they are stretched."[12]

Justice Louis Brandeis, in dissent, stressed the need for the Constitution to be adapted to changed circumstances and new technology. He said the failure of the Fourth Amendment's Framers to contemplate telephones or wiretapping should not exempt them from constitutional limits. The important issue, he wrote, was protecting citizens' privacy from government intrusion: the Framers had "sought to protect Americans in their beliefs, their thoughts, their emotions and their sensations. They conferred, as against the government, the right to be let alone — the most comprehensive of rights and the right most valued by civilized men."[13] He concluded that "to protect, that right, every unjustifiable intrusion by the government upon the privacy of the individual, whatever the means employed, must be deemed a violation of the Fourth Amendment."[14]

It was not until 1967, almost forty years after *Olmstead,* that the Court, in *Katz v. United States,* abandoned the originalist approach to the Fourth Amendment and held that it applies when there is a violation of the reasonable expectation of privacy.[15] In *Katz,* police had listened in to conversations over a pay phone in a phone booth in an effort to gather evidence of illegal gambling. The lower courts, following *Olmstead* and well-established law, said that no search had occurred and no warrant was required because there had been no physical trespass on Katz's property.

But the Supreme Court reversed the lower courts' decisions and overturned the earlier precedents. In an opinion by Justice Potter Stewart, the Court said that these earlier decisions "have been so eroded by our subsequent decisions that the 'trespass' doctrine there enunciated can no longer be regarded as controlling."[16] The government's listening to and recording Katz's words had violated his privacy, Stewart wrote, and "the fact that the electronic device employed to achieve that end did not happen to penetrate the wall of the booth can have no constitutional significance."[17]

The Fourth Amendment, Stewart went on, protects people, not property. A person's Fourth Amendment rights do not depend on where he or she is at the time of the government intrusion, nor do they depend on whether there is a physical trespass. "These considerations do not vanish," he explained, "when the search in question is transferred from the setting of a home, an office, or a hotel room to that of a telephone booth. Wherever a man may be, he is entitled to know that he will remain free from unreasonable searches and seizures."[18]

Stewart did not discuss how to determine whether a search exists under this standard. Justice John Marshall Harlan explained this in a concurring opinion that has been the controlling standard for the Fourth Amendment ever since. Harlan wrote that the Fourth Amendment creates "a twofold requirement" for protection: "first that a person have exhibited an actual (subjective) expectation of privacy and, second, that the expectation be one that society is prepared to recognize as 'reasonable.' "[19]

Defining the "reasonable expectation of privacy" raises great problems, but it is surely the right approach. In determining whether there is a "search" for purposes of the Fourth Amendment, Justice Harlan's test focuses the central inquiry on privacy, where it should be, and not on whether there has been a physical trespass. It means that wiretapping or electronic eavesdropping is a search even if the police do not enter a suspect's premises. It is why the Fourth

Amendment applies to the technology of the twenty-first century. But this approach cannot be justified under originalism. The original meaning of the Fourth Amendment was about limiting physical trespass by the police.

The originalist justices – Scalia, Thomas, and Gorsuch – have rejected the "reasonable expectation of privacy" standard and adhered to the view that the Fourth Amendment applies only when there is a physical trespass. This is the modernity problem; looking solely at original meaning in interpreting a constitutional provision leaves one no way to deal with modern problems that could not have been fathomed by the Constitution's drafters.

United States v. Jones, which the Court decided in 2012, was a case where the police put a global positioning system (GPS) device on the undercarriage of Antoine Jones's car without a valid warrant and tracked his movements for twenty-eight days.[20] The tracking information thus gained was the key evidence in Jones's conviction for drug trafficking. The Court unanimously held that the police had violated the Fourth Amendment. Justice Scalia wrote the opinion for the Court and held that putting the GPS device on the car was a trespass. He relied on *Entick v. Carrington,* the English law precedent from 1765 that had so impressed Justice Bradley in 1886.

I agree with the result in the case but find very troubling the return to the *Olmstead* approach of focusing solely on whether there was a trespass. What if the police had tracked Jones's movements through cellular or satellite technology rather than through a GPS device physically placed on his car? The result for the police would have been the same, but Scalia's approach would have meant that it was not a search and that the Fourth Amendment did not apply.

This is illustrated by a 2018 case, *Carpenter v. United States,* and especially by the dissents of the originalist justices, Thomas and

Gorsuch.[21] The Court held that police may obtain cellular location information — information that can be used to determine where a person was at a particular time — only if there is a warrant based on probable cause or there are emergency circumstances that justify allowing the search without a warrant.

Timothy Carpenter was suspected of committing a series of armed robberies; perhaps ironically, given the case, he had robbed Radio Shacks. These were stores, many of which have since gone out of business, that sold do-it-yourself electronic components. The Federal Bureau of Investigation went to Carpenter's cell phone company and, without a warrant from a judge, got the cell phone tower records — the cell site location information — that revealed his movements for 127 days.[22] This information was crucial evidence used to convict Carpenter; he was sentenced to 116 years in prison.

Every time we use our cell phone — to send or receive calls, texts, or emails or to access the internet — it connects to a cell tower. Even if we are not using the phone, if it is on, it is connected to a cell tower. The records of this connection — generated hundreds, sometimes thousands of times per day — include the precise GPS coordinates of each tower as well as the day and time the phone tried to connect to it. Someone can use these records to determine our location at almost any moment and track our movements. In 2016, Verizon and AT&T alone received about 125,000 requests for this information from law enforcement agencies.[23]

The issue before the Supreme Court in *Carpenter v. United States* was whether the Fourth Amendment requires the police to obtain a warrant in order to access this information. In reversing the lower courts and ruling in Carpenter's favor, the Court based its decision squarely on *Katz* and the Fourth Amendment's protection of a reasonable expectation of privacy. Chief Justice Roberts wrote the majority opinion, which was joined by Justices Ginsburg, Breyer, Sotomayor, and Kagan. Roberts stressed the intrusion into privacy from accessing a person's cellular location information over a long period of time. "Mapping a cell phone's location over the course of 127 days," he wrote, "provides an all-encompassing record of the holder's whereabouts," which reveal his "familial, political, professional, religious, and sexual associations."[24]

Under the originalist approach to the Fourth Amendment, the police's actions in *Carpenter* would not have been a search because there was no physical trespass; therefore no warrant or any kind of judicial protection would have been constitutionally required. Justice Thomas, in a vehement dissent, said he would overrule *Katz* and find a search only if the government invaded property rights. The *"Katz* test," he wrote, "has no basis in the text or history of the Fourth Amendment." Quoting those who called it "an unpredictable jumble," "a mass of contradictions and obscurities," "riddled with inconsistency and incoherence," "flawed to the core," and "inspired by the kind of logic that produced Rube Goldberg's bizarre contraptions," Thomas concluded that "the *Katz* test is a failed experiment."[25] Justice Gorsuch also dissented and agreed with Thomas that the Fourth Amendment applies only if there is a physical trespass of property.[26]

But it would make no sense to require an invasion of property rights for the Fourth Amendment to apply when the police rely so heavily on technology that gathers information without physical intrusion. The approach that preceded *Katz*, focusing on whether there was a police trespass, was problematic when it was created, but it is absurd in a world where the police can use stored cellular information and drones to gather information. That, of course, is originalism's modernity problem.

The Growth of Society and Government

In 1790, when the first census was taken, there were 3,893,635 people in the United States. The most populous state, Virginia, had 747,610. The total federal budget was about $640,000.[27] In 2021, the United States population is 331,449,281. The population of California is 39,466,917. President Biden's proposed budget for fiscal year 2022 is $6 trillion. Put another way, the population of the United States is about one hundred times larger than in 1787. The federal budget is vastly larger. In 1787 there were thirteen states, all on the East Coast. Now the country stretches across the continent and includes Alaska and Hawaii, as well as places as far as Guam.

It is absurd to define the powers of government from the perspective of the original meanings of 1787. The Framers could not have imagined a country as large physically, as populated, or as complex as the United States in 2021.

The need for federal government activity exists on a scale that could not have been conceived when the Constitution was written. A crucial example of that is federal administrative agencies. Although agencies and departments have existed in some form since the beginning of American history, it is only since the late nineteenth century, with the creation of the Interstate Commerce Commission in 1887, that Congress has routinely delegated broad legislative power to executive agencies. Over the next century, Congress created a vast array of federal agencies, including the Federal Communicatons Commission, the Securities and Exchange Commission, the Food and Drug Administration, the Environmental Protection Agency, the Nuclear Regulatory Commission, and many others. It's important to remember that all of these agencies were created out of public need: the Interstate Commerce Commission was needed to rein in the rapacious business practices of railroads and other firms exploiting the country's rapid and massive expansion, the Securities and Exchange Commission to prevent Wall Street from precipitating another Great Depression, the Environmental Protection Agency in response to increasing public alarm about pollution and other environmental damage.

The Constitution does not expressly mention such agencies, and in many ways they are in tension with basic constitutional principles. It is questionable, from an originalist perspective, whether they are constitutional at all. Virtually all of them possess rulemaking power, and their rules have the force of law. This seems to conflict with the notion that Congress alone possesses the federal legislative power. Yet there are many reasons why Congress has delegated broad legislative power to administrative agencies. The technical and legal complexity of many areas creates a need for complex regulations that are better handled by a specialized agency than by Congress. The sheer quantity of regulations exceeds Congress's capacity to manage. There is also a political dimension: delegating legislative power to administrative agencies allows Congress to avoid the political heat that some regulations might engender.[28]

Administrative agencies, however, do not possess only legislative power. They also have the executive power to enforce the regulations they have promulgated and the judicial power to adjudicate violations of their rules. Many agencies employ administrative law judges who hear cases brought by agency officials against those accused of violating the agency's regulations.

These agencies, and their power, arise from the need to govern a country that is exponentially larger and more complex than the drafters of the Constitution could ever have imagined. Originalism

---

is useless here, and efforts to apply it to these issues make effective governance more difficult.

One originalist answer to the constitutional problem posed by administrative agencies is the nondelegation doctrine: the principle that Congress may not delegate its legislative power to the executive branch. The height of the Supreme Court's enforcement of this doctrine came in the mid-1930s, in two decisions that invalidated New Deal legislation. The National Industrial Recovery Act of 1933, a key piece of New Deal legislation, authorized the president to approve "codes of fair competition" developed by boards of various industries. In *Panama Refining Co. v. Ryan,* in 1935, the Court struck down a provision of the act that authorized the president to prohibit the interstate shipment of oil produced in excess of state-imposed production quotas.[29] The Court concluded that the law was an impermissible delegation of legislative power to the president, and it emphasized the lack of any standards in the act to limit the president's discretion.[30]

In *Schechter Poultry Corp. v. United States,* also in 1935, the Court struck down another regulation adopted under the National Industrial Recovery Act: a Live Poultry Code for New York City that had presidential approval.[31] In part, the code required sellers to sell only entire coops of chickens or half coops of chickens and made it illegal for buyers to reject individual chickens. It also regulated employment by requiring collective bargaining, prohibiting child labor, and establishing a forty-hour workweek and a minimum wage.

The Court ruled that the regulation exceeded the scope of Congress's commerce power and was an impermissible delegation of legislative power: "Congress is not permitted to abdicate or to transfer to others the essential legislative function with which it is . . . vested."[32] The Court recognized the need for regulations to deal with the "host of details with which the national legislature cannot deal directly."[33] But "the constant recognition of the necessity and validity of such provisions, and the wide range of administrative authority which has been developed by means of them cannot be allowed to obscure the limitations of the authority to delegate, if our constitutional system is to be maintained."[34]

In the eight-plus decades since *Panama Oil* and *Schechter*, not a single federal law has been declared an impermissible delegation of legislative power. Although these decisions have not been expressly overruled, they have not been followed either. All delegations, no matter how broad, have been upheld. The Court says that when Congress delegates its legislative power it must provide criteria — "intelligible principles" — to guide the agency's exercise of discretion, but it has not struck down any delegation for a lack of criteria.[35] Undoubtedly, this reflects a judicial understanding that broad delegations are necessary in the complex modern world and that the judiciary is ill-equipped to draw meaningful lines.[36]

With the demise of the nondelegation doctrine, the issue arose as to how the power of administrative agencies would be checked and controlled. Congress, of course, could enact a law overturning an agency's rule, but requiring legislative action obviously limits the circumstances in which Congress can or will exercise its checking function.

In the 1930s, which not coincidentally saw a great proliferation of federal administrative agencies, Congress created the "legislative veto" as a check on these agencies' actions. Congress included in statutes provisions authorizing Congress or one of its houses or committees to overturn an agency's action by means less cumbersome than adopting a new law. A typical legislative veto provision authorized Congress to overturn an agency's decision by a resolution of one house of Congress. Other forms of legislative veto allowed Congress to overturn an agency rule by resolution of both houses of Congress or even by action of a congressional committee. Before 1983, more than two hundred federal laws contained legislative veto provisions.[37]

But in *Immigration and Naturalization Service (INS) v. Chadha,* the Supreme Court, in a highly originalist decision, declared the legislative veto unconstitutional.[38] Jagdish Rai Chadha was an East Indian who had been born in Kenya and held a British passport. After his visa expired, he was ordered to show cause as to why he should be allowed to remain in the United States. An immigration judge ruled in his favor and ordered that his deportation be stayed.

The House of Representatives then adopted a resolution overturning this decision and ordering Chadha's deportation. Federal law gave either house of Congress the authority to overturn an INS decision to suspend deportation.[39] Representative Joshua Eilberg, chair of the House Judiciary Subcommittee on Immigration, Citizenship, and International Law, introduced a resolution opposing the granting of citizenship to six individuals, including Chadha, on the ground that they "did not meet [the] statutory requirements, particularly as it relates to hardship."[40]

The Supreme Court declared this legislative veto unconstitutional. Chief Justice Warren Burger's majority opinion, originalist and formalistic, can be described as a syllogism. Its major premise is that Congress may legislate only if there is *bicameralism,* passage by both the House and the Senate, and *presentment,* a bill given to the president to sign or veto. Burger recited the constitutional provisions requiring bicameralism and presentment and quoted from the Federalist Papers as to the importance of these procedures.[41] It was an entirely originalist approach.

The minor premise of the syllogism was that the legislative veto was legislation without bicameralism or presentment. The action "was essentially legislative in purpose and effect" in that it "alter[ed] the legal rights, duties, and relations of persons, including the Attorney General, Executive Branch officials and Chadha."[42] Accordingly, Burger concluded, it was legislation that did not fit into any of the limited situations under the Constitution where one branch of government can act alone.[43]

The conclusion followed inevitably, as it always does in a syllogism: the legislative veto is unconstitutional. Chief Justice Burger expressly rejected the position that the legislative veto was necessary to ensure adequate checks and balances. He was explicit about his originalism: "The choices we discern as having been made in the Constitutional Convention impose burdens on governmental processes that often seem clumsy, inefficient, even unworkable, but those hard choices were consciously made by men who had lived under a form of government that permitted arbitrary governmental acts to go unchecked. There is no support in the Constitution or decisions of this Court for the proposition that the cumbersomeness and delays often encountered in complying with explicit Constitutional standards may be avoided, either by the Congress or the President."[44]

Justice White wrote a strong dissent that emphasized the need for the legislative veto as a check on the broad delegations of legislative power. He explained that although the legislative veto was not contemplated by the Framers of the Constitution, neither were the expansive delegations found in countless statutes creating administrative agencies, and he noted that "without the legislative veto, Congress is faced with a Hobson's choice: either to refrain from delegating the necessary authority, leaving itself with a hopeless task of writing laws with the requisite specificity to cover endless special circumstances across the entire policy landscape, or in the alternative, to abdicate its lawmaking function to the Executive Branch and independent agencies."[45]

There could hardly be a clearer contrast between the two justices' approaches. Burger emphasized the formal structure prescribed in the Constitution for adopting laws and dismissed the functional concern that the legislative veto was essential to check administrative power. White stressed that more than two hundred federal laws contained legislative vetoes, reflecting Congress's judgment that this was an essential tool for checking the exercise of delegated powers. He lamented that the majority in *Chadha* had invalidated "in one fell swoop provisions in more laws enacted by Congress than the Court had cumulatively invalidated in its history."[46]

Justice White is surely correct: it makes no sense to be non-originalist in allowing broad delegations to deal with the issues of modern society but originalist in limiting Congress's ability to check the powers of administrative agencies. I fear, though, that the originalists' response to this inconsistency will soon be something even worse: to revive the non-delegation doctrine and create chaos in essential federal regulation. In a 2019 case, *Gundy v. United States*, the conservative justices clearly signaled that this is coming.[47] The Sex Offender Registration and Notification Act of 2006 (SORNA) makes it a federal crime for a person who has been convicted of a sex crime to cross state lines if he or she has not registered as a sex offender as required by his or her state law. The act left it up to the attorney general to decide if and how the law applies to those convicted before its enactment. The attorney general issued a rule applying the statute to those convicted before the adoption of SORNA.

The year before SORNA was enacted, Herman Gundy pleaded guilty under Maryland law to sexually assaulting a minor. After his release from prison in 2012, he went to live in New York but never registered there as a sex offender. He was convicted under SORNA for failing to register. He argued that Congress unconstitutionally delegated legislative power when it authorized the attorney general to "specify the applicability" of SORNA's registration requirements to pre-act offenders.

The Supreme Court ruled against Gundy in a five-to-three decision without a majority opinion. (There were only eight justices because the case was argued in October 2018, before Justice Kavanaugh had been confirmed to replace Justice Kennedy.) Justice Kagan wrote the plurality opinion, joined by Justices Ginsburg, Breyer, and Sotomayor. She found that the statute contained a sufficient "intelligible principle" to guide the exercise of administrative discretion. But more importantly, she stressed the importance of allowing broad congressional delegations to deal with the needs of a modern, complex society. She wrote: "If SORNA's delegation is unconstitutional, then most of Government is unconstitutional—dependent as Congress is on the need to give discretion to executive officials to implement its programs. Consider again this Court's long-time recognition: 'Congress simply cannot do its job absent an ability to delegate power under broad general directives.' Among the judgments often left to executive officials are ones involving feasibility."[48]

Justice Alito wrote an enigmatic opinion in which he concurred in the judgment but made it clear that he would join an effort to revive the non-delegation doctrine. He wrote: "If a majority of this Court were willing to reconsider the approach we have taken for the past 84 years, I would support that effort. But because a majority is not willing to do that, it would be freakish to single out the provision at issue here for special treatment."[49]

Justice Gorsuch, joined by Roberts and Thomas, wrote a scathing dissent that gives us a sense of where the law is likely to go. He urged an immediate revival of the non-delegation doctrine and premised his argument on what the "framers understood" and the "framers' design."[50]

Since *Gundy*, Justices Kavanaugh and Barrett have joined the Court, and Ginsburg has passed away. There now seems to be a clear majority, maybe even six justices, willing to revive the non-delegation doctrine. But this will cause chaos because, as Justice Kagan observed, hundreds and even thousands of federal laws delegate power to administrative agencies. There is no apparent way to draw a distinction among federal laws and to decide which delegations are permissible and which go too far. It makes little sense to apply the notions of what the Framers thought about delegating power to a government and a society that are vastly larger and more complex than anything James Madison could have possibly imagined. It is absurd to even ask what the original understanding was in 1787 concerning delegating power to large administrative agencies because they were not contemplated at the time.

The First Amendment and New Speech Technology

The Supreme Court first considered how the First Amendment applies to new technology in 1915, in a case about state licensing of movies, *Mutual Film Corporation v. Industrial Commission of Ohio*.[51] Ohio had created a licensing board that had to approve the showing of any film and demanded that all films be submitted for "censoring."[52]

In rejecting the Mutual Film Corporation's challenge to the law, the Court made it clear that freedom of speech does not include movies. The unanimous opinion, written by Justice Joseph McKenna, said: "We need not pause to dilate upon the freedom of opinion and its expression, and whether by speech, writing, or printing. . . . Are moving pictures within the principle, as it is contended they are? They, indeed, may be mediums of thought, but so are many things. So is the theater, the circus, and all other shows and spectacles, and their performances may be thus brought by the like reasoning under the same immunity from repression or supervision as the public press."[53]

The Court said clearly that freedom of expression does not protect movies: "We immediately feel that the argument is wrong or strained which extends the guaranties of free opinion and speech to the multitudinous shows which are advertised on the billboards of our cities and towns, and which . . . seeks to bring motion pictures and other spectacle into practical and legal similitude to a free press and liberty of opinion. . . . The exhibition of moving pictures is a business, pure and simple, originated and conducted for profit, like other spectacles, not to be regarded, nor intended to be . . . part of the press of the country, or as organs of public opinion."[54]

Not until 1952, in *Burstyn v. Wilson,* did the Court hold that movies are protected as a form of speech under the First Amendment.[55] As a result, for much of the twentieth century, films had to be approved by licensing boards before they could be shown. This was clear prior restraint of speech, but it was not limited by the Constitution. Not until 1965 did the Court declare a licensing requirement for movies unconstitutional, and even then it indicated that it would be allowed with proper procedural protections. That case, *Freedman v. Maryland,* involved a Maryland statute that made it unlawful to exhibit a movie without having obtained a license.[56] The Court noted that Maryland's licensing system presented grave dangers for freedom of speech and that such a system was permissible "only if it takes place under procedural safeguards designed to obviate the dangers of . . . censorship."[57] It is stunning that licensing of movies was still allowed even after 1965, even though licensing of speech and press has always been thought to violate the very core of the First Amendment.

Yet from an originalist perspective, the Court's 1915 decision in *Mutual Film Commission* makes sense. The original understanding of the First Amendment obviously did not include protection of movies.

An originalist might respond that the protections for speech and press do not have to be limited to the media that existed in 1791. The problem with this argument is that originalism provides no way to assess the constitutionality of government regulation of media that did not yet exist. It offers no insights, for example, on any of the issues that arise with twentieth- and twenty-first-century media. To pick an example from a half century ago: in *Red Lion Broadcasting Co. v. FCC*, the Court unanimously upheld the constitutionality of the fairness doctrine, which required that broadcast stations present balanced discussion of public issues.[58] The law also provided that when the honesty or character of a person is attacked, he or she must be given notice, a transcript, and an opportunity to answer. Additionally, a station that endorsed a candidate in an election had to provide notice to the opponent and give that opponent a reasonable opportunity to respond.

The Court ruled that the government was justified in regulating broadcast frequencies' use in order to increase the range of voices available to the public. Justice White wrote: "In view of the scarcity of broadcast frequencies, the Government's role in allocating those frequencies, and the legitimate claims of those unable without governmental assistance to gain access to those frequencies for expression of their views, we hold the regulations . . . constitutional."[59]

One can agree or disagree with the Court's decision, but originalism surely provides no way to think about the scarcity of broadcast frequencies. More recently, the Court dealt with social media and the internet in *Packingham v. North Carolina*.[60] North Carolina law makes it a felony for a registered sex offender "to access a commercial social networking Web site where the sex offender knows that the site permits minor children to become members or to create or maintain personal Web pages." When he was twenty-one years old, Lester Packingham was convicted of taking indecent liberties with a minor and became a registered sex offender.

After he got a traffic ticket quashed by a judge, Packingham posted the message "God is Good" on Facebook. He was indicted under the North Carolina law for going on a website where minors can be present, was convicted, and received a suspended sentence. Thousands of other individuals had also been convicted under the same law.

The Court unanimously declared the North Carolina law unconstitutional. Justice Kennedy wrote the majority opinion, and Justice Alito wrote a concurring opinion that was joined by two other justices.

Kennedy began by emphasizing the importance of the internet as a place for speech. He spoke of the "vast democratic forums of the Internet" and of the importance of social media in particular.[61] Seven in ten American adults, he noted, use at least one internet social networking service, and more people are on Facebook than the entire population of North America. Acknowledging the unique importance of social media for free speech, he warned that "the Court must exercise extreme caution before suggesting that the First

Amendment provides scant protection for access to vast networks in that medium."[62]

Kennedy went on to say that even if the North Carolina law were assumed to be content-neutral, it still was unconstitutional and vastly overbroad. It would deny individuals access not just to Facebook but to washingtonpost.com, Amazon, and WebMD. He argued that the state could have written a narrower law, such as one that prevented registered sex offenders from having contact with minors over social media. "In sum, to foreclose access to social media altogether is to prevent the user from engaging in the legitimate exercise of First Amendment rights."[63] What makes this decision important is Justice Kennedy's strong language about protecting the internet as a medium of communication.

How could an originalist possibly analyze this case? The world in which the First Amendment was proposed and ratified contained nothing remotely like the internet or social media. And the Court will surely confront other questions concerning government regulation of speech over the internet. It is inherently different from any medium that existed in 1791 in that it gives virtually every person the ability to quickly reach a huge audience. This is a great benefit, but it also gives people the capacity to do great harm. Originalism provides no useful answers. It is therefore not surprising that originalist justices tend to ignore their constitutional theory in free speech cases. To return to the example at the beginning of this chapter, Justice Scalia's finding that violent video games are protected speech had no basis in the original understandings of the First Amendment.[64] How could it? Even if we could somehow explain the video game business — and the internet, and computers, and electricity, and signal transmission over metal wires — to James Madison or Patrick Henry or the New Jersey state ratifying convention, how could we possibly get them to grasp why the question was important?

The abhorrence problem and the modernity problem arise because changes in our society—in our basic values, in technology, in the nation's size and complexity—have made originalism unworkable as a method of constitutional interpretation. Sometimes, originalists try to have their cake and eat it, too: they avoid unacceptable outcomes by reading constitutional provisions in an abstract way, which they then label "originalism" even though it is not. But often, when it does not yield the results they want, they create yet another problem by abandoning their theory.

Chapter 7

THE HYPOCRISY PROBLEM

The main argument in support of originalism is that it constrains justices and judges, so that judicial decisions do not simply echo the values of whoever is on the bench. But this argument has a critical flaw: originalists often abandon the method when it fails to give them the results they want. Conservative justices use originalism when it justifies conservative decisions, but they become non-originalist when doing so serves their ideological agenda. This undermines any claim that originalism actually constrains judging and suggests instead that it is not a theory of judging at all but only a rhetorical ploy to make it appear that decisions are based on something other than political ideology.

To illustrate this, I will focus on four examples: the invalidation of a key provision of the Voting Rights Act, the Eleventh Amendment and sovereign immunity, the right of corporations to spend unlimited sums in election campaigns, and affirmative action programs. I chose these examples because of their importance in constitutional law and society. They clearly show how ready originalists are to abandon originalism to achieve conservative results.

I also chose these examples because they come from four very different areas of constitutional law. I am not saying, of course, that originalists never allow their methodology to lead to results contrary to their conservative ideology. But in crucial areas, where the conservative ideological position is clear and strongly held, that ideology, not the original meaning, controls these justices' rulings.

Shelby County v. Holder

The United States has a long, disgraceful history of discrimination against Black voters. After the Civil War, the Fourteenth Amendment was ratified in 1868; it includes a provision that no state may deny any person equal protection of the laws. The Fifteenth Amendment, ratified two years later, explicitly addressed the problem of race discrimination in voting. It states: "The right of citizens of the United States to vote shall not be denied or abridged by the United States or by any State on account of race, color, or previous condition of servitude." Section 2 of the Amendment authorizes Congress to adopt laws to enforce it and states: "The Congress shall have the power to enforce this article by appropriate legislation."

As a result of these amendments and Reconstruction, more than a half million African American men in the South became voters in the 1870s. (Women did not get the right to vote until the Nineteenth Amendment was ratified in 1920.) There was a dramatic effort to enfranchise Black men. In Mississippi, where former slaves made up more than half of the population, the state elected two Black United States senators and a number of Black state officials, including a lieutenant governor.[1]

As a result of the compromise that gave Rutherford B. Hayes the presidency in 1876, Reconstruction ended and northern troops withdrew from the South. Southern states quickly adopted laws to deny rights to former slaves and to segregate every aspect of life. They also enacted many laws designed to keep Blacks from voting.[2] Georgia initiated the poll tax – a fee one had to pay in order to vote – in 1871 and made it cumulative in 1877, meaning that citizens had to pay all back taxes before they could vote. Soon, every southern state had a poll tax. Georgia's poll tax is estimated to have reduced turnout by 16 to 28 percent, and Black turnout by half.[3]

Southern states also adopted literacy tests, requiring that a person seeking to register to vote had to read and explain a section of the state constitution to a county clerk. The clerk, who was always white, had discretion to decide whether the person was sufficiently literate. This excluded almost all Black men from voting because many could not read; for those who could, the clerk could still deem their literacy inadequate.[4] "Grandfather clauses" made those whose grandfathers were qualified to vote before the Civil War exempt from the literacy tests. This, of course, benefitted only white citizens.

These restrictions worked. In Mississippi, the percentage of Black voting-age men registered to vote fell from over 90 percent during Reconstruction to less than 6 percent in 1892.[5] Beyond the laws, there was intimidation directed at African Americans who tried to register to vote. By 1940, just 3 percent of voting-age Black men and women in the South were registered.[6] In Mississippi, fewer than 1 percent were registered.

The civil rights movement fought to combat race discrimination in many areas, including Black voter registration. Still, in 1964, only about 43 percent of adult Black men and women in the South were registered to vote.[7] In Alabama, only 23 percent were registered, and Mississippi had registered less than 7 percent of its voting-age Black citizens.[8]

The key change in voting access was the Voting Rights Act of 1965. Section 2 of this act prohibits voting practices or procedures that discriminate on the basis of race or against certain language minority groups. Under the 1982 amendments to section 2, the act is violated by state or local laws that have the effect of disadvantaging minority voters – intent to discriminate is not required. Both private citizens and the federal government can bring lawsuits to challenge state or local actions that are alleged to violate section 2.

But in passing the Voting Rights Act, Congress realized that allowing lawsuits to challenge election procedures was not adequate to stop discrimination in voting. Litigation is expensive and time consuming. Congress was aware that southern states could invent new ways of disenfranchising minority voters faster than these measures could be challenged, litigated, and struck down. Section 5 of the Voting Rights Act was adopted to prevent such actions.

Section 5 applies only to jurisdictions with a history of race discrimination in voting. It requires that the jurisdiction get preapproval – termed "preclearance" – of any attempt to change "any voting qualification or prerequisite to voting, or standard, practice, or procedure with respect to voting" in any covered jurisdiction.[9] The preapproval must come either from the attorney general of the United States, through an administrative procedure in the Department of Justice, or from a three-judge federal court in the District of Columbia through a request for a declaratory judgment.

In *South Carolina v. Katzenbach*, the Supreme Court upheld the constitutionality of section 5. Chief Justice Warren's majority opinion spoke of the "blight of racial discrimination in voting."[10] The Court found that section 5 was a constitutional exercise of Congress's power to enforce the Fifteenth Amendment. Section 4(B) of the act provides the formula that determines which jurisdictions are required to get preclearance.

Congress repeatedly extended section 5: for five years in 1970, for seven years in 1975, and for twenty-five years in 1982. In 1982, Congress revised section 4(B) and the method for determining which jurisdictions were required to obtain preclearance. After each of these reauthorizations, the Supreme Court again upheld the constitutionality of sections 4(B) and 5.[11]

These provisions were scheduled to expire again in 2007. In 2005–6, the House and Senate Judiciary Committees held twenty-one hearings, listened to ninety witnesses, and compiled a record of more than fifteen thousand pages. Representative Sensenbrenner, a Republican from Wisconsin and the chair of the House Judiciary Committee, described this record as "one of the most extensive considerations of any piece of legislation that the United States Congress has dealt with in the 27 1/2 years that I have been honored to serve as a Member of this body."[12]

Congress then voted overwhelmingly—98–0 in the Senate and 390–33 in the House—to extend section 5 for twenty-five years. It did not change section 4(B) or section 5. Congress expressly concluded that voting discrimination persisted in the covered jurisdictions and that without section 5, "minority citizens will be deprived of the opportunity to exercise their right to vote, or will have their votes diluted, undermining the significant gains made by minorities in the last 40 years."[13]

The record before Congress supported this conclusion. For example, between 1982 and 2006, the section 5 preclearance requirement blocked more than 700 discriminatory changes in election systems in covered jurisdictions.[14] Another 205 changes were withdrawn. Countless potential changes were not adopted because of

—

the recognition that preclearance was unlikely. The continued discrimination is further evidenced by 650 successful court challenges under section 2 of the Voting Rights Act in the covered jurisdictions. Professor Ellen Katz undertook extensive studies in which she found that covered jurisdictions have only 25 percent of the country's population but account for 56 percent of the successful suits under section 2.[15]

Nor is racial discrimination in voting over. Before the 2012 elections, of the twelve states with the largest Hispanic populations, seven adopted restrictive voting laws.[16] Of the ten states with the largest African American populations, five adopted restrictive voting laws.[17] In 2021 and 2022, we are seeing another flurry of laws to restrict voting in such states as Georgia, Florida, and Texas.

Despite the extensive record supporting preclearance, in *Shelby County v. Holder,* the Supreme Court declared section 4(B) of the Voting Rights Act unconstitutional.[18] This is the provision that determines which jurisdictions must get preclearance. Without section 4(B), section 5 is meaningless: no jurisdictions need preclearance.

Shelby County, Alabama, is a jurisdiction in a state with a long history of race discrimination in voting. Because of this history, it is covered by section 5. Shelby County challenged the constitutionality of these provisions of the Voting Rights Act, losing in both the district court and the federal court of appeals. The United States Court of Appeals for the District of Columbia Circuit, in a two-to-one decision, concluded that Congress found "widespread and persistent racial discrimination in voting in covered jurisdictions" and that section 5's "disparate geographic coverage is sufficiently related to the problem that it targets."[19]

But the Supreme Court, voting five to four, held section 4(B) unconstitutional and thereby nullified section 5 because it applies only to jurisdictions covered under section 4(B). It was the first time since the nineteenth century that the Court invalidated a federal civil rights statute. Chief Justice Roberts, writing for the Court, stressed that the formula in section 4(B), last modified in 1982, rests on data from the 1960s and the 1970s and that race discrimination in voting has changed since then. "Nearly 50 years later," he wrote, "things have changed dramatically. Shelby County contends that the preclearance requirement, even without regard to its disparate coverage, is now unconstitutional. Its arguments have a good deal of force. In the covered jurisdictions, voter turnout and registration rates now approach parity. Blatantly discriminatory evasions of federal decrees are rare. And minority candidates hold office at unprecedented levels. The tests and devices that blocked access to the ballot have been forbidden nationwide for over 40 years."[20] Thus, "coverage today is based on decades-old data and eradicated practices."[21]

Roberts pointed to the intrusion on the covered states, noting that they could not exercise the power to choose how to hold elections but instead "must beseech the Federal Government for permission to implement laws that they would otherwise have the right to enact and execute on their own, subject of course to any injunction in a § 2 action."[22] He also emphasized that sections 4(B) and 5, by requiring only some states to get preclearance, violated the principle of equal state sovereignty. "Not only do States retain sovereignty under the Constitution, there is also a 'fundamental principle of *equal* sovereignty' among the States. . . . Despite the tradition of equal sovereignty, the Act applies to only nine States (and several additional counties)."[23]

Justice Ginsburg's dissent, one of her most famous opinions, was joined by Justices Breyer, Sotomayor, and Kagan. The dissent emphasized that race discrimination in voting remains and was documented and acknowledged by Congress, and argued that the Court should defer to the judgment and exercise of power by Congress. Ginsburg wrote:

> In the Court's view, the very success of § 5 of the Voting Rights Act demands its dormancy. Congress was of another mind. Recognizing that large progress has been made, Congress determined, based on a voluminous record, that the scourge of discrimination was not yet extirpated. The question this case presents is who decides whether, as currently operative, § 5 remains justifiable, this Court, or a Congress charged with the obligation to enforce the post–Civil War Amendments "by appropriate legislation." With overwhelming support in both Houses, Congress concluded that, for two prime reasons, § 5 should continue in force, unabated. First, continuance would facilitate completion of the impressive gains thus far made; and second, continuance would guard against backsliding. Those assessments were well within Congress' province to make and should elicit this Court's unstinting approbation.[24]

What is most curious about the Court's majority opinion is that the Court never made it clear which constitutional provision or principle it thought section 4(B) of the Voting Rights Act violated. That Congress relied on old data does not make the law unconstitutional, especially given that it held exhaustive hearings in which it found continued discrimination in voting, particularly in the covered jurisdictions. The Court said that section 4(B) of the Voting Rights Act is unconstitutional because it fails to treat all the states the same, a concept the Court terms the principle of "equal state sovereignty." This is the only constitutional principle that the Court found violated.

But it is impossible to arrive at this principle from an originalist perspective. The text of the Constitution does not mention it. Nor can the original meaning of the Fourteenth and Fifteenth Amendments be seen as embodying such a requirement for equal state sovereignty. The Congress that ratified the Fourteenth and Fifteenth Amendments imposed Reconstruction on the South, literally creating military rule over former rebel states. It is hard to imagine a clearer instance of Congress treating some states differently from others. In fact, countless federal laws — now and throughout American history — treat some states differently from others.[25] The five most conservative justices, who regularly espouse the need for adherence to the text and to original meaning, invented a constitutional right for state governments that appears nowhere in the text and is contrary to the original understanding of the Fourteenth Amendment.

The Court's decision is having the predicted effect of encouraging race discrimination in voting. Soon after it was adopted, Texas and North Carolina put into place election systems that had been denied preclearance because of their discriminatory effects on minority voters. Other states quickly followed. In a recent voting rights case, *Brnovich v. Democratic National Committee,* Justice Kagan noted, "Although causation is hard to establish definitively, those post *Shelby County* changes appear to have reduced minority participation in the next election cycle. The most comprehensive study available found that in areas freed from Section 5 review, white turnout remained the same, but 'minority participation dropped by 2.1 percentage points' — a stark reversal in direction from prior elections. The results, said the scholar who crunched the numbers, 'provide early evidence that the Shelby ruling may jeopardize decades of voting rights progress.' "[26] In 2021, a wave of restrictive voting laws were adopted among states that would have had to get preclearance before *Shelby County.*

147

Chief Justice Roberts, in an opinion striking down a federal campaign finance law, wrote that "there is no right more basic in our democracy than the right to participate in electing our political leaders."[27] This certainly was the original meaning of the Fourteenth and especially Fifteenth Amendments, but it was not the majority's view in *Shelby County*. That decision was purely ideological and had no basis in the original meaning of anything.

The Eleventh Amendment and Sovereign Immunity

The Eleventh Amendment to the Constitution says, "The Judicial power of the United States shall not be construed to extend to any suit in law or equity, commenced or prosecuted against one of the United States by Citizens of another State, or by Citizens or Subjects of any foreign state." The text is clear: a federal court cannot hear a suit against a state *by citizens of other states or foreign countries*. It says absolutely nothing about limiting suits against a state by its own citizens.[28] As explained below, the original meaning is also evident: this provision was meant to preclude a suit against a state where the federal courts had jurisdiction only because the plaintiffs were from a state other than the one they were suing. It strikes out two clauses in Article III, section 2, of the Constitution that authorized suits against states by citizens of other states and of foreign countries. The Eleventh Amendment does not affect the provision of Article III, section 2, that allows federal courts to hear federal questions such as constitutional claims. Nothing in the text of this provision or the intent behind it supports construing it to bar such suits against state governments.

But the conservatives on the Supreme Court have interpreted the Eleventh Amendment to preclude virtually all suits against state governments, including claims that a state government has violated the Constitution. The Court has even held that sovereign immunity bars suits against state governments in *state* courts without their consent, though nothing whatsoever in the Constitution supports this view.[29]

In interpreting the Eleventh Amendment, the conservative justices have abandoned both textualism and originalism to implement a vision of protecting governments from suit, at the expense of accountability and of remedying constitutional violations. This is one of many instances where originalists abandon their methodology when it leads to results they do not want.

Article III of the Constitution defines the federal judicial power in terms of nine categories of cases and controversies. Two of the clauses of Article III, section 2, deal specifically with suits against state governments. These provisions permit suits "between a State and Citizens of another state" and "between a State . . . and foreign . . . Citizens." These are the clauses the Eleventh Amendment repealed.

A key dispute is whether Article III was meant to override the sovereign immunity that might have kept states from being sued in state courts. As Justice David Souter observed: "The 1787 draft in fact said nothing on the subject, and it was this very silence that occasioned some, though apparently not widespread, dispute among the Framers and others over whether ratification of the Constitution would preclude a State sued in federal court from asserting sovereign immunity as it could have done on any matter of nonfederal law litigated in its own courts."[30]

There is no record of any debate about this issue or these clauses at the Constitutional Convention. At the state ratification conventions, however, the question of suits against state governments in federal court received a great deal of attention. States had incurred substantial debts, especially during the Revolutionary War, and there was a great fear that suits could be brought against the states in federal court to collect on these debts.

The dispute over whether sovereign immunity survived Article III was presented to the Supreme Court soon after the Constitution was ratified. The Judiciary Act of 1789 gave the Supreme Court original jurisdiction in cases between states and citizens of another state or citizens of foreign states. In fact, the first case filed in the United States Supreme Court involved a suit by Dutch creditors trying to collect on Revolutionary War debts owed to them by Maryland.[31] The Court, however, did not address the relation of Article III to sovereign immunity until 1794, in *Chisholm v. Georgia*.[32] This decision is particularly important because the Eleventh Amendment was ratified specifically to overrule the Court's holding in *Chisholm*.

Chisholm involved an attempt by the estate of a South Carolina citizen, Robert Farquhar, to recover money owed him by the State of Georgia. Farquhar, a South Carolina citizen, had supplied materials to Georgia during the Revolutionary War. Although the Georgia legislature appropriated the funds, the Georgia commissaries refused to pay for the purchases. After Farquhar died, Alexander Chisholm, the executor of his estate, sued Georgia to recover the money. Chisholm, also a South Carolinian, sued in the Supreme Court based on the provision in the Judiciary Act of 1789 that created original jurisdiction for suits against a state by citizens of other states.

Chisholm was represented before the Court by Edmund Randolph, who was also serving at the time as attorney general of the United States. Randolph, who had been a delegate at the Constitutional Convention, argued that Article III of the Constitution clearly permitted suits against states by citizens of other states. The State of

Georgia chose not to appear, believing that federal courts had no jurisdiction over it unless it consented to be sued.

The Court, in a four-to-one decision, ruled in Chisholm's favor. Announcing their opinions seriatim, four justices seemed to have easily concluded that Article III clearly authorized suits like Chisholm's. Although later decisions by the Court criticized this view of Article III and the ruling in *Chisholm*, the four justices in the majority in *Chisholm* had impeccable credentials for discussing the intent behind constitutional provisions. Justices John Blair and James Wilson had been delegates to the Constitutional Convention. Justice William Cushing had presided over the state ratification convention in Massachusetts, and Chief Justice John Jay had been a delegate to the New York ratification convention and was one of the authors of the Federalist Papers.[33]

Only Justice James Iredell dissented in *Chisholm*. He argued that the Judiciary Act did not specifically authorize suits against states and that such suits were not permitted against the government in English common law. He concluded that the general language of Article III was insufficient to authorize such a suit against the State of Georgia without its consent.

State legislators and governors were outraged by the Court's decision in *Chisholm v. Georgia*. Georgia adopted a statute declaring that anyone attempting to enforce the decision was "hereby declared to be guilty of a felony, and shall suffer death, without the benefit of clergy by being hanged."[34] The intense reaction to *Chisholm* is reflected in the speed with which the nation adopted a constitutional amendment to overturn it. The Supreme Court decided *Chisholm* on February 14, 1794. By March 4, less than three weeks later, both houses of Congress had approved the Eleventh Amendment. The requisite number of states ratified it within a year, although it was

—

three more years before the president declared it to have been properly ratified. Scholars like William Fletcher make a compelling case that this provision was meant to keep states from being sued based on diversity of citizenship, not to bar constitutional or other federal claims.[35] The text of Article III clearly supports this conclusion.

Article III of the Constitution gives the federal courts jurisdiction over cases based on either the content of the litigation (such as questions involving federal law, known as "federal question jurisdiction") or the identity of the parties (such as suits between citizens of different states, known as "diversity jurisdiction"). One set of categories assigned to the federal courts is "Cases, in Law and Equity, arising under this Constitution, the Laws of the United States, and Treaties made, or which shall be made, under their Authority." This is the provision that authorizes federal question jurisdiction. A later passage of Article III, section 2, allows for "Controversies . . . between a State and Citizens of another state."[36] This is an authorization for suits against a state based on diversity of citizenship.

The language of the Eleventh Amendment modifies this latter provision. The amendment simply states: "The Judicial Power of the United States shall not be construed to extend to any suit . . . against one of the United States by Citizens of another state." Because *Chisholm* involved only this latter part of Article III, it makes sense to view the Eleventh Amendment as restricting only diversity suits against state governments. From an originalist perspective, the amendment does not bar suits against states based on other parts of Article III. Most notably, it says nothing about suits based on federal question jurisdiction. Thus all claims of state violations of the Constitution or federal laws should be able to be heard in federal courts.

But in countless five-to-four decisions, the conservative justices — including those who identify as originalists — have read the Eleventh Amendment as barring virtually all suits against state governments in federal court, including those claiming violations of the Constitution and federal law.[37] Justice Scalia declared that the Eleventh Amendment reflects a "broad constitutional principle of sovereign immunity," an abstract and non-originalist reading.[38] That is not what the amendment says. Furthermore, as Judge Fletcher and others have argued in detail, it is not what was understood or intended when the Eleventh Amendment was ratified.

Moreover, although the Eleventh Amendment speaks only of restrictions on the federal judicial power, in *Alden v. Maine* the Court held that state governments cannot be sued in *state* court without their consent.[39] Probation officers in Maine sued the state for overtime pay they claimed they were owed under the federal Fair Labor Standards Act. The suit was initially filed in federal court but was dismissed based on the Eleventh Amendment, and the probation officers then sued in Maine state court. The Supreme Court, in a five-to-four decision, ruled that the state had sovereign immunity and could not be sued in state court, even on a federal claim, without its consent. Justice Kennedy, writing for the majority, acknowledged that the Constitution and its Framers were silent about the ability to sue state governments in state courts. But he found it unthinkable that the states would have ratified the Constitution had they thought that it made them subject to suit without their consent. "We hold," he wrote, "that the powers delegated to Congress under Article I of the United States Constitution do not include the power to subject nonconsenting States to private suits for damages in state courts."[40] In one of the more astounding passages in the United States Reports, Kennedy declared:

The constitutional privilege of a State to assert its sovereign immunity in its own courts does not confer upon the State a concomitant right to disregard the Constitution or valid federal law. The States and their officers are bound by obligations imposed by the Constitution and by federal statutes that comport with the constitutional design. We are unwilling to assume the States will refuse to honor the Constitution or obey the binding laws of the United States. The good faith of the States thus provides an important assurance that "[t]his Constitution, and the Laws of the United States which shall be made in Pursuance thereof . . . shall be the supreme Law of the Land."[41]

Would the Court in the 1950s or the 1960s have said that there is no need to enforce desegregation orders because there can be trust in the "good faith of the States"? How could any originalist believe that the original meaning of the Constitution was that federal courts did not need to act to ensure the supremacy of federal law because they could trust in the good faith of state governments? Yet originalist Justices Scalia and Thomas both joined in Kennedy's opinion.

In *Federal Maritime Commission v. South Carolina State Ports Authority,* the Supreme Court held that states cannot be named as defendants in federal administrative agency proceedings.[42] A cruise ship company brought a claim against a state agency in the Federal Maritime Commission, claiming that it had been discriminated against in violation of federal maritime law. The Court, in a five-to-four decision, held that such actions are barred by sovereign immunity. In the majority opinion, Justice Thomas wrote that the "preeminent purpose" of sovereign immunity is to protect the "dignity" of state governments and that this dignity would be impermissibly offended by allowing states to be named as defendants in agency proceedings without their consent.[43] Where is that found in the Constitution, or in its original meaning?

In January 2019, I argued *Franchise Tax Board v. Hyatt* in the Supreme Court.[44] The issue was whether a state could be sued in another state court. Forty years earlier, in *Nevada v. Hall,* the Court had said that such suits are permitted.[45] Relying on *Nevada v. Hall,* my client, Gilbert Hyatt, sued the Franchise Tax Board of California in Nevada state court for what he claimed was egregious harassing conduct. Hyatt, an inventor, had moved from California to Nevada in 1991. Employees of the Franchise Tax Board, believing he had not actually moved, went to Nevada and broke into his house, sent letters with private information, including his Social Security number, and spread false rumors about him. The state court jury ruled in favor of Hyatt and awarded him $385 million in damages. After decades of proceedings and two prior trips to the Supreme Court, the judgment had been reduced to $100,000.

But the Supreme Court, in a five-to-four decision, overruled *Nevada v. Hall* and held that a state government cannot be sued in another state's court. Justice Thomas wrote the opinion for the Court. Repeatedly at oral argument, justices had asked the attorney for the Franchise Tax Board where the Constitution says anything about limiting the ability of a state to provide remedies for its citizens who are injured by another state. Thomas's opinion said that the absence of a constitutional provision creating such sovereign immunity did not matter: "Hyatt argues that we should find no right to sovereign immunity in another State's courts because no constitutional provision explicitly grants that immunity. But this is precisely the type of 'ahistorical literalism' that we have rejected when 'interpreting the scope of the States' sovereign immunity.' "[46]

It is stunning to see an originalist justice dismissing a focus on the Constitution's text and original understanding as "ahistorical literalism." Nor does history support Justice Thomas and the Court's majority. In *Nevada v. Hall,* when it allowed suits against states in other states' courts, the Court relied on precedent from the earliest days of the Republic: Chief Justice John Marshall's 1812 decision in *The Schooner Exchange v. McFaddon.*[47] *The Schooner Exchange* had been seen throughout American history as establishing the principle that a sovereign has no legal obligation to grant immunity to other sovereigns in its own courts.[48]

Sovereign immunity cannot be found in the Constitution from an originalist perspective. Justice Souter, reviewing the Eleventh Amendment's history in a majority opinion in 1987, rightly observed that "at most, . . . the historical materials show that . . . the intentions of the Constitution's Framers and Ratifiers were ambiguous."[49]

There is almost no evidence that the generation of the Framers thought sovereign immunity was fundamental in the sense of being unalterable. Whether one looks at the period before the framing, to the ratification controversies, or to the early republican era, the evidence is the same. Some Framers thought sovereign immunity was an obsolete royal prerogative inapplicable in a republic; some thought sovereign immunity was a common-law power defeasible, like other common-law rights, by statute; and perhaps a few thought, in keeping with a natural law view distinct from the common-law conception, that immunity was inherent in a sovereign because the body that made a law could not logically be bound by it. Natural law thinking on the part of a doubtful few will not, however, support the Court's position.[50]

The Court's more recent sovereign immunity decisions cannot be understood as anything other than a value choice by the conservative justices to protect state governments from being sued. The Court has invented a constitutional right of state governments that has no basis in the Constitution's text or original meaning and that precludes suits against states for remedies when they violate the Constitution. To create this right, the originalist justices, who were in the majority in all of these rulings, have abandoned their originalism.

Campaign Finance and *Citizens United*

Few Supreme Court decisions in history have affected our political system as profoundly as *Citizens United v. Federal Election Commission*. In *Citizens United,* the Court held that the First Amendment protects the right of corporations to spend unlimited amounts of money to support or oppose candidates in election campaigns.[51] Like the other examples in this chapter, *Citizens United* was a five-to-four decision split along ideological lines, with the conservative justices, including the originalists, in the majority. But it is risible to say that the original meaning of the First Amendment was to safeguard a right of corporations to spend unlimited money in election campaigns. Those who drafted and ratified the amendment could not have imagined campaign spending as it exists in the twenty-first century, let alone the wealth of modern corporations and their ability to spend that wealth to influence elections.

The Bipartisan Campaign Finance Reform Act of 2002, also known as the McCain-Feingold Act, came after years of hearings and debate. Congress sought to close loopholes and solve problems that had developed with campaign finance. It had long prohibited corporations and unions from contributing money directly to candidates

---

for federal office, but corporations and unions had recently found ways to get around this, including by taking out issue advertisements that did not expressly mention any candidate. The limits could be circumvented just by omitting the magic words "Elect Jane Doe" or "Vote for John Smith." As the Court noted in *McConnell v. Federal Election Commission,* "corporations and unions spent hundreds of millions of dollars of their general funds to pay for these ads, and those expenditures, like soft-money donations to the political parties, were unregulated."[52]

The McCain-Feingold Act applied campaign finance law to broadcast advertisements by corporations and unions that mentioned a federal candidate and were targeted to the relevant electorate within thirty days of a primary election or sixty days of a general election. It prohibited such "electioneering communication" by corporations and unions being paid for from their treasuries. In addition, coordinated electioneering communication had to be treated as contributions to candidates or parties.

In *McConnell v. Federal Election Commission,* the Supreme Court voted five to four to uphold these provisions as constitutionally permissible ways of preventing circumvention of federal campaign law. But seven years later, in *Citizens United,* it overruled this aspect of *McConnell* and held that restrictions on independent expenditures by corporations violated the First Amendment.[53] In a five-to-four decision, with Justice Kennedy writing for the conservative majority, the Court held that corporations and unions have free speech rights and that limits on independent expenditures are unconstitutional restrictions of core political speech. Kennedy wrote: "[T]he Government may not suppress political speech on the basis of the speaker's corporate identity. No sufficient governmental interest justifies limits on the political speech of nonprofit or for-profit corporations."[54]

What changed in those seven years? Justice O'Connor, who had been in the majority in *McConnell,* was replaced by Justice Alito, who joined the dissenters from *McConnell* to overrule it. Chief Justice Roberts also joined the Court in the interim, but he voted the same way as the man he replaced, Chief Justice Rehnquist.

In concluding that restrictions on independent expenditures by corporations and unions violated the First Amendment, the Court stated: "The censorship we now confront is vast in its reach. The Government has 'muffle[d] the voices that best represent the most significant segments of the economy.' And 'the electorate [has been] deprived of information, knowledge and opinion vital to its function.' By suppressing the speech of manifold corporations, both for-profit and nonprofit, the Government prevents their voices and viewpoints from reaching the public and advising voters on which persons or entities are hostile to their interests."[55]

Justice Stevens wrote a long, vehement dissent, which was joined by Justices Ginsburg, Breyer, and Sotomayor.[56] The dissent rejected the majority's premise that corporations are entitled to the same First Amendment rights as individuals. Stevens argued that the First Amendment was never intended to protect corporate speech:[57]

In the context of election to public office, the distinction between corporate and human speakers is significant. Although they make enormous contributions to our society, corporations are not actually members of it. They cannot vote or run for office. Because they may be managed and controlled by nonresidents, their interests may conflict in fundamental respects with the interests of eligible voters. The financial resources, legal structure, and instrumental orientation of corporations raise legitimate concerns about their role in the electoral process. Our lawmakers have a compelling constitutional basis, if not also a democratic duty, to take measures designed to guard against the potentially deleterious effects of corporate spending in local and national races.[58]

Stevens stressed that even under the McCain-Feingold Act, corporations and unions could engage in campaign spending through political action committees. The limits on spending directly from corporate and union treasuries was justified, he argued, to prevent corruption and the appearance of corruption, to counter the distorting effects of corporate wealth in elections, and to protect corporate shareholders from having their funds spent against their beliefs. He concluded his dissent by declaring:

> At bottom, the Court's opinion is . . . a rejection of the common
> sense of the American people, who have recognized a need to
> prevent corporations from undermining self-government since
> the founding, and who have fought against the distinctive
> corrupting potential of corporate electioneering since the days of
> Theodore Roosevelt. It is a strange time to repudiate that com-
> mon sense. While American democracy is imperfect, few outside
> the majority of this Court would have thought its flaws included
> a dearth of corporate money in politics.[59]

Which approach, the majority's or the dissent's, seems more closely aligned with originalism? The answer is clear: there is no way, from an originalist perspective, to say that corporations have a First Amendment right to spend unlimited sums in election campaigns. Campaign spending simply did not exist in 1791, when the First Amendment was adopted. There is no plausible argument that the original meaning of freedom of speech was not only that corporations have the free speech rights of individuals – something the Court did not recognize until 1978, in *First National Bank of Boston v. Bellotti* – but that this includes a right to spend freely from the corporate treasury to elect or defeat political candidates.[60] Justice Stevens made this point in his dissenting opinion in *Citizens United*, noting that the majority "makes only a perfunctory attempt to ground its analysis in the principles or understandings of those who drafted and ratified the Amendment. Perhaps this is because there is not a scintilla of evidence to support the notion that anyone believed it would preclude regulatory distinctions based on the corporate form. To the extent that the Framers' views are discernible and relevant to the disposition of this case, they would appear to cut strongly against the majority's position."[61]

Justice Scalia responded that there was no exclusion in the First Amendment for corporations. He wrote: "The lack of a textual exception for speech by corporations cannot be explained on the ground that such organizations did not exist or did not speak. To the contrary, colleges, towns and cities, religious institutions, and guilds had long been organized as corporations at common law and under the King's charter. . . . [B]oth corporations and voluntary associations actively petitioned the Government and expressed their views in newspapers and pamphlets."[62]

But corporations as they exist today were unknown in 1791. Far more important, corporate campaign spending in elections was unknown. Nor was there any analogous form of expression in existence that might justify an originalist finding that it deserves constitutional protection. Justice Scalia suggests nothing to the contrary. Neither he nor anyone else can justify the decision in *Citizens United* based on the original understanding of free speech. Of course, he could try to explain his position under the First Amendment's abstract goal of facilitating political speech. But once that step is taken, anything can be justified under originalism, and it becomes indistinguishable from non-originalism.

Affirmative Action

One more example – a particularly powerful one of originalists abandoning originalism when it does not serve their ideological goals – is affirmative action. The originalists who have been on the Court, like Justices Scalia and Thomas, are fervent in their opposition to affirmative action. Never have they voted to uphold an affirmative action program. This position, of course, is completely consistent with the strong conservative opposition to affirmative action, but it is not sustainable under originalism.

In *Grutter v. Bollinger* (2003), which upheld colleges' and universities' use of affirmative action to achieve diversity, Justice Thomas wrote an impassioned dissent arguing against affirmative action, joined by Justice Scalia.[63] Thomas concluded his dissent by declaring: "For the immediate future, however, the majority has placed its *imprimatur* on a practice that can only weaken the principle of equality embodied in the Declaration of Independence and the Equal Protection Clause. 'Our Constitution is color-blind, and neither knows nor tolerates classes among citizens.' "[64] The quoted line came from Justice Harlan's famous dissent in *Plessy v. Ferguson*.[65]

Scalia likewise was adamant in his opposition to affirmative action. In a 1995 case, for example, he wrote:

In my view, government can never have a "compelling interest" in discriminating on the basis of race in order to "make up" for past racial discrimination in the opposite direction. Individuals who have been wronged by unlawful racial discrimination should be made whole; but under our Constitution there can be no such thing as either a creditor or a debtor race. . . . To pursue the concept of racial entitlement – even for the most admirable and benign of purposes – is to reinforce and preserve for future mischief the way of thinking that produced race slavery, race privilege and race hatred. In the eyes of government, we are just one race here. It is American.[66]

What is striking, however, is that from an originalist perspective, affirmative action is clearly constitutional. There is no basis for concluding that those who wrote the Constitution, or who drafted and ratified the Fourteenth Amendment, ever meant to create a requirement for color blindness. Professor Stephen Siegel thoroughly examined the constitutional history and concluded that originalism provides no grounds for limiting the federal government's ability to enact programs to benefit racial minorities.[67] He argues that "when interpreted through originalist jurisprudence, nothing in the Founding era Constitution limits federal power to enact race-based classifications. . . . Under the Founding era Constitution the federal government has plenary power (within its limited jurisdiction) to enact color-conscious laws, both invidious and benign."[68]

Perhaps more importantly for understanding the Civil War Amendments, Siegel shows that "the Reconstruction era Congresses produced a vast array of laws treating blacks preferentially, indicating its view that federal affirmative action violated no constitutional norms."[69] One of the most significant examples was the Freedmen's Bureau, which implemented a massive federal assistance program. Originally established in March 1865 for one year, the bureau was renewed by subsequent Congresses and operated until July 1872. It was seen at the time as a program primarily intended to benefit Blacks. As Siegel notes: "While active, the Bureau provided its charges with clothing, food, fuel, and medicine; it built, staffed, and operated their schools and hospitals; and it wrote their leases and labor contracts, rented them land, and interceded in legal proceedings to protect their rights. The Bureau even provided courts in unreconstructed states in order to secure civil and criminal justice and equal rights in cases involving freedmen."[70]

This is but one example of many race-conscious programs adopted by the same Congresses that ratified the Thirteenth, Fourteenth, and Fifteenth Amendments. Professor Siegel writes: "Beyond the Freedmen's Bureau laws, Reconstruction era Congresses enacted a mass of express race-conscious preferences for blacks. Some dealt with black soldiers. . . . Other Reconstruction era benign race-conscious laws involved charitable payments restricted to black recipients or payments and property transfers to institutions restricted to serving the black community. In each instance, there were no corresponding payments or transfers to whites, who received their share of governmental charity through legally unrestricted transfers."[71]

Originalists frequently look to practices at the time a constitutional provision was adopted to determine its original meaning. By this measure, the original meaning of the Fourteenth Amendment as it relates to affirmative action could not be clearer. Yet originalists such as Scalia and Thomas pay no attention to this original meaning. They make no effort to justify their opposition to affirmative action in originalist terms because it can't plausibly be done. As Professor Eric Segall noted, "Neither Justice Scalia nor Justice Thomas addressed this specific history or even the original meaning of the

Fourteenth Amendment as applied to limited racial preferences."[72] Affirmative action is a very powerful example of how conservative political ideology is far more important to these justices than their commitment to originalism.

The remarkable willingness of originalists to abandon originalism when it fails to produce conservative results shows that the theory was never the constraint on the judiciary that its boosters promised. It is simply convenient rhetoric, used by conservatives to make it seem that their decisions are a product of something other than their political views. To be sure, there are a few examples where original-ists do follow originalism even when they dislike its results. But the important examples in this chapter – voting rights, the Eleventh Amendment and sovereign immunity, campaign finance laws, and affirmative action – show that in the areas conservatives care deeply about, they are unwilling to let a mere theory stand in the way of the outcomes they desire.

Chapter 8

IN DEFENSE OF NON-ORIGINALISM

When confronted with criticisms of originalism, Justice Antonin Scalia often fell back on a familiar defense: I have a theory, however flawed, and they don't.[1] I have tried to show that originalism is more than flawed: it is not a defensible theory at all. The historical record is so incomplete and inconsistent, and the choice of the level of abstraction so arbitrary, that on many issues justices and judges can find evidence to justify almost any result. On other questions, following originalism would lead to repugnant results, and on still others, originalists forsake it when it does not generate the conservative outcomes they favor. Originalism fails on its own terms to provide a constraint on judging. It is only a fig leaf allowing a justice to pretend to adhere to a neutral method while advancing a conservative political ideology. If taken literally, it calls for its own abandonment.

Yet what is the alternative? Throughout American history the Supreme Court has rejected originalism. Never has a majority of the justices professed to believe in it. They have always looked to multiple sources in interpreting the text of the Constitution, which rarely provides simple answers to the matters that come before the

Court: the Framers' intent if it can be known, the original meaning to the extent that it can be ascertained, the structure of the Constitution, historical practices, constitutional and social traditions, precedent, and what is best for society. All those who interpret the Constitution — originalists and non-originalists alike — seek to advance what they see as the objectives of a constitutional provision, but for non-originalists these objectives are stated in a general as opposed to a very specific way.

Admittedly, non-originalism does not yield determinate results. It gives justices great discretion in deciding constitutional cases. But this is just as true for originalism or for any theory of interpretation. Formalism is impossible in constitutional law.

A belief in formalism dominated jurisprudence in the nineteenth century. The principles of law were seen as part of the natural law, and the role of judges was to discover them. Judging was conceived as a relatively mechanical act of applying law to the facts of the particular case. Formalism has enormous allure, and it is easy to understand why people would want to believe in it. It promises objectivity and relieves judges of the grave moral weight of their decisions.

During the early twentieth century, legal realists demolished formalism as the dominant legal theory.[2] They demonstrated that all legal rules are value choices. For instance, a tort law that made recovery difficult for injured workers because of such doctrines as assumption of risk, contributory negligence, and the fellow servant rule reflected judges' choices to favor employers over employees. Benjamin Cardozo said that "the demon of formalism tempts the intellect with the lure of scientific order," and when "judges are called upon to say how far existing rules are to be extended or restricted, they must let the welfare of society fix the path, its direction and its distance."[3]

The legal realists taught us that judging is inherently discretionary. This hardly seems like a profound point, yet it threatened the very foundations of jurisprudence. I have always thought that the power of the realists' critique of formalism came from its confirming what people already knew: that the emperor really had no clothes. Any nineteenth-century reader of *Marbury v. Madison, Dred Scott v. Sandford,* and *Plessy v. Ferguson* surely recognized that the justices in those cases made value choices.

Now, a century after the legal realists' attack on formalism, there is a strong consensus that formalism is alluring but impossible. My law students find it hard to grasp that people really believed in it. It is widely recognized, though not always admitted, that the values of the judges making the decisions often matter (frequently enormously), particularly in constitutional law. Yet originalists continue to champion a formalist approach to constitutional law that, despite their claims, is just as indeterminate as non-originalism and very undesirable.

I will defend non-originalism with three primary arguments: it is desirable to examine many different sources and considerations in deciding the meaning of a constitutional provision; it is desirable that the Constitution be a living document that evolves by interpretation as well as amendment; and it is desirable to make constitutional decisions with candor and transparency.

The primary criticism of non-originalism is that it does not yield conclusively right or wrong results. But no theory of constitutional interpretation can do this. Quite contrary to Justice Kagan's declaration that "we are all originalists," we are all non-originalists, always have been, and always will be.

Ultimately, the question is whether the benefits of originalism — assuming that following the theory would actually yield those benefits — outweigh its costs, or outweigh the gains from a non-originalist approach. Originalists do not do this analysis, being content to assert the benefits of originalism in constraining judicial decision-making. But even if originalism actually limited judges, it still imposes great unnecessary costs and deprives us of the great benefits of a non-originalist approach.

What Should Be Considered

Originalists say that the *only* thing relevant to constitutional interpretation is that which helps us discern the original meaning of a given provision. By this definition, nothing that happened after its adoption is pertinent, other than subsequent actions by the ratifiers that reflect on what they understood they were ratifying. But this standard dismisses the insights from other sources that might aid our interpretation. Originalists, if they are true to their theory, would reject all the wisdom and experience gained since a constitutional provision was adopted.

It is hard to fathom why one would prefer such ignorance. The history that occurred since the provision's adoption can be useful in deciding what meaning to give it. That is why the Supreme Court, from its earliest days, has looked to historical practices in interpreting the Constitution.

Take as an example the creation of the national bank.[4] One of the most powerful scenes in the musical *Hamilton* is when Alexander Hamilton and Thomas Jefferson debate the constitutionality of creating a national bank, with George Washington watching. Ultimately, Washington sides with Hamilton.

Congress did approve the plan for a Bank of the United States.[5] The bank existed for twenty-one years, until its charter expired in

1811. But after the War of 1812, the country experienced serious economic problems, and in 1816 the Bank of the United States was re-created. Even though he had opposed such a bank a quarter of a century earlier, when he was a congressman from Virginia, as president, James Madison endorsed its re-creation. The United States government owned only 20 percent of this new bank.

The new Bank of the United States did not solve the country's economic problems, and many even blamed the bank's monetary policies for aggravating the depression that followed the War of 1812. State governments were particularly angry, especially because the bank called in loans the states owed. Many states adopted laws designed to limit the operation of the bank. Some outright prohibited it from operating within their borders. Others taxed it. Maryland required that any bank not chartered by the state pay an annual tax of either $15,000 or 2 percent on all its notes, which had to be printed on special stamped paper.

The bank refused to pay, and John James sued for himself and the State of Maryland in the County Court of Baltimore to recover the money owed under the tax. The defendant, James W. McCulloch, was the cashier of the bank's Baltimore branch. The trial court ruled that the bank had to pay the tax, and the Maryland Court of Appeals affirmed.

The constitutionality of this tax came to the Supreme Court in *McCulloch v. Maryland*, which became one of the most important Supreme Court decisions in American history.[6] It defined the scope of Congress's power and the relation between the federal government and the states.

Chief Justice Marshall began his majority opinion by considering whether Congress had the authority to create a Bank of the United States. He did not invoke what the Constitution's Framers intended or try to ascertain its original meaning. Instead, he started his opinion by declaring: "It has been truly said, that this can scarcely be considered as an open question, entirely unprejudiced by the former proceedings of the nation respecting it. The principle now contested was introduced at a very early period of our history, has been recogni[z]ed by many successive legislatures, and has been acted upon by the judicial department, in cases of peculiar delicacy, as a law of undoubted obligation."[7] In other words, historical practice – the creation of the first Bank of the United States after the ratification of the Constitution, and the ongoing acceptance of that action – established Congress's power to make it. The history of the first Bank of the United States was the authority for the constitutionality of the second bank.

Marshall expressly noted that the First Congress enacted the bank after much debate and that it was approved by an executive "with as much persevering talent as any measure has ever experienced, and being supported by arguments which convinced minds as pure and as intelligent as this country can boast."[8] Without mentioning James Madison by name, Marshall noted that even those who opposed the first bank endorsed creating the second. He concluded that "it would require no ordinary share of intrepidity, to assert that a measure adopted under these circumstances, was a bold and plain usurpation, to which the constitution gave no countenance."[9] Notice that he uses history and tradition *after the adoption of the Constitution* – non-originalist reasoning – to justify his conclusion.

The Supreme Court has repeatedly looked to historical practices. It is what Justice Frankfurter meant when he said, "[I]t is an inadmissibly narrow conception of American constitutional law to confine it to the words of the Constitution and to disregard the gloss which life has written upon them."[10] It is what Justice Brennan had in mind when he said, "[T]he Constitution carries the gloss of history."[11]

Although everything after the adoption of a constitutional provision should be irrelevant for originalists, they, too, invoke subsequent history when it serves their purposes. *District of Columbia v. Heller*, in which the Court found a Second Amendment right to have guns in the home, is regarded as the quintessential originalist decision.[12] But Justice Scalia, who wrote the majority opinion, spent many pages reviewing what happened after the ratification of the Second Amendment to support his interpretation, implicitly conceding the relevance of such material.

Closely related to post-ratification history is the importance of looking at social traditions. For decades, the Court has said the Due Process Clause protects those fundamental rights and liberties that are "deeply rooted in this Nation's history and tradition."[13] As Justice Harlan famously wrote:

> Due process has not been reduced to any formula; its content cannot be determined by reference to any code. The best that can be said is that through the course of this Court's decisions it has represented the balance which our Nation, built upon postulates of respect for the liberty of the individual, has struck between that liberty and the demands of organized society. . . . The balance of which I speak is the balance struck by this country, having regard to what history teaches are the traditions from which it developed as well as the traditions from which it broke. That tradition is a living thing. A decision of this Court which radically departs from it could not long survive, while a decision which builds on what has survived is likely to be sound. No formula could serve as a substitute, in this area, for judgment and restraint.[14]

On countless occasions, the Court has stressed the importance of looking at traditions when interpreting the Constitution.

There is, of course, a danger to relying on traditions as the basis for decisions. Racism, sexism, and homophobia are American traditions too, at least as much as egalitarianism. The Supreme Court invoked tradition in *Bowers v. Hardwick*, in 1986, to uphold a Georgia law that prohibited private adult consensual same-sex sexual activity.[15] As Justice Harry Blackmun pointed out in his dissent, quoting Justice Harlan, "it is revolting to have no better reason for a rule of law than that so it was laid down in the time of Henry IV. It is still more revolting if the grounds upon which it was laid down have vanished long since, and the rule simply persists from blind imitation of the past."[16] Seventeen years later, the Court overruled *Bowers* in *Lawrence v. Texas*.[17]

Tradition should not limit the meaning of the Constitution, but it is an important source that can inform decisions. For an originalist, nothing matters except what was thought when the provision was adopted. This limitation denies our ability to learn from all that has happened since, including from long-standing traditions of protecting rights and advancing equality, as well as from rethinking traditions that we should renounce.

Closely related to history and tradition, but perhaps even more crucial to judicial decision-making, is the role of precedent. Stare decisis — respect for precedent — matters in all areas of law, including constitutional law. Justice Kagan wrote for the Court in *Kimble v. Marvel Entertainment* in 2015 that

> Stare decisis — in English, the idea that today's Court should stand by yesterday's decisions — is "a foundation stone of the rule of law." Application of that doctrine, although "not an inexorable

command," is the "preferred course because it promotes the evenhanded, predictable, and consistent development of legal principles, fosters reliance on judicial decisions, and contributes to the actual and perceived integrity of the judicial process." It also reduces incentives for challenging settled precedents, saving parties and courts the expense of endless relitigation. Respecting *stare decisis* means sticking to some wrong decisions. The doctrine rests on the idea, as Justice Brandeis famously wrote, that it is usually "more important that the applicable rule of law be settled than that it be settled right."[18]

But under originalism, precedent and stare decisis properly play no role in interpretation because they base decisions on something other than the original meaning of the Constitution. Originalist scholars have made exactly that argument. Professor Gary Lawson has argued that justices and judges violate their oaths of office when they follow precedent rather than what they understand the Constitution to require.[19] Professor Michael Stokes Paulson argues that reliance on stare decisis is unconstitutional because it

would have judges apply, in preference to the Constitution, that which is not consistent with the Constitution. That violates the premise on which judicial review rests, as set forth in *Marbury*. If one accepts the argument for judicial review in *Marbury* as being grounded, correctly, in the supremacy of the Constitution (correctly interpreted) over anything inconsistent with it, and as binding the judiciary to enforce and apply the Constitution (correctly interpreted) in preference to anything inconsistent with it, then courts must apply the correct interpretation of the Constitution, *never* a precedent inconsistent with the correct

---

interpretation. It follows, then, that if *Marbury* is right (and it is), *stare decisis* is unconstitutional.[20]

It is stunning that these scholars not only want to reject stare decisis—a foundation of the American legal system—but claim that it is unconstitutional. Under originalism, this claim makes sense because the duty of the justice or judge is solely to follow the original meaning of the Constitution; anything that happened after ratification, including Supreme Court rulings, is irrelevant. Justice Scalia was never willing to go that far and, for that reason, called himself a "faint-hearted originalist."[21] But Justice Thomas isn't faint-hearted at all. Like Professors Lawson and Paulson, he believes that stare decisis is incompatible with originalism and is prepared to vote this conviction. In *Gamble v. United States,* in 2019, he wrote: "Our judicial duty to interpret the law requires adherence to the original meaning of the text. For that reason, we should not invoke *stare decisis* to uphold precedents that are demonstrably erroneous."[22] This amounts to an assertion that precedent should play no role in constitutional law. In the same opinion, he went on:

> In my view, the Court's typical formulation of the *stare decisis* standard does not comport with our judicial duty under Article III because it elevates demonstrably erroneous decisions—meaning decisions outside the realm of permissible interpretation—over the text of the Constitution and other duly enacted federal law. . . . By applying demonstrably erroneous precedent instead of the relevant law's text—as the Court is particularly prone to do when expanding federal power or crafting new individual rights—the Court exercises "force" and "will," two attributes the People did not give it. We should restore our *stare decisis* jurisprudence to

ensure that we exercise "mer[e] judgment," which can be achieved through adherence to the correct, original meaning of the laws we are charged with applying. In my view, anything less invites arbitrariness into judging.[23]

Another self-proclaimed originalist, Justice Amy Coney Barrett, as a law professor took the same radical position as Thomas. She wrote in 2013: "I tend to agree with those who say that a justice's duty is to the Constitution and that it is thus more legitimate for her to enforce her best understanding of the Constitution rather than a precedent she thinks clearly in conflict with it."[24] She, too, argued that following precedent is unconstitutional, writing that "rigid application" of stare decisis "unconstitutionally deprives a litigant of the right to a hearing on the merits of her claim."[25]

Thus at least two members of the Supreme Court have told us that precedent and stare decisis should not matter in constitutional law. Their position is another reason why non-originalism is preferable to originalism: precedent should matter. It has been a core feature of common law countries for centuries because, as Justice Kagan explained, it creates stability and predictability. It allows citizens to rely on the law.

Another source that non-originalists consult that originalists consider irrelevant is foreign law and practices. These sources are much more controversial, and the Court rarely invokes them, I think, because doing so would draw attacks from originalists. But Justice Stephen Breyer has persuasively argued that the United States does not have a monopoly on wisdom about governance and that we can learn from the experience of other nations.[26] In the 2005 case of *Roper v. Simmons,* in which the Court found that the death penalty for crimes committed by juveniles is unconstitutional, Justice Kennedy's majority opinion pointed to the elimination of this practice by virtually every other country.[27] He noted "that the laws of other countries and . . . international authorities [are] instructive for . . . interpretation of the Eighth Amendment's prohibition of 'cruel and unusual punishments.' "[28] Only seven countries in the world—not ones whose human rights records we want to emulate—allow the death penalty for crimes committed by juveniles.[29] To be clear, he did not say subjecting juveniles to the death penalty is unconstitutional because this is not done by other countries, only that international practice is a relevant consideration in deciding what is cruel and unusual punishment.

Kennedy explained that the "prohibition against 'cruel and unusual punishments,' like other expansive language in the Constitution, must be interpreted according to its text, by considering history, tradition, and precedent, and with due regard for its purpose and function in the constitutional design. To implement this framework we have established the propriety and affirmed the necessity of referring to 'the evolving standards of decency that mark the progress of a maturing society' to determine which punishments are so disproportionate as to be cruel and unusual."[30]

"Evolving standards of decency" is a profoundly non-originalist criterion. The alternative would be that only punishments deemed unacceptable in 1791 could be outlawed today. As Justice Brennan pointed out, that would mean that "pillorying, branding, and cropping and nailing of the ears" would all be permissible.[31]

My point is that it is desirable for justices interpreting the Constitution to take into account history and tradition and precedent and foreign practice. Originalism precludes thinking about any of this. There are many sources of wisdom and insight about constitutional provisions; it is a virtue of non-originalism in that it allows us to consider all of them.

The Benefits of a Living Constitution

Most of all, non-originalism allows the Constitution to evolve by interpretation and thus for decisions to consider changes in social values, technology, and society's needs. In this book I have given many examples, one of the most important of which is equal protection. Under the social values of 1868, when the Fourteenth Amendment was ratified, state-mandated segregation, laws prohibiting interracial marriage, and discrimination against women and gays and lesbians were all constitutional. Our values regarding equal protection are enormously different today, and for the Constitution to remain relevant, it must be interpreted to reflect those differences.

Technology is also vastly different today. It is impossible to discern an original understanding that can guide us on how the government should regulate the internet, social media, or video games under the First Amendment. Whether obtaining criminal suspects' cellular location data or tracking their actions through thermal imaging devices counts as a "search" can't plausibly be analyzed based on the original understanding of the Fourth Amendment. Nor does original meaning help us decide whether the police can take DNA from a suspect arrested for a crime to see if it matches an unsolved crime in their database.

To take another example, the analysis of whether a gun regulation is constitutional must include the harms done by particular weapons. That need not be the decisive consideration, but it should be relevant in assessing the constitutionality of government actions.

The views and practices of 1791 cannot tell us whether the government can ban assault rifles. Nothing like an AR-15 existed when the Second Amendment was ratified.

Society's needs have changed dramatically since the Constitution was written. To understate the obvious, both our society and government are vastly larger than in 1787. A living Constitution allows this growth and the changes it brings to influence the Court's thinking on the scope of federal powers. Decisions are worse if they are made for the twenty-first century on the basis of eighteenth- or nineteenth-century experiences. The constitutional amendment process is highly unlikely to be used, and a minority's rights should not depend on the willingness of a supermajority to enact an amendment.

Candor

There is another, more subtle benefit of non-originalism. It leads the Court to be much more candid about the value choices it is making and why. A major theme of this book is how originalist justices make value choices every bit as much as non-originalists do, but the originalists pretend they are reflecting the original meaning of the Constitution. Take, for example, the Establishment Clause of the First Amendment. Justices must decide to what extent it should be interpreted to require the government be as secular as possible, or interpreted to accommodate religion, so that the government violates the clause only if it coerces religious participation. The historical record is unclear, with many different understandings and views in 1791, though I think there is a persuasive case that the Framers intended separation of church and state.[32] Rather than defend the desirability of their own view, originalists present it as reflecting the original meaning of the First Amendment.[33] But the original meaning does not actually support an originalist's version of the Establishment Clause. Conservatives are just hiding their value choice about the appropriate role of religion in government, rather than defending it.

To take another example I've already discussed, consider state sovereign immunity. The conservatives on the Court, in a series of five-to-four decisions, have insulated state governments from being sued even when they violate fundamental constitutional rights. They have made a value choice to favor the immunity of state governments over holding them accountable. They never defend that value choice but instead present their rulings as based on the original understanding of the Constitution, even though the text provides no foundation for a broad protection of sovereign immunity and the historical basis for it is dubious.

One must ask why we have judicial opinions at all. There are many benefits to having judges explain their decisions. Written opinions show that the rulings stem from reasoning, not fiat. Supreme Court opinions provide guidance to lower courts, to legislatures, and to government officials at all levels as to what is permissible or impermissible and why. They explain the Court's rulings to the public, often through intermediaries. They contribute to public discourse about important and divisive issues.

Society benefits from open discussion about values. To ignore them because the conversation is difficult is to risk undermining what we regard as most important. That the dialogue cannot be resolved, that it is inherently open-ended, is what makes it essential that the discussion occur. Constitutional law is ultimately a discourse about what values should be protected from majoritarian decision-making, why, and how.

Conflicts among constitutional values are inevitable. Society has many different objectives that often conflict. There is an inherent tension between liberty and equality. There is a tension between majority rule and protecting certain fundamental rights from majority rule. It is important that these competing values be clearly identified and choices among them be explained.

The Constitution is where society states its most important values about how governing is to be done and how individuals are to be protected. It is better, in constitutional cases, for courts to identify those values and elaborate the basis for their choices. Non-originalism does this. Originalists insist that the answers are in what people thought hundreds of years ago, so their value choices are hidden rather than explained.

Indeterminacy

The primary objection to non-originalism is its indeterminacy. Letting interpretation be guided by multiple sources – history, tradition, precedent, foreign law, modern social needs – can only yield indeterminate results. Originalists purport to avoid this by having a less open-ended method for determining the meaning of constitutional provisions. But just as formalism can never eliminate judicial discretion, so any method of constitutional interpretation must be indeterminate. Originalism and non-originalism both leave justices and judges tremendous discretion in deciding constitutional cases.

The Constitution is written in broad, open-textured language that rarely provides explicit answers to the issues that come before the Court. Justices and judges must decide what is an "unreasonable" search, what is a "taking," what is "due process," and what is "cruel and unusual punishment." Rarely does any constitutional provision have a clear original meaning or provide an unequivocal basis for deciding a specific case.

———

Even originalists have largely come to reject basing their idea of original meaning on Framers' intent. So many people were involved in drafting and ratifying that it was fiction to claim a clear intent behind any provision. Justice Scalia described the need to look at many different sources in determining original meaning.[34] Inevitably, these point in different directions, and the justice has to choose.

Not only must justices choose how to determine an original meaning, but they must choose the level of abstraction at which to state a right. Is it at the most specific level, or can it be stated more generally? Should equal protection be seen as protecting only racial minorities from discrimination, as protecting all historically discriminated-against groups, or as protecting everyone from arbitrary treatment? Any of those choices can be justified from an originalist perspective, yet the level of abstraction makes a crucial difference in determining what is constitutional or unconstitutional. Originalists often try to avoid the undesirable consequences of their theory, such as in making *Brown v. Board of Education* a wrong decision, by articulating the meaning of a provision at a more abstract level.

Beyond all such choices, determinacy is impossible because balancing is inherent in constitutional law. Virtually no right in the Constitution is absolute. The government can infringe the most fundamental rights or even discriminate based on race if its action is necessary to achieve a compelling interest. But what is compelling? Originalists never have claimed that is determined by original meaning. Nor has the Court ever articulated criteria for determining what interests are compelling. It is a value choice made by justices and judges. Any discrimination or infringement of liberty, even if not against a suspect class or involving a fundamental right, must be rationally related to a legitimate purpose. But what purposes are legitimate? Again, deciding this requires a value choice by justices and judges.

———

Examples make this less abstract.[35] No one – liberal or conservative – can deny that laws prohibiting same-sex marriages discriminated against gays and lesbians; heterosexuals could marry the people they loved, but homosexuals could not. Under equal protection, at the very least, these laws would have to meet rational basis review and be rationally related to a legitimate government interest. Unless the originalist would say that gays and lesbians are not entitled to equal protection, originalists and non-originalists would have to determine whether any legitimate state interest is served by prohibiting same-sex marriage. There is no way for the Court to avoid making a value choice in resolving that issue.

Or take the example of affirmative action by colleges and universities.[36] All of the justices have agreed that the central question in deciding the constitutionality of affirmative action is whether diversity in the classroom is a compelling government interest. Answering that question inescapably requires a value choice by the justices.

Or consider the issue of whether the government can restrict political expenditures by corporations in election campaigns.[37] A crucial question before the justices was whether lessening corporate influence was a compelling government interest. The justices split five to four along ideological lines, not over anything that original meaning could answer.

More than thirty years ago, in my conclusion to the *Harvard Law Review* "Foreword" in 1989, I wrote that "constitutional law is now, will be, and always has been . . . largely a product of the views of the Justices."[38] No theory of constitutional law can avoid that. That, of course, is why there are intense fights over Supreme Court nominations. It is why the Republicans blocked the consideration of Chief Judge Merrick Garland and rammed through Judge Amy Coney Barrett's confirmation. Everyone knows that Supreme Court justices have great discretion and that how it is exercised is a product of who is on the bench, their values, their ideology, and their life experience. Originalists only pretend to avoid this discretion.

What Is Constitutional Law?

Ultimately, the Supreme Court should be able to consult any relevant source to decide the meaning of a constitutional provision, and then apply that meaning to the specific issue in any given case. This is an inherently indeterminate process, which is why justices so often disagree, especially along ideological lines.

I am often asked whether this makes judges indistinguishable from politicians. Yet there are many ways in which judges differ from other public officials. It is completely acceptable to lobby a legislator or mayor or governor. But our judicial system makes it unheard of for parties to try and lobby judges at any level. It is generally considered acceptable for legislators to trade votes. That same practice would be condemned if justices did it, and reports of it are unheard of.

At the same time, justices and judges, like all who hold public office, make value choices, and their ideology very often informs those choices. When I have an argument in a court of appeals, I want to know my panel as soon as possible, because the identity of the judges can matter enormously in the case's outcome. Every lawyer knows that. It is even more true of cases that make it to the Supreme Court.

Ultimately, our society has decided that we are better off allowing an institution like the Supreme Court, largely insulated from direct majoritarian control, to interpret the Constitution and apply it to the cases before it. We certainly can continue to debate whether we actually are better off with a judiciary having the power to declare laws and executive actions unconstitutional. But it seems inarguable that as long as this power exists – and it has since *Marbury v. Madison* in 1803 – justices and judges will make value choices. Non-originalism recognizes this; originalism hides it. It is far better to acknowledge the reality of how constitutional decisions are made.

Chapter 9

WE SHOULD BE AFRAID

I have no illusions that this book will have any effect on those who believe in the originalist approach to constitutional law.[1] Non-originalists have launched devastating attacks on originalism for decades, but other than pressuring originalists to modify their theory, these criticisms have had little effect. The election of Donald Trump in 2016 meant that three conservative justices — two of them self-avowed originalists — were appointed to the Supreme Court, along with many lower federal court judges with a similar jurisprudence. Originalism is accepted among conservative law professors and has the enthusiastic endorsement of the Federalist Society. The conservative majority on the Supreme Court will likely remain in place for many years to come.

Where will originalism take the Court? Obviously, unexpected issues will arise, but I feel safe in making several predictions of the dramatic changes on the horizon. I will focus on three areas: rights of privacy and autonomy, the scope of congressional power, and the Constitution's religion clauses. Political conservatives likely will cheer these changes, but the rest of us should be afraid. More than a decade ago, Professor Cass Sunstein, in the title of a book, described originalist jurists as "Radicals in Robes."[2] In coming years we will see their radicalism on full display and will, with great pain, learn what originalism means for constitutional law and, most important-ly, for people's lives.

Privacy and Autonomy

Originalists are adamant that *Roe v. Wade* was wrongly decided and that the Constitution does not protect reproductive rights what-soever.[3] Justice Clarence Thomas has said plainly: "Because we can reconcile neither *Roe* nor its progeny with the text of our Constitu-tion, those decisions should be overruled."[4]

As I write this, the Supreme Court has before it a case that could overturn *Roe v. Wade*. *Dobbs v. Jackson Women's Health Organi-zation* involves a Mississippi law that prohibits abortion after the fif-teenth week of pregnancy.[5] For months after it was filed in the fall of 2020, the justices took no action on the petition for a writ of certio-rari, raising hopes that perhaps the Court's conservative majority was not ready to take up the issue. But then it agreed to review the Mississippi statute, an action that should frighten all who believe that women have a right to reproductive autonomy.

Under existing law, this should be an easy case. There is no reason for the Supreme Court to hear it unless a majority of the justices are prepared to dramatically change the law of abortion. In *Roe v. Wade,* in 1973, the Court held that the government cannot prohibit abortions before viability, the time at which the fetus can survive outside the womb. In 1992, in *Planned Parenthood v. Casey,* the Court reaffirmed this and called it the "essential holding" of *Roe.*[6]

It is generally accepted that viability is about the twenty-third or twenty-fourth week of pregnancy. The Mississippi law, with its fifteen-week ban, prohibits abortions before viability. Lower federal courts had no hesitation in declaring it unconstitutional.[7] Similar laws prohibiting abortions before viability have been repeatedly invalidated without the Supreme Court granting review.

If the Court overrules that aspect of *Roe* and *Casey* and allows states to prohibit abortions before viability, nothing will stop them from outlawing abortions even earlier in pregnancy. Many states now have adopted laws that ban abortions once a fetal heartbeat can be detected, which is about the sixth week of pregnancy. That would effectively outlaw most abortions, because many women do not even know they are pregnant at six weeks. And some states, such as Alabama, have adopted laws prohibiting all abortions, period.

It seems all but certain that a majority on the Court is willing to overturn *Roe* and *Casey*. In 2016, the Court invalidated a Texas law requiring that doctors performing abortions have admitting privileges at hospitals within thirty miles of the clinic. The five justices in the majority were Kennedy, Ginsburg, Breyer, Sotomayor, and Kagan.[8] In June 2020, the Court struck down an identical Louisiana law, but four justices—Thomas, Alito, Gorsuch, and Kavanaugh—dissented with a foreboding notice that they would not only uphold that law but radically change the Constitution's protection of abortion rights. Kennedy, who was part of the majority in the former decision, and Ginsburg who was in the majority in both, are no longer on the bench.

In October 2020, Justice Amy Coney Barrett joined the Court's conservative wing. As a Notre Dame law professor, she expressed strong opposition to *Roe;* as a federal court of appeals judge, she voted to uphold restrictions on abortion.[9] Her presence gives the

Court five apparently reliable votes to overrule *Roe*. Chief Justice Roberts could be a sixth. Since coming on the Court in 2005, he has voted to strike down a restriction on abortion only once: the June 2020 Louisiana case, where he made his vote on the narrow grounds of following the recent prior decision.[10]

None of this should surprise anyone. Overruling *Roe* has been an increasingly central aspect of conservative ideology. Originalism was embraced by conservatives, in part, because it provided an argument against abortion rights. Robert Bork, one of the original originalists, was also one of the first conservative legal scholars to speak out against *Roe*. Republican presidents have for years picked conservatives who were perceived as likely to overrule it. Now there are at least five justices ready and likely eager to do so. The Mississippi case provides the vehicle.

I expect that the Court will uphold the Mississippi law, saying that abortion is not mentioned in the Constitution and is not part of its original meaning. They will say that *Roe v. Wade* invented a new constitutional right and usurped the political process. Because the Constitution is silent about abortion, they will argue that the matter should be resolved politically, not by the judiciary. They will say, as conservative justices have urged for decades, that states may regulate and even outlaw abortions so long as the action is rationally related to a legitimate government purpose, and that protecting fetal life is such a purpose.[11]

To be clear, the Court's reasoning in *Roe* was sound. There is no basis for overruling it other than ideology. No basis exists for a court or state government to decide when human personhood begins; there is no moral, theological, or legal consensus on this. The *Roe* Court wisely drew the line at viability, ruling that states cannot prohibit abortions until the fetus can survive outside the womb. Women have relied on this case for their reproductive rights ever since.

In some states, such as California and New York, nothing will change if *Roe* is overruled – abortion will remain a legal right. But many women will face a reality not seen in this country for almost fifty years. Nearly half the states will likely criminalize most or all abortions almost immediately.[12] Many states already have such laws on the books, which will be triggered into effect if *Roe* is invalidated. Women across the country will feel the consequences instantly.

Wealthy women desiring abortions who live where abortions are banned will travel to places where the procedure is allowed. But poor women and teenagers will not have this ability. These women will have no option but to choose between a cheap, unsafe, back-alley abortion and an unwanted pregnancy.

Nor will overruling *Roe* be the end of the story. We can expect that the next time there is a Republican president and a Republican Congress, they will push to adopt a federal law prohibiting all or almost all abortions across the entire United States. Keep in mind that the Supreme Court upheld a federal law, the Federal Partial Birth Abortion Act, that prohibited a specific abortion procedure nationally.[13] A Court that overrules *Roe* would presumably uphold a much broader federal law ending abortions, even if, as explained below, the originalists on the Court want to greatly limit the scope of Congress's powers.

Overruling *Roe*, explicitly or effectively, will put in jeopardy many of the other rights the Supreme Court has protected under the word "liberty" in the Due Process Clause. For example, it has interpreted the word to protect the right to marry, the right to procreate, the right to custody of one's children, the right to keep one's family together, the right to control the upbringing of one's children, the right to purchase and use contraceptives, the right to engage in private adult consensual same-sex sexual activity, and the right of competent adults to refuse medical treatment.[14] Some of these liberties, like the right of parents to control their children's upbringing, have been recognized by the Court for almost a century. Yet none of them are enumerated in the Constitution's text or can be said to be part of its original meaning. From an originalist perspective, all of them are unjustifiable. When these rights have been involved in cases before the Supreme Court in recent years, the conservative justices have consistently dissented and denied their existence. These dissents foretell what is likely to happen to unenumerated rights now that a conservative supermajority sits on the highest court.

A few examples illustrate why we should be concerned. In *Troxel v. Granville*, in 2000, the Court reaffirmed the right of parents to control the upbringing of their children and held that it was unconstitutional for a court in Washington State to grant grandparent visitation over a fit mother's objections.[15] Justice O'Connor, in a plurality opinion, emphasized the fundamental nature of the right involved: "The liberty interest at issue in this case — the interest of parents in the care, custody, and control of their children — is perhaps the oldest of the fundamental liberty interests recognized by this Court."[16] The plurality found that the Washington law, as applied in this case, was unconstitutional as infringing on this fundamental right. Justice Scalia vehemently dissented, saying the courts should not recognize such a right:

> While I would think it entirely compatible with the commitment
> to representative democracy set forth in the founding documents
> to argue, in legislative chambers or in electoral campaigns, that
> the State has *no power* to interfere with parents' authority over the

---

191

rearing of their children, I do not believe that the power which the Constitution confers upon me *as a judge* entitles me to deny legal effect to laws that (in my view) infringe upon what is (in my view) that unenumerated right. . . . If we embrace this unenumerated right, I think it obvious . . . that we will be ushering in a new regime of judicially prescribed, and federally prescribed, family law. I have no reason to believe that federal judges will be better at this than state legislatures; and state legislatures have the great advantages of doing harm in a more circumscribed area, of being able to correct their mistakes in a flash, and of being removable by the people.[17]

In *Lawrence v. Texas*, Justices Scalia and Thomas forcefully dissented when the Court held that states cannot prohibit private adult consensual same-sex sexual activity, or punish adults for sexual activity in the privacy of their own bedroom.[18] Justice Thomas made clear that under originalism, no such right exists, and the matter is left to the political process:

Punishing someone for expressing his sexual preference through noncommercial consensual conduct with another adult does not appear to be a worthy way to expend valuable law enforcement resources. Notwithstanding this, I recognize that as a Member of this Court I am not empowered to help petitioners and others similarly situated. My duty, rather, is to "decide cases 'agreeably to the Constitution and laws of the United States.' " . . . I "can find [neither in the Bill of Rights nor any other part of the Constitution a] general right of privacy," or as the Court terms it today, the "liberty of the person both in its spatial and more transcendent dimensions."[19]

In *Obergefell v. Hodges*, Chief Justice Roberts and Justices Scalia, Thomas, and Alito dissented to the Court's holding that the right to marry is infringed by state laws that prohibit same-sex marriage.[20] None of these justices wanted to accept long-standing precedents protecting a right to marry; all said the matter should be left to the political process. Justice Scalia's objection to such constitutional protection was notably vehement: "If, even as the price to be paid for a fifth vote, I ever joined an opinion for the Court that began: 'The Constitution promises liberty to all within its reach, a liberty that includes certain specific rights that allow persons, within a lawful realm, to define and express their identity,' I would hide my head in a bag. The Supreme Court of the United States has descended from the disciplined legal reasoning of John Marshall and Joseph Story to the mystical aphorisms of the fortune cookie."[21]

Under the originalist view, there is no constitutional limit on how governments can restrict marriage, impose involuntary sterilization, remove children from their parents, interfere with parental decisions, regulate contraceptives and abortion, prohibit private consensual sexual activity, or limit people's ability to refuse medical care. All have been regarded as fundamental aspects of liberty by the Supreme Court, but not for originalists.

The Commerce Power

Although the Court's decisions on the Commerce Clause are less high profile, they are nonetheless enormously important. The originalist view of Congress's power to regulate commerce among the states is likely to endanger many key federal laws, including statutes protecting the environment and civil rights. The Commerce Clause is the basis for virtually all federal regulation, most federal criminal laws, almost all environmental statutes, and many civil rights laws. Early in American history, the Supreme Court broadly defined the scope of Congress's powers under the provision and held that it allows Congress to regulate any commerce that affects more than one state.[22]

But from the 1890s until 1937, a conservative Supreme Court interpreted the commerce power narrowly, striking down many federal laws as exceeding Congress's authority.[23] The measures it struck down included federal laws outlawing child labor, providing employees a minimum wage, breaking up monopolies, and regulating business practices.

But in 1937 there was a dramatic shift in the Court's jurisprudence, perhaps in response to President Franklin Delano Roosevelt's threat of Court packing, which was then followed by a rapid change in the composition of the Court. Between that year and 1995, not a single federal law was invalidated as exceeding Congress's commerce power. The Supreme Court allowed Congress to regulate any activity that, taken cumulatively, had a substantial effect on interstate commerce. The Court recognized the need for Congress to exercise broad authority to regulate all aspects of the economy in the complex world of the twentieth century.[24]

But in two ideologically divided five-to-four decisions in 1995 and 2000, the Court again changed course and struck down federal laws as exceeding the scope of Congress's commerce power. In both cases, the conservative justices who professed judicial restraint comprised the majority.

The first case was *United States v. Lopez*.[25] Alfonso Lopez was a twelfth-grade student at Edison High School in San Antonio, Texas, in 1992 when he was arrested for carrying a concealed .38-caliber handgun and five bullets. He was charged with violating the Gun-

Free School Zones Act of 1990, which made it a federal offense "for any individual knowingly to possess a firearm at a place that the individual knows, or has reasonable cause to believe, is a school zone."[26] The law defined a school zone as "in, or on the grounds of, a public, parochial or private school" or "within a distance of 1,000 feet from the grounds of a public, parochial or private school."[27] Lopez was convicted of violating this law and sentenced to six months' imprisonment and two years of supervised release.

The Supreme Court ruled that the Gun-Free Schools Zone Act exceeded the scope of Congress's commerce powers. It found that the presence of a gun near a school did not substantially affect interstate commerce and that the federal law was therefore unconstitutional. The Court specifically rejected the federal government's claim that regulation was justified under the Commerce Clause because possession of a gun near a school may result in violent crime that can adversely affect the economy.

The second case, *United States v. Morrison,* presented the question of whether the civil damages provision of the federal Violence Against Women Act was constitutional.[28] The provision authorized victims of gender-motivated violence to sue for money damages. Congress enacted the Violence Against Women Act based on detailed findings about the inadequacy of state laws in protecting female victims of domestic violence and sexual assault. It found that gender-motivated violence costs the American economy billions of dollars per year and is a substantial constraint on women's freedom to travel throughout the country.

The case was brought by Christy Brzonkala, who was allegedly raped by football players while a freshman at Virginia Polytechnic Institute. The players were not criminally prosecuted, and they ultimately avoided sanctions from the university. Brzonkala sued her

---

assailants and the university under the civil damages provision of the Violence Against Women Act.

The issue before the Supreme Court was whether Congress had the constitutional authority to enact the civil damages provision, and in another five-to-four decision, it declared the law unconstitutional. The split was the same as in *Lopez*: Chief Justice Rehnquist wrote the opinion for the Court, joined by Justices O'Connor, Scalia, Kennedy, and Thomas, while Justices Stevens, Souter, Ginsburg, and Breyer dissented.

Many thought this was just the beginning. These rulings, they predicted, would lead the Court to strike down other federal laws as exceeding Congress's authority. So far it has not; but the much more conservative majority now on the Court is significantly more likely to do so. The originalist view of the Commerce Clause could place countless laws in jeopardy. In both *Lopez* and *Morrison*, Justice Thomas wrote concurring opinions expressing his very narrow view, based on originalism, of Congress's legislative powers. I worry that the new composition of the Court will turn his concurrences into majority opinions, and the consequences feared after *Lopez* and *Morrison* will come to pass.

In *Lopez*, Thomas wrote: "In an appropriate case, I believe that we must further reconsider our 'substantial effects' test with an eye toward constructing a standard that reflects the text and history of the Commerce Clause without totally rejecting our more recent Commerce Clause jurisprudence."[29] He noted that "at the time the original Constitution was ratified, 'commerce' consisted of selling, buying, and bartering, as well as transporting for these purposes."[30] This definition would return the Court to the approach that led it, in the early twentieth century, to strike down laws ranging from regulating antitrust to requiring pay of a minimum wage.

—

Thomas then went even further: "The Constitution not only uses the word 'commerce' in a narrower sense than our case law might suggest, it also does not support the proposition that Congress has authority over all activities that 'substantially affect' interstate commerce."[31]

In his concurring opinion in *Morrison*, Thomas again objected to the "substantial effects" test as a way of justifying congressional action under the commerce power. He wrote:

> The very notion of a "substantial effects" test under the Commerce Clause is inconsistent with the original understanding of Congress' powers and with this Court's early Commerce Clause cases. By continuing to apply this rootless and malleable standard, however circumscribed, the Court has encouraged the Federal Government to persist in its view that the Commerce Clause has virtually no limits. Until this Court replaces its existing Commerce Clause jurisprudence with a standard more consistent with the original understanding, we will continue to see Congress appropriating state police powers under the guise of regulating commerce.[32]

In other words, Justice Thomas would go significantly further than the Court already has in restricting the scope of Congress's commerce power. While the majority in *Morrison* would allow Congress to regulate economic activities based on their cumulative impact on the economy, Thomas would not.

To say that Congress cannot regulate activities that have a substantial effect on interstate commerce would overrule two hundred years of precedent and imperil countless federal laws. This radically restrictive view is at odds with how John Marshall and the Supreme Court interpreted the Commerce Clause early in American history.

It is a view that conflicts with the need for Congress to legislate for our complex modern society. For instance, almost every federal environmental law is based on Congress's power to regulate activities that, taken cumulatively, have a substantial effect on interstate commerce. If the other originalists on the Court follow Justice Thomas's lead and strike down federal laws ranging from environmental protections to labor regulations to civil rights, American government would become vastly different.

Religion and the Constitution

Of all the areas of constitutional law where the new, more conservative Court will bring great changes, the most certain are the religion clauses of the First Amendment.[33] The First Amendment begins: "Congress shall make no law respecting an establishment of religion, or prohibiting the free exercise thereof."[34] These two clauses are commonly called, respectively, the Establishment Clause and the Free Exercise Clause. Conservatives on the Court, including the originalists, are dramatically changing the law regarding both clauses. None of these changes can be attributed to following originalism.

For decades, the Supreme Court interpreted the Establishment Clause as mandating a separation of church and state. The idea of a wall that separates church and state comes from Thomas Jefferson.[35] In 1947, when the Court extended the Establishment Clause to state and local governments, all nine justices saw this separation as the provision's central mission.[36] Under this view, the government should be secular, to the greatest realistic extent. The appropriate places for religion are in the private realm: the home, places of worship, and people's daily lives. This view would limit the presence of religion in government activities (such as through prayer or religious symbols) and restrict government support for religious institutions. Based on this interpretation, the Supreme Court outlawed prayers in public schools, limited religious symbols on government property, and restricted government aid to religious schools.[37]

But now a majority on the Court rejects the idea of a wall separating church and state. These judges believe that the Establishment Clause should be interpreted to accommodate religion in government and government support for religion and that government violates the clause only if it coerces religious participation or discriminates among religions in awarding government benefits. For example, Justice Scalia wrote that "the coercion that was a hallmark of historical establishments of religion was coercion of religious orthodoxy and of financial support *by force of law and threat of penalty*."[38] Justice Kennedy, though not an originalist, took this approach as well, writing that "the Establishment Clause . . . guarantees at a minimum that a government may not coerce anyone to support or participate in religion or its exercise, or otherwise act in a way which 'establishes a [state] religion or religious faith, or tends to do so.' "[39]

This approach sees no constitutional limit on making religion a part of government activities, such as through prayer or religious symbols, provided that there is no coercion. Judges using this approach not only are untroubled by government aid to religious institutions but believe that it violates free exercise of religion to deny religious institutions benefits that are provided to secular private institutions.

We have already seen the Court shift toward this view. In *Town of Greece v. Galloway,* for example, the Court held that it did not violate the Establishment Clause for a town board to begin virtually every meeting over a ten-year period with a prayer by a Christian minister.[40] The Town of Greece is a suburb of Rochester, New York, of just under one hundred thousand people. Its town board opened meetings with a moment of silence until 1999, when the town supervisors began inviting ministers to start meetings each month with a prayer. From 1999 to 2007, the town invited exclusively Christian ministers, most of whom gave explicitly Christian prayers. In 2007, after complaints were made to the town board, clergy from other religions were invited for about four months. But then for the next eighteen months, the town board reverted to inviting only Christian clergy, and their prayers almost always had explicitly Christian content.

The Court, in a five-to-four decision, held that the Town of Greece did not violate the Establishment Clause. Justice Kennedy, in his majority opinion, expressed great deference to the government's wish to have prayers before legislative sessions: "Absent a pattern of prayers that over time denigrate, proselytize, or betray an impermissible government purpose, a challenge based solely on the content of a prayer will not likely establish a constitutional violation."[41] Justice Thomas gave the originalist perspective in a concurring opinion: "To the extent coercion is relevant to the Establishment Clause analysis, it is actual legal coercion that counts — not the 'subtle coercive pressures' allegedly felt by respondents in this case."[42] Even highly sectarian prayers can now become a regular part of government meetings throughout the country.

Another recent example of this shift is the Court's 2019 decision in *American Legion v. American Humanist Association,* in which it reversed a lower court and allowed a thirty-two-foot cross on a large pedestal (about forty feet high altogether) to remain at a busy intersection on public property in Prince George's County, Maryland.[43] In concluding that the cross did not violate the First Amendment, the Court stressed that it was put there after World War I as a tribute to those who died in military service and thus should be considered a tribute to fallen soldiers.

Justice Alito's majority opinion said that the cross "has also taken on a secular meaning. Indeed, there are instances in which its message is now almost entirely secular."[44] In this instance, Alito wrote, it was a symbol for those who died in a war: "The Bladensburg Cross carries special significance in commemorating World War I. Due in large part to the image of the simple wooden crosses that originally marked the graves of American soldiers killed in the war, the cross became a symbol of their sacrifice, and the design of the Bladensburg Cross must be understood in light of that background."[45] A cross is a quintessentially Christian symbol; it is not found on graves in Jewish cemeteries even of those who died in military service. Yet the Court had no trouble with its prominent display on public property.

Again, Justice Thomas wrote a concurring opinion to express the originalist perspective, arguing that the Establishment Clause does not apply to state and local governments at all and that these governments may mandate official state religions and coerce religious participation:

> The text and history of this Clause suggest that it should not be incorporated against the States. Even if the Clause expresses an individual right enforceable against the States, it is limited by its text to "law[s]" enacted by a legislature, so it is unclear whether the Bladensburg Cross would implicate any incorporated right. And even if it did, this religious display does not involve the type of actual legal coercion that was a hallmark of historical establishments of religion. Therefore, the Cross is clearly constitutional.[46]

Though the originalists claim that their approach to the Establishment Clause reflects its original meaning, a true originalist perspective actually provides a stronger case for interpreting the clause to require separation of church and state.[47] The result of the present majority's rulings will be a far greater presence of prayers at public events, no limit on religious symbols on government property, and the government being constitutionally required to subsidize religious schools when it funds private secular schools.[48]

We are also seeing a shift with regard to the Free Exercise Clause. For decades, the Court took the position that government should stay out of the business of worship and the internal operations of religious institutions; that is, the Free Exercise Clause requires that the government not act with animus toward religion. It did not require special accommodations for religious people when the government passes neutral laws of general applicability. Instead, the Court expected all people to live by the same rules when the government was acting in its secular capacity.

This approach is reflected in the Court's 1990 decision in *Employment Division v. Smith*.[49] *Smith* involved a challenge by Native Americans to an Oregon law prohibiting use of peyote, a hallucinogenic substance they used in certain religious rituals. The Native Americans challenged the state's determination that this use of peyote, for which they were fired from their jobs, was misconduct disqualifying them from receiving unemployment compensation benefits.

Justice Scalia, writing for the majority, rejected the claim that free exercise of religion required an exemption from an otherwise valid law. He said that "we have never held that an individual's religious beliefs excuse him from compliance with an otherwise valid law prohibiting conduct that the State is free to regulate."[50] Scalia declared "that the right of free exercise does not relieve an individual of the obligation to comply with a 'valid and neutral law of general applicability on the ground that the law proscribes (or prescribes) conduct that his religion prescribes (or proscribes).' "[51] To rule otherwise would force courts to "determine the 'centrality' of religious beliefs before applying a 'compelling interest' test in the free exercise field." But, Scalia asked, "what principle of law or logic can be brought to bear to contradict a believer's assertion that a particular act is 'central' to his personal faith?"[52] This sentiment echoed Justice Stevens's earlier objections to offering special accommodations to religious practitioners, where he emphasized "the overriding interest in keeping the government—whether the legislature or the courts—out of the business of evaluating the relative merits of differing religious claims." To do otherwise, Stevens warned, ran the risk that "governmental approval of some and disapproval of others will be perceived as favoring one religion over another" in violation of the Establishment Clause.[53]

This analysis makes sense for many reasons. In a society with enormous religious pluralism, it would be unwieldy to create an exception any time a law burdened someone's beliefs. Also, if exceptions are granted for religion, courts will have the impossible task of defining what is a "religion." The Constitution does not create exceptions to general laws for other exercises of conscience; preferring religious beliefs over other kinds of belief would violate the First Amendment prohibition against government's taking any action respecting an establishment of religion.

But a majority of the justices appear ready to do just that. Most notably, it is the originalist justices who want to give special preference to religion, even though Justice Scalia wrote the opinion in *Employment Division v. Smith*. In June 2021, in *Fulton v. City of Philadelphia*, Justice Alito, joined by Justices Thomas and Gorsuch, urged that *Smith* be overruled.[54] Justice Barrett, joined by Justice Kavanaugh, expressed support for this position, though they saw no need to go that far in that case. These justices believe that strict scrutiny is required when the government substantially burdens religion and that the government must, whenever possible, take the approach that imposes the least restriction on religious liberty, even if that means exempting religious practitioners from laws that everyone else has to obey.

In practical terms, this will give people the ability to violate laws, including antidiscrimination statutes, in the name of their religion. The *Fulton* case involved Philadelphia's refusal to contract with organizations that engage in forbidden discrimination. The city routinely contracts with private social service agencies to help place children in foster homes. Those agencies are "delegated" the power of the government in determining whether individuals satisfy the state requirements for becoming foster parents. Every contract explicitly prohibits these agencies from discriminating on the basis of race, sex, religion, and sexual orientation.

Catholic Social Services had long participated in this program, but in recent years it had declined to do so because of the contractual requirement that it not discriminate based on sexual orientation. The organization claimed that its religious beliefs do not allow it to provide inspections of same-sex couples to determine their eligibility as foster parents, or to place children with those couples.

Catholic Social Services challenged the nondiscrimination requirement as violating its First Amendment rights. The federal district court and the United States Court of Appeals for the Third Circuit rejected these arguments, but the Supreme Court reversed those decisions and ruled in favor of Catholic Social Services. Chief Justice Roberts, writing for the court, said that the Philadelphia law allowed city officials to grant exceptions from the antidiscrimination requirement in the law and that this discretion meant it was not a sufficiently general law. The *possibility* of discrimination in exercising this discretion, he wrote, made Philadelphia's requirement a violation of the free exercise of religion. But there was no evidence that Philadelphia actually treated Catholic Social Services differently from other social service agencies or used its discretion in an impermissible way.

The *Fulton* decision is part of a broader trend of expanding the protection of free exercise of religion at the expense of other crucial government interests. Earlier in the year, the court found that California violated the free exercise of religion when it limited the size of religious gatherings in homes as a public health measure during the pandemic, even though secular gatherings were restricted in exactly the same way.[55]

In 2018, the Court ruled in favor of a baker who refused to design and bake a cake for a same-sex couple due to his religious beliefs, in violation of a Colorado law prohibiting discrimination by places of public accommodation.[56] Many cases now pending raise the same issue, involving florists, photographers, and stationery stores that refuse to serve same-sex couples because of the business owners' religious beliefs. In 2020, the Court held in *Bostock v. Clayton County* that Title VII of the 1964 Civil Rights Act protects employees against discrimination based on sexual orientation or gender identity.[57] Now, many employers have gone to court, claiming a religious right to discriminate against LGBTQ individuals. Justices Alito and Thomas dissented in *Bostock*, stressing the right to discriminate based on religion.[58]

The underlying issue is profoundly important. There is an inherent tension between liberty and equality. Any law that prohibits discrimination limits the freedom to discriminate. For over half a century, the Supreme Court has found that stopping discrimination is more important than protecting a right to discriminate. In *Newman v. Piggie Park Enterprises*, in 1968, the court rejected a challenge to the 1964 Civil Rights Act, which prohibits race discrimination by places of public accommodation, on the ground that it interfered with the "free exercise of the Defendant's religion." The Court called the claim "patently frivolous."[59]

At the oral argument in *Fulton*, Justices Breyer and Kagan asked the lawyer for Catholic Social Services whether Philadelphia could refuse to contract with a social services agency that, because of its religious beliefs, refused to place children with interracial couples. The lawyer immediately said that the city could refuse to contract because that would involve race discrimination, whereas this case concerned sexual orientation discrimination. But there is no basis for this distinction: government has a compelling interest in stopping both forms of discrimination.

The conservative majority on the Court will most likely continue to use the Free Exercise Clause to permit religiously based discrimination. But despite what originalist justices may suggest, nothing in the original meaning of the Free Exercise Clause implies that it was meant to provide exceptions from general laws on account of religious beliefs.

It is urgent that we realize how radical the transformations in constitutional law are likely to be in the years ahead, and especially the degree to which these changes will be due to originalism.[60] Many conservatives will cheer these shifts: the end of constitutional protections of privacy, the narrowing of congressional powers, the end of the separation of church and state, and the aggressive protection of free exercise of religion even when it involves discrimination.

———

But ultimately, we must ask whether these are desirable ways to interpret the Constitution. The endless fight between originalists and non-originalists — in which this book admittedly takes part — obscures that issue. Originalism is a fallacy. It is a rhetorical shield that conservatives use to pretend they are not making value judgments, when that is exactly what they are doing.[61] Rather than defend those value choices, originalists assert that their answers are based on "original meaning" — except when that supposedly sacred meaning fails to give the conservative results they desire.

Justice Scalia, perhaps the foremost champion of originalism, found in the Constitution robust protection for gun rights, no limit on prayer in public schools or at government events, no right to contraception or abortion, and a prohibition on affirmative action. All this, of course, is the modern Republican Party platform, not what those in 1787, 1791, or 1868 had in mind.

Now is the time to get past the debate over originalism and non-originalism and focus instead on a far more consequential question. What meaning for the words of the Constitution would advance the noblest goals of a modern, democratic, pluralistic society, and how should that meaning be applied in specific cases? The Constitution has always been, and will always be, about balancing the majority's values against the values that should be protected from society's majorities. That is what every Supreme Court opinion concerning the Constitution should be about, and what scholars and commentators on constitutional matters should consider first and last. Everything else is a distraction.

NOTES

PREFACE

1. Robert Bork, *Neutral Principles and Some First Amendment Problems*, 47 IND. L.J. 1, 2–3 (1971).

2. Roe v. Wade, 410 U.S. 113 (1973).

3. Paul Brest, *The Misconceived Quest for the Original Understanding*, 60 B.U. L. Rev. 204 (1980); RONALD DWORKIN, TAKING RIGHTS SERIOUSLY (1977); JOHN HART ELY, DEMOCRACY AND DISTRUST (1980); LAURENCE TRIBE, CONSTITUTIONAL CHOICES (1985).

4. STEVEN G. CALABRESI, ED., ORIGINALISM: A QUARTER CENTURY OF DEBATE 6 (2007).

5. Antonin Scalia, *Foreword, id.* at 44.

6. *See, e.g.,* JACK BALKIN, LIVING ORIGINALISM (2011).

7. For excellent criticisms of originalism, *see* ERIC SEGALL, ORIGINALISM AS FAITH (2018); FRANK CROSS, THE FAILED PROMISE OF ORIGINALISM (2013).

CHAPTER 1. THE RISE OF ORIGINALISM

1. Plessy v. Ferguson, 163 U.S. 537 (1896); RICHARD KLUGER, SIMPLE JUSTICE: THE HISTORY OF BROWN V. BOARD OF EDUCATION AND BLACK AMERICA'S STRUGGLE FOR EQUALITY 605–6 (1975) (describing Rehnquist's memo to Justice Robert Jackson).

2. *See* ERWIN CHEMERINSKY, PRESUMED GUILTY: HOW THE SUPREME COURT EMPOWERED THE POLICE AND SUBVERTED CIVIL RIGHTS (2021); San Antonio Indep. Sch. Dist. v. Rodriguez, 411 U.S. 1, 35 (1973).

3. Roe v. Wade, 410 U.S. 113 (1973).

---

4. Robert Bork, *Neutral Principles and Some First Amendment Problems*, 47 IND. L.J. 1 (1971).

5. *See* JOHN HART ELY, DEMOCRACY AND DISTRUST: A THEORY OF JUDICIAL REVIEW 1 (1980) (contrasting originalism and non-originalism).

6. Robert J. Delahunty & John Yoo, *Saving Originalism*, 113 MICH. L. REV. 1081, 1089 (2015). Justice Hugo Black was famous for claiming that he was following the literal language of the Constitution. But he did not express the view that the Constitution's meaning was limited to what its drafters intended.

7. Bork, *supra* note 4, at 7.

8. Griswold v. Connecticut, 381 U.S. 479, 499 (1965) (declaring unconstitutional a Connecticut law prohibiting the sale, distribution, or use of contraceptives as violating the right to privacy).

9. *See, e.g.,* John Hart Ely, *The Wages of Crying Wolf: A Comment on* Roe v. Wade, 82 YALE L.J. 920 (1973). Although Ely was not an originalist, his criticism of *Roe v. Wade* was very much written in originalist language.

10. *Nomination of Robert H. Bork to Be Associate Justice of the Supreme Court of the United States: Hearing Before the S. Comm. on the Judiciary,* 100th Cong. (1987) (opening statement of Sen. Edward Kennedy, S. Comm. on the Judiciary).

11. Bolling v. Sharpe, 347 U.S. 497, 500 (1954) (holding that equal protection applies to the federal government through the Due Process Clause of the Fifth Amendment and declaring unconstitutional the federal law requiring segregation of the District of Columbia public schools).

12. *See, e.g.,* Reynolds v. Sims, 377 U.S. 533 (1964) (articulating the rule of one person – one vote).

13. *Bork* MERRIAM-WEBSTER, https://www.merriam-webster.com/dictionary/bork.

14. Bork, *supra* note 4, at 9.

15. Jason Silverstein, *Here's What Mitch McConnell Said About Not Filing a Supreme Court Vacancy in an Election Year,* CBS NEWS (Sept. 19, 2020, 1:32 PM), https://www.cbsnews.com/news/mitch-mcconnell-supreme-court-vacancy-election-year-senate/.

16. RUTH MARCUS, SUPREME AMBITION: BRETT KAVANAUGH AND THE CONSERVATIVE TAKEOVER 69 (2019).

17. *Id.*

18. Marcia Coyle, *Amy Barrett Touts Scalia in Remarks from Rose Garden,* LAW. COM: THE NATIONAL LAW JOURNAL (Sept. 26, 2020, 5:27 PM), https://www.law.com/nationallawjournal/2020/09/26/his-judicial-philosophy-is-mine-amy-barrett-touts-scalia-in-remarks-from-rose-garden/.

19. *Nomination of Amy Coney Barrett for Supreme Court of the United States: Hearing Before the S. Comm. on the Judiciary*, 116th Cong. (2020) (statement from Hon. Amy Coney Barrett, J., then nominee).

20. Amy C. Barrett, *Precedent and Jurisprudential Disagreement*, 91 Tex. L. Rev. 1711, 1728 (2012–13).

21. Amy Coney Barrett, *Stare Decisis and Due Process*, 74 U. Colo. L. Rev. 1011, 1013 (2003).

22. John O. McGinnis, *Which Justices Are Originalists?*, Law & Liberty (Nov. 9, 2018), https://lawliberty.org/which-justices-are-originalists/.

23. The Hon. Neil M. Gorsuch, *Of Lions and Bears, Judges and Legislators, and the Legacy of Justice Scalia*, 66 Case W. Res. L. Rev. 905, 906 (2016).

24. Jamal Greene, *On the Origins of Originalism*, 88 Texas L. Rev. 1, 2–3 (2009).

25. *Nomination of Elena Kagan to Be an Associate Justice of the Supreme Court of the United States: Hearing Before the S. Comm. on the Judiciary*, 111th Cong. (2010) (statement from Hon. Elena Kagan, J., then nominee).

26. McCulloch v. Maryland, 17 U.S. 316, 407 (1819).

27. Eric J. Segall, Originalism as Faith 7 (2018).

28. *Id.* at 8.

29. Katie Glueck, *Scalia: The Constitution Is "Dead,"* Politico (Jan. 29, 2013, 8:26 AM), https://www.politico.com/story/2013/01/scalia-the-constitution-is -dead-086853.

30. Scott K. Petersen, *The Punishment Need Not Fit the Crime:* Harmelin v. Michigan *and the Eighth Amendment*, 20 Pepp. L. Rev. 747, 767–71 (1993).

31. Glossip v. Gross, 576 U.S. 863, 894 (2015) (Scalia, J., concurring).

32. Trop v. Dulles, 356 U.S. 86, 101 (1958).

33. *Glossip, supra* note 31, at 908 (Breyer, J., dissenting).

34. *See Roe, supra* note 3, at 163–65.

35. Raoul Berger, Government by Judiciary: The Transformation of the Fourteenth Amendment 383 (President and Fellows of Harvard College eds., 1971); Bork, *supra* note 5, at 13–14; Segall, *supra* note 28, at 10; Jeremy K. Kessler & David E. Pozen, *Working Themselves Impure: A Life Cycle Theory of Legal Theories*, 83 U. Chi. L. Rev. 1819, 1844 (2016).

36. Richard H. Fallon Jr., *Are Originalist Constitutional Theories Principled, or Are They Rationalizations for Conservatism?*, 34 Harv. J.L. & Pub. Pol'y 5, 7, 8 (2011).

37. John Wofford, *The Blinding Light: The Uses of History in Constitutional Interpretation*, 31 U. Chi. L. Rev. 502, 508–9 (1964).

38. *See, e.g.,* United States v. Butler, 297 U.S. 1, 65–66 (1936) (describing Madison as believing that Congress could tax and spend only to carry out specific powers enumerated in the Constitution, while Hamilton believed that Congress could tax and spend for the "general welfare").

39. Kessler & Pozen, *supra* note 35, at 1845.

40. Antonin Scalia, *Address Before the Attorney General's Conference on Economic Liberties in Washington, D.C.* (June 14, 1986), *in* ORIGINAL MEANING JURISPRUDENCE: A SOURCEBOOK 101, 106 (1987); Antonin Scalia, *Common-Law Courts in a Civil-Law System: The Role of United States Federal Courts in Interpreting the Constitution and Laws, in* A MATTER OF INTERPRETATION: FEDERAL COURTS AND THE LAW 3, 38 (Amy Gutmann ed., 1997).

41. *See* Kessler & Pozen, *supra* note 35, at 1846; Fallon Jr., *supra* note 36, at 8.

42. *See, e.g.,* Thomas R. Lee & Stephen C. Mouritsen, *Judging Ordinary Meaning,* 127 YALE L.J. 788 (2018); Thomas R. Lee & Stephen C. Mouritsen, *The Corpus and the Critics,* 88 U. CHI. L. REV. (2021).

43. Kessler & Pozen, *supra* note 35, at 1844, 1845.

44. Brown v. Bd. of Educ. of Topeka, Shawnee Cnty. Kan., 347 U.S. 483, 495 (1954); Plessy, *supra* note 1.

45. Korematsu v. United States, 323 U.S. 214, 223–24 (1944) (upholding the evacuation of Japanese Americans from the West Coast during World War II).

46. Trump v. Hawaii, 138 S. Ct. 2392, 2423 (2018).

47. District of Columbia v. Heller, 554 U.S. 570, 627–34 (2008).

48. Citizens United v. Fed. Election Com'n, 558 U.S. 310, 333–36 (2010).

49. Keith E. Whittington, *The New Originalism,* 2 GEO. J.L. & PUB. POL'Y 599, 609 (2004).

50. Shelby County, Ala. v. Holder 570 U.S. 529, 548–51 (2013).

51. *Id.* at 593–94 (Ginsburg, J., dissenting).

52. United States v. Windsor, 570 U.S. 744, 772–75 (2013).

53. *Id.* at 778 (Scalia, J., dissenting).

54. *Id.* at 804 (Alito, J., dissenting).

55. Frederick Schauer, *Formalism,* 97 YALE L.J. 509, 510 (1988).

56. Scalia, *Common-Law Courts, supra* note 40.

57. For an excellent description of this, *see* EDWARD PURCELL, THE CRISIS OF DEMOCRATIC THEORY (2d ed. 2014).

58. Southern Pac. Co. v. Jensen, 244 U.S. 205, 222 (1917) (Holmes, J., dissenting).

CHAPTER 2. THE ALLURE OF ORIGINALISM

1. Walter Benn Michaels, *Response to Perry and Simon*, 58 S. CAL. L. REV. 673, 673 (1985).

2. *Id.*

3. Edward Melvin, *Judicial Activism: The Violation of an Oath*, 27 CATH. L. REV. 283, 284 (1982).

4. Letter from Thomas Jefferson to William Johnson (June 12, 1823), *in Founders Online*, NATIONAL ARCHIVES, https://founders.archives.gov /documents/Jefferson/98-01-02-3562.

5. John Choon Yoo, *Marshall's Plan: The Early Supreme Court and Statutory Interpretation*, 101 YALE L.J. 1607, 1616 (1992).

6. South Carolina v. United States, 199 U.S. 437, 448 (1905).

7. ERIC J. SEGALL, ORIGINALISM AS FAITH 172 (2018).

8. U.S. v. Classic, 313 U.S. 299, 316 (1941).

9. Home Bldg. & Loan Ass'n v. Blaisdell, 290 U.S. 398, 442-43 (1934).

10. Brown v. Bd. of Educ. of Topeka, Shawnee Cnty. Kan., 347 U.S. 483, 492 (1954).

11. Harper v. Va. Bd. of Elec., 383 U.S. 663, 669 (1996).

12. Obergefell v. Hodges, 576 US. 644, 663-64 (2015).

13. ALEXANDER BICKEL, THE LEAST DANGEROUS BRANCH: THE SUPREME COURT AT THE BAR OF POLITICS 17-18 (1962).

14. Robert Bork, *Neutral Principles and Some First Amendment Problems*, 47 IND. L.J. 1, 2-3 (1971).

15. Randy Barnett, *Original Ideas on Originalism: The Misconceived Assumption About Constitutional Assumptions*, 103 NW. U. L. REV. 615, 660 (2009).

16. David Strauss, *Why Conservatives Shouldn't Be Originalists*, 31 HARV. J.L. & PUB. POL'Y 969, 973 (2008).

17. Bork, *supra* note 14, at 5-6.

18. *Id.* at 6-8.

19. RAOUL BERGER, GOVERNMENT BY JUDICIARY: THE TRANSFORMA-TION OF THE FOURTEENTH AMENDMENT (1997).

20. Douglas Martin, *Raoul Berger, 99, an Expert on Constitution in 2nd Career*, N.Y. TIMES, Sept. 28, 2000, at C27.

21. BERGER, *supra* note 19, at 457.

22. *Id.* at 461.

23. Transcript of *Firing Line* with guest Raoul Berger (1977), *available at* https://digitalcollections.hoover.org/internal/media/dispatcher/82207/full.

24. *Id.* at 6.

25. *Id.* at 8.

26. *Id.* at 3.

27. Edwin Meese III, *Construing the Constitution*, 19 U.C. DAVIS L. REV. 22 (1985).

28. Michael Kruse, *The Weekend at Yale That Changed American Politics*, POLIT-ICO (Sept./Oct. 2018), https://www.politico.com/magazine/story/2018/08/27/federalist-society-yale-history-conservative-law-court-219608.

29. Meese, *supra* note 27, at 29.

30. *Id.* at 27.

31. *Nomination of Robert H. Bork to Be Associate Justice of the Supreme Court of the United States: Hearing Before the S. Comm. on the Judiciary*, 100th Cong. 103 (1987).

32. *Id.* at 104.

33. *Id.* at 249; *see also* Kurt T. Lash, *Inkblot: The Ninth Amendment as Textual Justification for Judicial Enforcement of the Right to Privacy*, 80 U. CHI. L. REV. DIA-LOGUE 219, 220 (2013).

34. Mark Pulliam, *The Original Originalist*, CITY JOURNAL (2018), https://www.city-journal.org/html/robert-bork-16039.html.

35. SEGALL, *supra* note 7, at 175.

36. Bork, *supra* note 14, at 8.

37. Paul Brest, *The Misconceived Quest for the Original Understanding*, 60 B.U. L. REV. 204 (1980).

38. SEGALL, *supra* note 7, at 176.

39. Alfred Avins, *Literacy Tests, the Fourteenth Amendment, and District of Columbia Voting: The Original Intent*, WASH. U. L.Q. 429, 429–30 (1965) ("[T]he amending power as set forth in article V of the United States Constitution . . . [is] exclusive, and . . . any changes made in a constitution must be made in accordance with such provisions, and not otherwise. As a corollary, this author's position is that a constitution is exactly what its framers intended it to be, . . . and that the intent of the framers is the beginning, middle, and end of all inquiry as to meaning"); *see also* MCGINNIS & RAPPAPORT, ORIGINALISM AND THE GOOD CONSTITUTION 88–94 (2013) ("Judicial updating . . . undermines the constitutional amendment process. Consequently, one cannot, to a significant degree, employ both judicial updating and constitutional amendments. One must choose between them").

40. Melvin, *supra* note 3, at 384.

41. Eric Posner, *The U.S. Constitution Is Impossible to Amend*, SLATE (May 5, 2014), https://slate.com/news-and-politics/2014/05/amending-the-constitution-is-much-too-hard-blame-the-founders.html.

42. Jamal Greene, *Selling Originalism,* GEO. L.J. 657, 716 (2009); *see also* LEE J. STRANG, ORIGINALISM'S PROMISE: A NATURAL LAW ACCOUNT OF THE AMERICAN CONSTITUTION 2 (2019) ("Originalism promises that the Framing, Ratification, and subsequent following of the Constitution was a rational process, one that then and today gives Americans sound reasons to follow").

43. FRANK CROSS, THE FAILED PROMISE OF ORIGINALISM 5 (2013).

44. *Id.* at 11.

45. Mitchell Berman, *Originalism Is Bunk,* 84 N.Y.U. L. REV. 1, 8 (2009).

46. CROSS, *supra* note 43, at 6.

47. *Id.* at 4.

48. *See* JACK M. BALKIN, LIVING ORIGINALISM 21 (2011).

49. Justice Neil Gorsuch, *Why Originalism Is the Best Approach to the Constitution,* TIME (Sept. 6, 2019), https://time.com/5670400/justice-neil-gorsuch-why-originalism-is-the-best-approach-to-the-constitution/.

50. Jack M. Balkin, *Abortion and Original Meaning,* 24 CONST. COMMENT. 291, 293 (2007) (emphasis added).

51. *Id.*

52. Balkin, *The New Originalism and the Uses of History,* 82 FORDHAM L. REV. 641, 652 (2013).

53. Balkin, *supra* note 48, at 352.

54. *Id.* at 292.

55. SEGALL, *supra* note 7, at 96.

56. William Baude, *Is Originalism Our Law,* 115 COLUM. L. REV. 2349, 2355 (2015) (emphasis omitted).

57. *Id.* at 2356.

58. *Id.*

59. *Id.* at 2358.

60. *Id.* at 2360.

61. *Obergefell, supra* note 12, at 680–81 .

62. Baude, *supra* note 56, at 2382.

63. *Obergefell, supra* note 12, at 717 (Scalia, J., dissenting) ("[The majority] discovered in the Fourteenth Amendment a 'fundamental right' overlooked by every person alive at the time of ratification, and almost everyone else in the time since"). SEGALL, *supra* note 7, at 108.

64. Baude, *supra* note 56, at 2352.

65. Lawrence Lessig, *Fidelity and Constraint,* 65 FORDHAM L. REV. 1365, 1366 (1997).

66. Antonin Scalia, *Originalism: The Lesser Evil*, 57 U. CIN. L. REV. 849 (1989); *see also* Eric Segall, *Scalia Speaks Well: But Not About Originalism*, DORF ON LAW (Nov. 10, 2017), http://www.dorfonlaw.org/2017/11/scalia-speaks -well-but-not-about.html (quoting Scalia, non-originalists "explode into a hundred different groups, or indeed as many groups as there are academics. . . . The fact is that no principle of interpretation other than originalism has even the shadow of a chance of attracting a general adherence. As a practical matter, there is no alternative to originalism but standardless judicial constitution-making"); *see also* Elain McArdle, *In Inaugural Vaughan Lecture, Scalia Defends the "Methodology of Originalism,"* HARV. L. TODAY (Oct. 3, 2008): "But all of these questions pose enormous difficulty for non-originalists, who must agonize over what the modern Constitution ought to mean with each of these subjects, and then agonize again five or 10 years later because times change."

CHAPTER 3. THE EPISTEMOLOGICAL PROBLEM

1. Woo v. Superior Court, 83 Cal. App. 4th 967 (2000).

2. *Id.* at 970.

3. *See, e.g.*, Paul Brest, *The Misconceived Quest for the Original Understanding*, 60 B.U. L. REV. 204, 209–22 (1980).

4. United States v. Butler, 297 U.S. 1, 65 (1936).

5. *Id.*

6. Jeffrey Shaman, *The Constitution, the Supreme Court, and Creativity*, 9 HASTINGS CONST. L.Q. 257, 267 (1982).

7. Youngstown Sheet & Tube v. Sawyer, 343 U.S. 579, 634 (1952) (Jackson, J., concurring).

8. WILLIAM WINSLOW CROSSKEY, POLITICS AND THE CONSTITUTION IN THE HISTORY OF THE UNITED STATES 1009 (1953).

9. The Records of the Federal Convention of 1787.

10. THE FEDERALIST NO. 78 (Alexander Hamilton).

11. Marbury v. Madison, 5 U.S. (1 Cranch) 137, 180 (1803).

12. United States v. Nixon, 418 U.S. 683 (1974).

13. Goldwater v. Carter, 444 U.S. 996 (1979) (the Court dismissed a challenge to President Carter's rescission of a treaty on the grounds that the case posed a political question; whether the president can do this thus remains unresolved).

14. John Wofford, *The Blinding Light: The Uses of History in Constitutional Interpretation*, 31 U. CHI. L. REV. 502, 508–9 (1964).

15. Note, *Original Meaning and Its Limits*, 120 HARV. L. REV. 1279 (2007).

16. ANTONIN SCALIA, A MATTER OF INTERPRETATION: FEDERAL COURTS AND THE LAW 47 (Amy Gutmann ed., 1997).

17. Caroline Mala Corbin, *Opportunistic Originalism and the Establishment Clause,* 54 WAKE FOREST L. REV. 617, 649 (2019).

18. *See, e.g.,* Thomas R. Lee & Stephen C. Mouritsen, *Judging Ordinary Meaning,* 127 YALE L.J. 788 (2018); Thomas R. Lee & Stephen C. Mouritsen, *The Corpus and the Critics,* 88 U. CHI. L. REV. (2021).

19. District of Columbia v. Heller, 554 U.S. 570 (2008).

20. Randy Barnett, Opinion, *News Flash: The Constitution Means What It Says,* WALL ST. J., June 27, 2008, at A13; *Heller, supra* note 19, at 576.

21. *Heller, supra* note 19, at 643 (Stevens, J., dissenting).

22. *Id.* at 646.

23. *Id.* at 576-77.

24. Mark Tushnet, *Heller and the New Originalism,* 69 OHIO ST. L.J. 609, 621 (2008).

25. Caroline Mala Corbin, *Opportunistic Originalism and the Establishment Clause,* 54 WAKE FOREST L. REV. 617, 623 (2019).

26. Lee v. Weisman, 505 U.S. 577, 640 (1992) (Scalia, J., dissenting).

27. Town of Greece v. Galloway, 572 U.S. 565, 610 (2014) (Thomas, J., concurring) (as discussed in the next chapter, Justice Thomas does not believe, based on originalism, that the Establishment Clause applies to the states at all).

28. *See* HOWARD GILLMAN & ERWIN CHEMERINSKY, THE RELIGION CLAUSES: THE CASE FOR SEPARATING CHURCH AND STATE (2020).

29. NIGEL ASTON, RELIGION AND REVOLUTION IN FRANCE, 1780-1804, at 187-88 (2000).

30. John K. Wilson, *Religion Under the State Constitutions, 1776-1800,* 32 J. CHURCH & STATE 753, 754-73 (1990).

31. Trinity Lutheran Church of Columbia Inc. v. Comer, 137 U.S. 2012, 2017 (2017).

32. *Id.* at 2018; *see also* MO. CONST. art. I, § 7 ("[N]o money shall ever be taken from the public treasury, directly or indirectly, in aid of any church, sect or denomination of religion").

33. *See* Keith E. Whittington, *Originalism: A Critical Introduction,* 82 FORDHAM L. REV. 375, 378 (2013).

34. *Trinity Lutheran, supra* note 31, at 2020 ("[T]he [McDaniel] Court struck down under the Free Exercise Clause a Tennessee statute disqualifying ministers from serving as delegates to the State's constitutional convention").

35. THOMAS BUCKLEY, CHURCH AND STATE IN REVOLUTIONARY VIRGINIA 108 (1977).

36. *Id.*, at 109.

37. Vincent Phillip Muñoz, *James Madison's Principle of Religious Liberty*, 97 AM. POL. SCI. REV. 17–32, 21–24 (2003).

38. *See* Noah Feldman, *The Intellectual Origins of the Establishment Clause*, 77 N.Y.U. L. REV. 346, 352 (2002) ("[T]he Framers cared mostly about dissenters' liberty of conscience from paying taxes").

39. *Trinity Lutheran*, *supra* note 31, at 2023 ("[O]nly a state interest 'of the highest order' can justify the Department's discriminatory policy. Yet the Department offers nothing more than Missouri's policy preference for skating as far as possible from religious establishment concerns" [quoting McDaniel v. Paty, 435 U.S. 618, 628 (1978)]).

40. Antonin Scalia, *Originalism: The Lesser Evil*, 57 U. CIN. L. REV. 849, 856 (1989).

41. Wilson v. Arkansas, 514 U.S. 927 (1995).

42. *See, e.g.*, Lange v. California, 141 S. Ct. 2011 (2021) (reviewing common law practices in deciding whether police can enter a home without a warrant in hot pursuit when they are chasing someone suspected of a misdemeanor).

43. Printz v. United States, 521 U.S. 898 (1997).

44. Alfred H. Kelly, *Clio and the Court: An Illicit Love Affair*, 1965 SUP. CT. REV. 119, 122 (1965).

45. *See, e.g.*, Stump v. Sparkman, 435 U.S. 349 (1978); Mireles v. Waco, 502 U.S. 9 (1991).

46. J. Randolph Block, *Stump v. Sparkman and the History of Judicial Immunity*, 1980 DUKE L.J. 879 (1980).

47. *See* New Prime Inc. v. Oliveria 139 U.S. 532, 539–43 (2019); Iancu v. Brunetti 139 U.S. 2294, 2299–301 (2019).

48. FRANK B. CROSS, THE FAILED PROMISE OF ORIGINALISM, 56–57 (2013).

49. *See, e.g.*, Michael H. v. Gerald D., 491 U.S. 110, 128 n.6 (1989) (Scalia, J., plurality opinion); for the broad view, *see* Jack M. Balkin, *Abortion and Original Meaning*, 24 CONST. COMMENT. 291, 304–5 (2007); *see also* Jack M. Balkin, *Framework Originalism and the Living Constitution*, 103 NW. U. L. REV. 549, 553 (2009); Randy E. Barnett, *Trumping Precedent with Original Meaning: Not as Radical as It Sounds*, 22 CONST. COMMENT. 257, 264 (2005).

50. Peter J. Smith, *How Different Are Originalism and Non-Originalism*, 62 HASTINGS L.J. 707, 709 (2010).

51. *See* United States v. Virginia, 518 U.S. 515, 566–601 (1996) (Scalia, J., dissenting).

52. Robert H. Bork, *Neutral Principles and Some First Amendment Problems*, 47 IND. L.J. 1, 14 (1971); BORK, THE TEMPTING OF AMERICA: THE POLITICAL SEDUCTION OF THE LAW 82 (1990).

53. *See* GEOFFREY R. STONE ET AL., CONSTITUTIONAL LAW 476 (5th ed. 2005).

54. *See* RICHARD KLUGER, SIMPLE JUSTICE: THE HISTORY OF BROWN V. BOARD OF EDUCATION AND BLACK AMERICA'S STRUGGLE FOR EQUAL-ITY, 633–34 (1976); *see also* STONE, *supra* note 53, at 476 (The states permitting segregated schools were California, Kansas, Missouri, Nevada, New York, Ohio, Pennsylvania, and West Virginia. The states entirely excluding Black children from public education were Delaware, Indiana, Illinois, Kentucky, and Maryland.)

55. *See* RAOUL BERGER, GOVERNMENT BY JUDICIARY: THE TRANS-FORMATION OF THE FOURTEENTH AMENDMENT 125 (1977); *see also* Stone, *supra* note 53, at 476.

56. *See* Stone, *supra* note 53, at 476; John P. Frank & Robert F. Munro, *The Original Understanding of "Equal Protection of the Laws,"* WASH. U. L. Q. 421, 460–62 (1972).

57. Bork, *supra* note 52, at 6.

58. Edwin Meese, Speech to American Bar Association on "Jurisprudence of Original Intention" (July 9, 1985), https://www.justice.gov/sites/default/files/ag/legacy/2011/08/23/07-09-1985.pdf.

59. *Id.*

60. *Michael H., supra* note 49, at 148 n.6.

61. *Confirmation Hearing on the Nomination of John G. Roberts, Jr. to Be Chief Justice of the United States: Hearings Before the Comm. on the Judiciary*, 109th Cong. 55–56 (2005), http://www.uscourts.gov/educational-resources/educational-activities/chief-justice-roberts-statement-nomination-process.

62. Chuck Grassley, *Grassley Statement on the President's Nomination of Merrick Garland to the U.S. Supreme Court* (Mar. 16, 2016), https://www.grassley.senate.gov/news/news-releases/grassley-statement-presidents-nomination-merrick-garland-us-supreme-court.

63. Maryland v. King, 569 U.S. 435, 441 (2013).

64. *See* Grutter v. Bollinger, 539 U.S. 306, 317–34 (2003) (I discuss affirmative action in detail in chapter 8).

65. Fisher v. Univ. of Texas, Austin, 570 U.S. 297, 308–16 (2013).

66. Erwin Chemerinsky, *The Vanishing Constitution*, 103 HARV. L. REV. 43, 100 (1989).

CHAPTER 4. THE INCOHERENCE PROBLEM

1. ALEXANDER BICKEL, THE LEAST DANGEROUS BRANCH 1 (1962).

2. THE FEDERALIST NO. 78 (Alexander Hamilton).

3. Marbury v. Madison, 5 U.S. (1 Cranch) 137, 180 (1803).

4. JAMES MACGREGOR BURNS, PACKING THE COURT: THE RISE OF JUDICIAL POWER AND THE COMING CRISIS OF THE SUPREME COURT 253 (2009).

5. Max Lerner, *The Constitution and Court as Symbols*, 46 YALE L.J. 1290, 1296 (1937).

6. H. Jefferson Powell, *The Original Understanding of Original Intent*, 98 HARV. L. REV. 885, 948 (1985).

7. Boris I. Bittker, *Interpreting the Constitution: Is the Intent of the Framers Controlling? If Not, What Is?*, 19 HARV. J.L. & PUB. POL'Y 9, 21–30 (1995); 5 ANNALS OF CONG. 776 (1796).

8. Bittker, *supra* note 7, at 31.

9. *Id.*

10. *Id.* at 32.

11. *Id.*

12. *Id.*; 5 ANNALS OF CONG. 776 (1796).

13. Bittker, *supra* note 7, at 32.

14. Powell, *supra* note 6, at 888.

15. Bittker, *supra* note 7, at 32.

16. *Id.*

17. *Id.* at 32–33. *See also* 1 JOSEPH STORY, COMMENTARIES ON THE CONSTITUTION OF THE UNITED STATES § 398 (Thomas Cooley ed., 4th ed. 1873).

18. Bittker, *supra* note 7, at 33.

19. *Id.*

20. *Id.* at 33, 34; LEONARD W. LEVY, ORIGINAL INTENT AND THE FRAMERS' CONSTITUTION 293 (1988).

21. Bittker, *supra* note 7, at 34.

22. *Id.*

23. Nat'l Mut. Ins. Co. v. Tidewater Transfer Co., 337 U.S. 582, 646 (1949) (Frankfurter, J., dissenting); RONALD DWORKIN, TAKING RIGHTS SERIOUSLY 135–36 (1977).

24. Gerard E. Lynch, *The Constitution, the Courts, and Human Rights,* 84 COLUM. L. REV. 537, 546 (1984).

25. McCulloch v. Maryland, 17 U.S. (4 Wheat.) 316, 407, 415 (1819).

26. ZACHARIAH CHAFFEE, HOW HUMAN RIGHTS GOT INTO THE CON-STITUTION 12 (1952); BERNARD BAILYN, THE IDEOLOGICAL ORIGINS OF THE AMERICAN REVOLUTION 77–78 (1968).

27. Robert N. Clinton, *Judges Must Make Law: A Realistic Appraisal of the Judicial Function in a Democratic Society,* 67 IOWA L. REV. 711, 734 (1982).

28. *See* Bond Almand, *The Supreme Court of Georgia: An Account of Its Delayed Birth,* 6 GA. B.J. 95 (1943) (explaining that Georgia lacked a Supreme Court until the mid-1800s, suggesting there was no high court to exercise constitutional judicial review of state legislative acts); JULIUS GOEBEL, HISTORY OF THE SUPREME COURT OF THE UNITED STATES: ANTECEDENTS AND BEGINNINGS TO 1801 125–42 (1971) (detailing history of state courts exercising judicial review in the years before the Constitution was adopted).

29. JONATHAN GIENAPP, THE SECOND CREATION: FIXING THE AMERICAN CONSTITUTION IN THE FOUNDING ERA 5 (2018).

30. *Id.* at 1; 1 ANNALS OF CONG. 425 (Joseph Gales ed., 1789).

31. THE FEDERALIST NO. 37, at 182 (James Madison) (Ian Shapiro ed., 2009).

32. *Id.* at 183.

33. H. Jefferson Powell, *Rules for Originalists,* 73 VA. L. REV. 659, 670 (1987).

34. *Id.* at 670.

35. JOSEPH J. ELLIS, THE QUARTET: ORCHESTRATING THE SECOND AMERICAN REVOLUTION, 1783–1789 218 (2015).

36. *Id.* at 219.

37. *See id.* at 219–20 (quoting Thomas Jefferson to Samuel Kercheval, July 12, 1816).

38. JACK M. BALKIN, LIVING ORIGINALISM 28 (2011).

39. U.S. CONST. amend. XIV, § 1.

40. U.S. CONST. amend. X.

41. United States v. Darby, 312 U.S. 100, 124 (1941).

42. New York v. United States, 505 U.S. 144 (1992).

43. *Id.* at 153.

44. *Id.* at 175.

45. *Id.* at 188.

46. For an excellent analysis of the commandeering principle and its implications, *see* Vicki C. Jackson, *Federalism and the Uses and Limits of Law: Printz and Principle,* 111 HARV. L. REV. 2180 (1998); Evan H. Caminker, *State Sovereignty and Subordinacy: May Congress Commandeer State Officers to Implement Federal Laws?,* 95 COLUM. L. REV. 1001 (1995).

47. Printz v. United States, 521 U.S. 898 (1997). For an excellent analysis of *Printz, see* Evan H. Caminker, *Printz, State Sovereignty, and the Limits of Formalism,* 1997 SUP. CT. REV. 199 (1997).

48. *Printz, supra* note 46, at 907.

CHAPTER 5. THE ABHORRENCE PROBLEM

1. In Bolling v. Sharpe, 347 U.S. 497 (1954), the Court held that the Due Process Clause of the Fifth Amendment applies equal protection to the federal government. But this cannot be justified from an originalist perspective. I discuss this more fully later in this chapter at text accompanying notes 87–89.

2. William J. Brennan Jr., *Foreword: Neither Victims nor Executioners,* 8 NOTRE DAME J. L., ETHICS & PUB. POL'Y 1, 5 (1994).

3. LAURENCE H. TRIBE & MICHAEL C. DORF, ON READING THE CONSTITUTION (1991).

4. Brown v. Bd. of Educ. of Topeka, Shawnee Cnty. Kan., 347 U.S. 483 (1954).

5. Plessy v. Ferguson, 163 U.S. 537 (1896).

6. *Id.* at 540.

7. *Id.* at 550–51.

8. McCabe v. Atchison, Topeka & Santa Fe Ry. Co., 235 U.S. 151 (1914).

9. Cumming v. Bd. of Educ., 175 U.S. 528 (1899).

10. Berea Coll. v. Kentucky, 211 U.S. 45 (1908).

11. Gong v. Rice, 275 U.S. 78 (1927).

12. *Id.* at 87.

13. *See* RICHARD KLUGER, SIMPLE JUSTICE: THE HISTORY OF BROWN V. BOARD OF EDUCATION AND BLACK AMERICA'S STRUGGLE FOR EQUALITY (Vintage Books ed. 2004) (1975) (for a superb discussion of this litigation and its history).

14. *Id.* at 327.

15. Briggs v. Elliott, 342 U.S. 350 (1952) (decided with Brown v. Bd. of Educ., 347 U.S. 294 [1954]).

16. KLUGER, *supra* note 13, at 332.

17. Michael C. Dorf, *Equal Protection Incorporation*, 88 VA. L. REV. 951, 958 (2002).

18. *See* Plessy v. Ferguson, 163 U.S. 537, 545 (1896) ("Similar laws have been enacted by Congress under its general power of legislation over the District of Columbia").

19. *See* KLUGER, *supra* note 13, at 694–99.

20. *Brown, supra* note 4, at 483.

21. *Id.* at 489–90. *But see* Michael McConnell, *Originalism and the Desegregation Decisions,* 81 VA. L. REV. 947 (1995) (arguing that the framers of the Fourteenth Amendment meant to prohibit "separate but equal" laws).

22. *Id.* at 492–93.

23. Richard A. Posner & Eric J. Segall, *Faux Originalism*, 20 GREEN BAG 2D 109 (2016).

24. Adam Liptak, *From 19th-Century View, Desegregation Is a Test*, N.Y. TIMES, Nov. 9, 2009, at A16.

25. Margaret Talbot, *Supreme Confidence*, NEW YORKER, Mar. 28, 2005, at 54.

26. McConnell, *supra* note 21, at 985–86.

27. *Id.* at 956.

28. The Federalist Society, *What About Brown v. Board of Education?* (Dec. 10, 2019), https://fedsoc.org/no86/module/originalism-and-the-courts/video /4?course=originalism.

29. Michael McConnell, *The Originalist Justification for Brown: A Reply to Professor Klarman,* 81 VA. L. REV. 1937, 1938–39 (1995).

30. *See* Ronald Turner, *On Brown v. Board of Education and Discretionary Originalism,* 2015 UTAH L. REV. 1143, 1198 (2015).

31. JACK BALKIN, LIVING ORIGINALISM 229 (2011).

32. Turner, *supra* note 30, at 1148 n.30 (provides summaries of originalist scholarship on *Brown*).

33. DAVID A. STRAUSS, THE LIVING CONSTITUTION 79 (Geoffrey R. Stone et al. eds., 2010).

34. *Id.*

35. Michael C. Dorf, *Equal Protection Incorporation*, 88 VA. L. REV. 951, 958 (2002).

36. *See Anti-Amalgamation Law Passed*, AFR. AM. REGISTRY (Sept. 9, 2020), https://aaregistry.org/story/anti-amalgamation-law-passed/.

37. Loving v. Virginia, 388 U.S. 1, 6 (1967).

38. Pace v. Alabama, 106 U.S. (16 Otto) 583 (1883).

39. *Id.* at 584.

40. McLaughlin v. Florida, 379 U.S. 184, 196 (1964).

41. *Id.* at 188.

42. *Loving, supra* note 37, at 1.

43. *Id.* at 11-12.

44. United States v. Virginia, 518 U.S. 515, 568-69 (1996) (Scalia, J., dissenting) ("[I]t is my view that 'when a practice not expressly prohibited by the text of the Bill of Rights bears the endorsement of a long tradition of open, widespread, and unchallenged use that dates back to the beginning of the Republic, we have no proper basis for striking it down.' The same applies, mutatis mutandis, to a practice asserted to be in violation of the post–Civil War Fourteenth Amendment") (internal citations omitted); *id.* at 570 ("Today . . . change is forced upon Virginia, and reversion to single-sex education is prohibited nationwide, not by democratic processes but by order of this Court. . . . This is not the interpretation of a Constitution, but the creation of one"); *see* Richard H. Fallon Jr., *Are Originalist Constitutional Theories Principled, or Are They Rationalizations for Conservatism?*, 34 HARV. J.L. & PUB. POL'Y 5, 17 (2011) (further discussion on the matter).

45. Slaughter-House Cases, 83 U.S. (16 Wall.) 36, 81 (1873).

46. Bradwell v. Illinois, 83 U.S. (16 Wall.) 130 (1872).

47. *Id.* at 141-42 (Bradley, J., concurring).

48. *Id.* at 142.

49. *In re* Lockwood, 154 U.S. 116 (1894).

50. Minor v. Happersett, 88 U.S. (21 Wall.) 162 (1874).

51. *See, e.g.*, against women, United States v. Virginia, 518 U.S. 515 (1996), Reed v. Reed, 404 U.S. 71 (1971); against gays and lesbians, United States v. Windsor 570 U.S. 744 (2013), Romer v. Evans, 517 U.S. 620 (1996); against people with disabilities, City of Cleburne v. Cleburne Living Ctr., 473 U.S. 432 (1985); against noncitizens, Plyler v. Doe, 457 U.S. 202 (1982), Graham v. Richardson, 403 U.S. 365 (1971); against nonmarital children, Clark v. Jeter, 486 U.S. 456 (1988), Lalli v. Lalli, 439 U.S. 259 (1978).

52. Steven G. Calabresi & Julia T. Rickert, *Originalism and Sex Discrimination*, 90 TEX. L. REV. 1, 6-7 (2011).

53. *Id.* at 7-10.

54. Michael C. Dorf, *The Undead Constitution,* 125 HARV. L. REV. 2011, 2031–32 (2012).

55. SCOTT DOUGLAS GERBER, FIRST PRINCIPLES: THE JURISPRUDENCE OF CLARENCE THOMAS 193 (1999).

56. *Id.*

57. Thomas B. Colby & Peter J. Smith, *Living Originalism,* 59 DUKE L.J. 239, 304 (2009).

58. New York Times Co. v. Sullivan, 376 U.S. 254, 283–84 (1964) (the Court held that damages in defamation actions must comport with the First Amendment).

59. PHILLIP I. BLUMBERG, REPRESSIVE JURISPRUDENCE IN THE EARLY AMERICAN REPUBLIC: THE FIRST AMENDMENT AND THE LEGACY OF ENGLISH LAW 323 (2010).

60. *Id.* at 319, 327.

61. *Id.* at 8.

62. *Id.* at 321.

63. *Id.* at 327.

64. WILLIAM E. NELSON, THE COMMON LAW IN COLONIAL AMERICA: VOLUME IV: LAW AND THE CONSTITUTION ON THE EVE OF INDEPENDENCE, 1735–1776 50–51 (2018).

65. BLUMBERG, *supra* note 63, at 327–28.

66. *Id.*

67. Robert H. Bork, *Neutral Principles and Some First Amendment Problems,* 47 IND. L.J. 1 (1971).

68. David A. Anderson, *Freedom of the Press,* 80 TEX. L. REV. 429, 520 n.494 (2002).

69. William T. Mayton, *Seditious Libel and the Lost Guarantee of a Freedom of Expression,* 84 COLUM. L. REV. 91, 105 (1984).

70. *Id.*

71. *Id.* at 108.

72. *Id.* at 107.

73. *Id.*

74. *Id.*

75. *Id.* at 108.

76. Alien and Sedition Acts of July 14, 1798, 1 Stat. 596 (one law was repealed by the Naturalization Law of 1802, and the other three were left until they expired).

77. *Id.*

78. *New York Times,* 376 U.S. at 276.

79. Justice Thomas has argued that *New York Times v. Sullivan* was wrong and should be overruled, McKee v. Cosby, 139 S. Ct. 675 (2019) (Thomas, J., concurring in the denial of certiorari).

80. Brennan, *supra* note 2.

81. Harmelin v. Michigan, 501 U.S. 957 (1991) (under the precedent set in *Harmelin,* Solem v. Helm, 463 U.S. 277 (1983), was wrongly decided).

82. *Bolling, supra* note 1, at 497.

83. *See* Kenneth Karst, *The Fifth Amendment's Guarantee of Equal Protection,* 55 N.C. L. Rev. 541 (1977).

84. *Bolling, supra* note 1, at 499.

85. Buckley v. Valeo, 424 U.S. 1, 93 (1976).

86. Charles Fairman, *Does the Fourteenth Amendment Incorporate the Bill of Rights?,* 2 Stan. L. Rev. 5, 137 (1949).

87. Zelman v. Simmons-Harris, 536 U.S. 639, 678 (2002) (Thomas, J., concurring).

88. Elk Grove Unified School Dist. v. Newdow, 542 U.S. 1, 45 (2004) (Thomas, J., concurring); *see also* Town of Greece v. Galloway, 572 U.S. 565, 603–9 (2014) (Thomas, J., concurring in part and concurring in the judgment).

89. Thomas Jefferson, The Papers of Thomas Jefferson: Retirement Series, vol. 10, at 367–69 (J. Jefferson Looney et al. eds., 2013) (Jefferson said, "[W]ere our state a pure democracy . . . there would yet be excluded from our deliberations . . . women, who, to prevent deprivation of morals and ambiguity of issues, should not mix promiscuously in public meetings of men").

90. John O. McGinnis & Michael B. Rappaport, Originalism and the Good Constitution 2, 12–13 (2013).

91. *Id.* at 85–86.

92. *Id.* at 88–90.

93. *Id.* at 88–89.

94. *Id.* at 89–90.

95. *Id.* at 90.

96. Stephen Carter, *Constitutional Interpretation and the Indeterminate Text: A Preliminary Defense of an Imperfect Muddle,* 94 Yale L.J. 821, 842 (1985).

97. Sanford Levinson, Our Undemocratic Constitution: Where the Constitution Goes Wrong (and How We the People Can Correct It) 21 (2006).

98. *96 Congressmen's Declaration on Integration*, N.Y. TIMES, Mar. 12, 1956, at 19 (the "Southern Declaration of Independence").

99. Edmund Cahn, *Jurisprudence*, 30 N.Y.U. L. REV. 150, 156 (1955).

CHAPTER 6. THE MODERNITY PROBLEM

1. Brown v. Entertainment Merchants, 564 U.S. 786, 799–805 (2011).

2. BRUCE ALLEN MURPHY, SCALIA: COURT OF ONE 437 (2015).

3. Boyd v. United States, 116 U.S. 616, 623 (1886).

4. Justice Scalia cited to *Entick v. Carrington* as a basis for his decision in United States v. Jones, 565 U.S. 400 (2012), in explaining why it was a search for the police to put a GPS device on a car without a warrant.

5. *Boyd, supra* note 2, at 626.

6. *Id.* at 626–27.

7. *Id.*

8. Olmstead v. United States, 277 U.S. 438 (1928).

9. *Id.* at 456–57.

10. *Id.* at 457.

11. *Id.* at 464.

12. *Id.* at 465.

13. *Id.* at 478.

14. *Id.*

15. Katz v. United States, 389 U.S. 347, 353 (1967); *see also id.*, at 360 (Harlan, J., concurring).

16. *Id.* at 353.

17. *Id.* at 353.

18. *Id.* at 359.

19. *Id.* at 369 (Harlan, J., concurring).

20. *Jones, supra* note 4, at 403.

21. Carpenter v. United States, 138 S. Ct. 2206, 2235, 2261 (2018) (Thomas & Gorsuch, JJ., dissenting).

22. *Id.* at 2209. The officers had obtained a court order pursuant to the federal Stored Communications Act. The key difference is that probable cause, which is required for a warrant, is not needed under the Stored Communications Act.

23. Erwin Chemerinsky, *A Quartet of Fourth Amendment Cases to Watch*, ABA J. (Mar. 8, 2018, 8:00 AM CST), https://www.abajournal.com/news/article /chemerinsky_a_quartet_of_fourth_amendment_cases_to_watch_for.

24. *Carpenter, supra* note 20, at 2217.

25. *Id.* at 2244–46 (Thomas, J., dissenting).

26. *Id.* at 2268 (Gorsuch, J., dissenting).

27. *Act for 1789 Federal Government Appropriations,* DOCSTEACH (June 17, 2021), https://www.docsteach.org/documents/document/1789-federal -appropriations

28. These and other justifications for broad delegations of power are discussed in Richard Stewart, *The Reformation of American Administrative Law,* 88 HARV. L. REV. 1667, 1681 (1975).

29. Panama Refining Co. v. Ryan, 293 U.S. 388, 430 (1935).

30. *Id.* at 431–32.

31. A.L.A. Schechter Poultry Corp. v. United States, 295 U.S. 495, 542 (1935).

32. *Id.* at 529.

33. *Id.* at 530.

34. *Id.*

35. *See, e.g.,* Whitman v. Am. Trucking Ass'ns, Inc., 531 U.S. 457, 463–65 (2001); Nat'l Cable Television Ass'n v. United States, 415 U.S. 336, 342 (1974).

36. *See* Stewart, *supra* note 27, at 1695–97.

37. Immigration and Naturalization Servs. (INS) v. Chadha, 462 U.S. 919, 967 (1983) (White, J., dissenting).

38. *Id.* at 959.

39. *Id.* at 925 (quoting 8 U.S.C. §1254(c)(2)).

40. *Id.* at 926 (quoting Representative Eilberg).

41. *Id.* at 945–50.

42. *Id.* at 952.

43. *Id.*

44. *Id.* at 959.

45. *Id.* at 968 (White, J., dissenting).

46. *Id.* at 1002.

47. Gundy v. United States, 139 S. Ct. 2116, 2130–31 (2019).

48. *Id.* at 2130.

49. *Id.* at 2131 (Alito, J., dissenting).

50. *Id.* at 2133 (Gorsuch, J., dissenting).

51. Mut. Film Corp. v. Indus. Comm'n of Ohio, 236 U.S. 230, 244 (1915).

52. *Id.* at 245.

53. *Id.* at 243.

54. *Id.* at 243–44, 244.

55. Burstyn v. Wilson, 343 U.S. 495, 499–502 (1952).

56. Freedman v. Maryland, 380 U.S. 51, 59–60 (1965).

57. *Id.* at 58.

58. Red Lion Broad. Co. v. FCC, 395 U.S. 367, 386–401 (1969).

59. *Id.* at 400–401.

60. Packingham v. North Carolina, 137 S. Ct. 1730, 1738 (2017).

61. *Id.* at 1735.

62. *Id.* at 1736.

63. *Id.* at 1737.

64. *Brown, supra* note 1, at 799–805.

CHAPTER 7. THE HYPOCRISY PROBLEM

1. *Race and Voting,* CONSTITUTIONAL RIGHTS FOUNDATION, http://www.crf-usa.org/brown-v-board-50th-anniversary/race-and-voting.html.

2. Michael J. Pitts, *The Voting Rights Act and the Era of Maintenance,* 59 ALA. L. REV. 903, 909–10 (2008).

3. *Techniques of Direct Disenfranchisement, 1880–1965,* http://www.umich.edu/~lawrace/disenfranchise1.htm.

4. *Id.*

5. *Id.*

6. *Id.*

7. *Id.*

8. *Id.*

9. Voting Rights Act, 89 Pub. L. No. 89-110, § 5, 79 Stat. 437, 439 (1965).

10. South Carolina v. Katzenbach, 383 U.S. 301, 308 (1966).

11. Georgia v. United States, 411 U.S. 526 (1973); City of Rome v. United States, 446 U.S. 156 (1980); Lopez v. Monterey Cnty., 525 U.S. 266 (1999).

12. *Fannie Lou Hamer, Rosa Parks, and Coretta Scott King Voting Rights Act Reauthorization and Amendments Act of 2006: Hearing on H.R. 9 Before the Comm. of the Whole H. on the State of the Union,* 109th Cong. 5143 (2006) (statement of Jim Sensenbrenner, U.S. Rep. from Wis.).

13. Fannie Lou Hamer, Rosa Parks, and Coretta Scott King Voting Rights Act Reauthorization and Amendments Act, 109 Pub. L. No. 246, § 2(b)(9), 120 Stat. 577, 578 (2006).

14. Shelby Cnty. v. Holder, 133 S. Ct. 2612, 2639 (2013) (Ginsburg, J., dissenting) (citing to H.R. Rep. No. 109-478, at 21).

15. *Id.* at 2643.

16. *Election 2016: Restrictive Voting Laws by the Numbers,* BRENNAN CENTER FOR JUSTICE (Sept. 28, 2016), https://www.brennancenter.org/analysis/election -2016-restrictive-voting-laws-numbers.

17. *Id.*

18. *Shelby Cnty.,* 133 S. Ct. at 2631.

19. Shelby Cnty. v. Holder, 679 F.3d 848, 864, 873 (D.C. Cir. 2012).

20. *Shelby Cnty.,* 133 S. Ct. at 2625 (citations omitted).

21. *Id.* at 2617.

22. *Id.* at 2624.

23. *Id.* at 2623-24.

24. *Id.* at 2632-33 (Ginsburg, J., dissenting).

25. *Id.* at 2649 (Ginsburg, J., dissenting) (giving several examples of federal laws that treat some states differently from others).

26. Brnovich v. Democratic Nat'l Comm., 141 S. Ct. 2321, 2353 (2021) (Kagan, J., dissenting).

27. McCutcheon v. Fed. Election Comm'n, 134 S. Ct. 1434, 1440-41 (2014).

28. The Court held that a state cannot be sued by its own citizens in Hans v. Louisiana, 134 U.S. 1 (1890).

29. Alden v. Maine, 527 U.S. 706 (1999). Also, the Court has held that sovereign immunity bars actions against states in federal administrative agencies. Fed. Mar. Comm'n v. S.C. State Ports Auth., 535 U.S. 743 (2002).

30. Seminole Tribe v. Florida, 517 U.S. 44, 104 (1996) (Souter, J., dissenting).

31. Vanstophorst v. Maryland, 2 U.S. (2 Dall.) 401 (1791).

32. Chisholm v. Georgia, 2 U.S. (2 Dall.) 419 (1793).

33. JOHN V. ORTH, THE JUDICIAL POWER OF THE UNITED STATES: THE ELEVENTH AMENDMENT IN AMERICAN HISTORY 22-23 (1987).

34. PETER W. LOW, JOHN C. JEFFRIES JR., & CURTIS A. BRADLEY, FEDERAL COURTS AND THE LAW OF FEDERAL-STATE RELATIONS 1096 (9th ed. 2018).

35. William A. Fletcher, *The Diversity Explanation of the Eleventh Amendment: A Reply to Critics,* 56 U. CHI. L. REV. 1261, 1264 (1989); William A. Fletcher, *A Historical Interpretation of the Eleventh Amendment: A Narrow Construction of an*

Affirmative Grant of Jurisdiction Rather Than a Prohibition Against Jurisdiction, 35 Stan. L. Rev. 1033 (1983); *see also* John J. Gibbons, *The Eleventh Amendment and State Sovereign Immunity: A Reinterpretation,* 83 Colum. L. Rev. 1889 (1983).

36. Fletcher, *Diversity Explanation,* at 1264.

37. *See, e.g., Seminole Tribe, supra* note 30, at 44.

38. Pennsylvania v. Union Gas Co., 491 U.S. 1, 39 (1989) (Scalia, J., concurring in part and dissenting in part) (citations omitted).

39. Alden v. Maine, 527 U.S. 706 (1999).

40. *Id.* at 712.

41. *Id.* at 754–55 (citing U.S. Const. art. VI).

42. *Fed. Mar. Comm'n, supra* note 29, at 743.

43. *Id.* at 760.

44. Franchise Tax Bd. v. Hyatt, 139 S. Ct. 1485 (2019).

45. Nevada v. Hall, 440 U.S. 410 (1979).

46. *Franchise Tax Bd., supra* note 44, at 1498.

47. The Schooner Exch. v. McFaddon, 11 U.S. (7 Cranch) 116 (1812).

48. *See, e.g.,* The Santissima Trinidad, 20 U.S. (7 Wheat.) 283, 352 (1822); *see also* William Baude, *Sovereign Immunity and the Constitutional Text,* 103 Va. L. Rev. 1, 23–24 (2017) (quoting *Nevada, supra* note 45, at 414) ("Immunity in one's own courts, the Court wrote, 'has been enjoyed as a matter of absolute right for centuries,' while immunity in another sovereign's courts was a matter of mutual agreement or comity").

49. Welch v. Texas Dep't of Highways & Public Transp., 483 U.S. 468, 483–84 (1987).

50. Alden v. Maine, 527 U.S. 706, 764 (1999) (Souter, J., dissenting).

51. Citizens United v. Fed. Election Comm'n, 130 S. Ct. 876 (2010).

52. McConnell v. Fed. Election Comm'n, 540 U.S. 93, 128–29 (2003).

53. *Citizens United, supra* note 51, at 876.

54. *Id.* at 913.

55. *Id.* at 907 (citations omitted).

56. *Id.* at 929 (Stevens, J., dissenting).

57. *Id.* at 948–49. Justice Scalia wrote a separate concurring opinion that responded to this and defended the protection of corporate political spending from an originalist perspective. *Id.* at 925 (Scalia, J., concurring).

58. *Id.* at 930.

59. *Id.* at 979 (Stevens, J., dissenting).

60. First Nat'l Bank v. Bellotti, 435 U.S. 765 (1978).

61. *Citizens United, supra* note 51, at 425–26 (Stevens, J., concurring in part and dissenting in part).

62. *Id.* at 388–89 (Scalia, J., concurring).

63. Grutter v. Bollinger, 539 U.S. 306 (2003).

64. *Id.* at 378 (Thomas, J., dissenting).

65. Plessy v. Ferguson, 163 U.S. 537, 559 (1896) (Harlan, J., dissenting).

66. Adarand Constructors v. Pena, 515 U.S. 200, 239 (1995) (Scalia, J., dissenting) (citations omitted).

67. Stephen A. Siegel, *Federal Government's Power to Enact Color-Conscious Laws: An Originalist Inquiry,* 92 Nw. U.L. Rev. 477 (1997–98).

68. *Id.* at 481.

69. *Id.* at 556.

70. *Id.* at 558–59.

71. *Id.* at 560–61.

72. Eric J. Segall, Originalism as Faith 128 (2018).

CHAPTER 8. IN DEFENSE OF NON-ORIGINALISM

1. Antonin Scalia, *Originalism: The Lesser Evil,* 57 U. Cin. L. Rev. 849, 864–65 (1989).

2. For an excellent summary of the legal realists' critique of formalism, see Morton J. Horwitz, The Transformation of American Law, 1870–1960: The Crisis of Legal Orthodoxy, 183–230 (1992).

3. Benjamin Cardozo, The Nature of the Judicial Process 66–67 (1921), quoted in Horwitz, *supra* note 2, at 190.

4. McCulloch v. Maryland, 17 U.S. 316, 354 (1819).

5. A thorough discussion of the history of the Bank of the United States can be found in Charles Warren, The Supreme Court in United States History, 499–540 (1922).

6. *McCulloch, supra* note 4, at 318.

7. *Id.* at 401.

8. *Id.* at 402.

9. *Id.*

10. Youngstown Sheet & Tube v. Sawyer, 343 U.S. 579, 611 (1952).

11. Richmond Newspapers, Inc. v. Virginia, 448 U.S. 555, 589 (1980) (Brennan, J., concurring in judgment).

12. Saul Cornell, *Originalism on Trial: The Use and Abuse of History in District of Columbia v. Heller,* 69 OHIO ST. L.J. 625, 625–26 (2008).

13. Snyder v. Massachusetts, 291 U.S. 97, 105 (1934).

14. Poe v. Ullman, 397 U.S. 497, 542 (1961) (Harlan, dissenting).

15. Bowers v. Hardwick, 478 U.S. 186, 215 (1986).

16. *Id.* at 199 (Blackmun, J., dissenting), quoting Oliver Wendell Holmes, *The Path of the Law,* 10 HARV. L. REV. 457, 469 (1897).

17. Lawrence v. Texas, 539 U.S. 558, 578 (2003).

18. Kimble v. Marvel Entm't, LLC, 576 U.S. 446, 455 (2015).

19. See Gary Lawson, *Stare Decisis and Constitutional Meaning: Panel II—The Constitutional Case Against Precedent,* 17 HARV. J.L. & PUB. POL'Y 23, 27–28 (1994).

20. Michael Stokes Paulsen, *The Intrinsically Corrupting Influence of Precedent,* 22 CONST. COMMENT. 289, 291 (2005).

21. Scalia, *supra* note 1, at 864 ("I hasten to confess that in a crunch I may prove a faint-hearted originalist").

22. Gamble v. United States, 139 S. Ct. 1960, 1989 (2019).

23. *Id.* at 1981.

24. Amy C. Barrett, *Precedent and Jurisprudential Disagreement,* 91 TEX. L. REV. 1711, 1728 (2013).

25. Amy Coney Barrett, *Stare Decisis and Due Process,* 74 U. COLO. L. REV. 1011, 1013 (2003).

26. STEPHEN BREYER, THE COURT AND THE WORLD: AMERICAN LAW AND THE NEW GLOBAL REALITIES 83 (2016).

27. Roper v. Simmons, 543 U.S. 551, 560 (2005).

28. *Id.* at 575.

29. *Id.* at 577.

30. *Id.* at 560–61; *see also* Trop v. Dulles, 356 U.S. 86, 100–101 (1958) (noting that cruel and unusual punishment is defined based on "evolving standards of decency").

31. William J. Brennan Jr., *Foreword: Neither Victims nor Executioners,* 8 NOTRE DAME J.L. ETHICS & PUB. POL'Y 1, 5 (1994).

32. *See* HOWARD GILLMAN & ERWIN CHEMERINSKY, THE RELIGION CLAUSES: THE CASE FOR SEPARATING CHURCH AND STATE 21–42 (2020).

33. *See* Andrew Koppelman, *Phony Originalism and the Establishment Clause,* 103 NW. U. L. REV. 727, 733–34 (2009), discussing Scalia's dissent argument in Edwards v. Aguillard, 482 U.S. 578 (1987). *Edwards* was a "case involving the teaching of creation science in public schools." Scalia proposed that the Court should not require the law to have a secular purpose but did not present any evidence of original intent of the Establishment Clause to support his argument. He instead argued that the current secular requirement simply was not workable, which seems much more non-originalistic. However, in Lee v. Weisman, 505 U.S. 577, Scalia's dissent instead argued to uphold prayer in schools by using history and justified his argument by saying that traditionally the government has sponsored endorsement of religion but that the endorsement is "sectarian." He used this to justify his interpretation of the Establishment Clause, saying that the Founders would have supported public religious ceremonies without citing any historical source showing that they would have endorsed it.

34. Scalia, *supra* note 1, at 856.

35. *See* Obergefell v. Hodges, 576 U.S. 644 (2015).

36. *See, e.g.,* Fisher v. Univ. of Texas at Austin, 136 S. Ct. 2198, 2203 (2016); Grutter v. Bollinger, 539 U.S. 306, 333 (2003).

37. Citizens United v. Fed. Election Comm'n, 558 U.S. 310, 322 (2010).

38. Erwin Chemerinsky, *Foreword: The Vanishing Constitution,* 103 HARV. L. REV. 43, 100 (1989).

CHAPTER 9. WE SHOULD BE AFRAID

1. Robert Post & Reva Siegel, *Originalism as a Political Practice: The Right's Living Constitution,* 75 FORDHAM L. REV. 545, 573–74 (2006) ("[O]riginalism cannot be dented by attacks on its jurisprudence. Originalism has appeal because it imbues citizens with motive and authority to assert their understanding of the Constitution. . . . To counter originalism, progressives need more than a logical critique").

2. CASS SUNSTEIN, RADICALS IN ROBES (2005).

3. Roe v. Wade, 410 U.S. 113 (1973).

4. June Med. Servs. LLC v. Russo, 140 S. Ct. 2103, 2152–53 (2020) (Thomas, J., dissenting).

5. Dobbs v. Jackson Women's Health Org., 945 F.3d 265 (5th Cir., 2019).

6. Planned Parenthood v. Casey, 505 U.S. 833, 846 (1992).

7. *Dobbs, supra* note 5, at 269.

8. Whole Woman's Health v. Hellerstedt, 136 S. Ct. 2292 (2016).

9. Josh Salman and Kevin McCoy, *Supreme Court Nominee Amy Barrett Signed Anti-Abortion Letter Accompanying Ad Calling to Overturn Roe v. Wade,* USA TODAY, Oct. 1, 2020, https://www.usatoday.com/story/news/2020/10/01/amy-barrett -signed-anti-abortion-letter-alongside-anti-roe-v-wade-ad/5880595002/. *See*

Planned Parenthood of Ind. & Ky. v. Box, 949 F.3d 997 (7th Cir. 2019) (Kanne, J., dissenting).

10. *Russo, supra* note 4, at 2133 (Roberts, C.J., concurring). In September 2021, the Court, five to four, refused to issue a preliminary injunction against a Texas law that prohibited abortions once the fetal heartbeat can be detected (about the sixth week of pregnancy) and created civil liability for those who violate it. Chief Justice Roberts dissented from the denial of the preliminary injunction. Whole Women's Health v. Jackson, 141 S. Ct. ___ (Sept. 1, 2021) (Roberts, C.J., dissenting).

11. For example, this was exactly the approach urged by Chief Justice William Rehnquist in Webster v. Reprod. Health Servs., 492 U.S. 490 (1989).

12. Quoctrung Bui, Claire Cain Miller, and Margot Sanger-Katz, *What Happens If Roe v. Wade Is Overturned?*, THE UPSHOT, N.Y. TIMES, Oct. 15, 2020, https://www.nytimes.com/interactive/2020/10/15/upshot/what-happens-if-roe-is-overturned.html.

13. Gonzales v. Carhart, 550 U.S. 124 (2007).

14. On the right to marry, Loving v. Virginia, 388 U.S. 1 (1967), Obergefell v. Hodges, 576 U.S. 644 (2015); on the right to procreate, Skinner v. Oklahoma, 316 U.S. 535 (1942); on the right to custody of one's children, Stanley v. Illinois, 405 U.S. 645 (1972); on the right to keep one's family together, Moore v. City of East Cleveland, 431 U.S. 494 (1977); on the right to control the upbringing of one's children, Troxel v. Granville, 530 U.S. 57 (2000), Meyer v. Nebraska, 262 U.S. 390 (1923), Pierce v. Soc'y of Sisters, 268 U.S. 510 (1925); on the right to purchase and use contraceptives, Griswold v. Connecticut, 381 U.S. 479 (1965); on the right to engage in private adult consensual same-sex sexual activity, Lawrence v. Texas, 539 U.S. 558 (2003); on the right of competent adults to refuse medical treatment, Cruzan v. Dir., Mo. Dep't of Health, 497 U.S. 261 (1990).

15. *Troxel, supra* note 14, at 58.

16. *Id.* at 65.

17. *Id.* at 91-92 (Scalia, J., dissenting).

18. *Lawrence, supra* note 14, at 558.

19. *Id.* at 605-6 (Thomas, J., dissenting) (citations omitted).

20. *Obergefell, supra* note 14, at 686 (Roberts, C.J., dissenting).

21. *Id.* at 742 n.22.

22. Gibbons v. Ogden, 22 U.S. (9 Wheat.) 1 (1824).

23. *See, e.g.*, United States v. EC Knight Co., 156 U.S. 1 (1895); Carter v. Carter Coal Co., 298 U.S. 238 (1936).

24. *See, e.g.*, Wickard v. Filburn, 317 U.S. 111 (1942); United States v. Darby, 312 U.S. 100 (1941).

25. United States v. Lopez, 514 U.S. 549 (1995).

26. 18 U.S.C. § 922(q)(2)(A).

27. 18 U.S.C. § 921(a)(25)(A), (B).

28. United States v. Morrison, 529 U.S. 598 (2000); 34 U.S.C. § 12361.

29. *Lopez, supra* note 25, at 585 (Thomas, J., concurring).

30. *Id.*

31. *Id.* at 587.

32. *Morrison, supra* note 29, at 627 (Thomas, J., concurring).

33. I develop this argument more fully in ERWIN CHEMERINSKY & HOW-ARD GILLMAN, THE RELIGION CLAUSES: THE CASE FOR SEPARATING CHURCH AND STATE (2020).

34. U.S. CONST. amend. I.

35. Thomas Jefferson, Letter to Messrs. Nehemiah Dodge and Others, a Committee of the Danbury Baptist Association, WRITINGS 510 (1984).

36. Everson v. Bd. of Educ., 330 U.S. 1 (1947).

37. On outlawing prayers in public schools, Engel v. Vitale, 370 U.S. 421 (1962); on limiting religious symbols on government property, *see, e.g.,* Stone v. Graham, 449 U.S. 39 (1980); on restricting government aid to religious schools, *see, e.g.,* Lemon v. Kurtzman, 403 U.S. 602 (1971).

38. Lee v. Weisman, 505 U.S. 577, 640 (1992) (Scalia, J., dissenting).

39. *Id.* at 587-88.

40. Town of Greece v. Galloway, 134 S. Ct. 1811 (2014).

41. *Id.* at 1814.

42. *Id.* at 1838 (Thomas, J., concurring).

43. Am. Legion v. Am. Humanist Ass'n, 139 S. Ct. 2067 (2019).

44. *Id.* at 2074.

45. *Id.* at 2089.

46. *Id.* at 2095 (Thomas, J., concurring).

47. *See* CHEMERINSKY & GILLMAN, *supra* note 33, at Ch. 2.

48. *See* Espinoza v. Mon. Dep't of Revenue, 140 S. Ct. 2246 (2020); Trinity Lutheran Church of Columbia, Inc. v. Comer, 137 S. Ct. 2012 (2017).

49. Emp. Div. Dep't of Human Res. of Or. v. Smith, 494 U.S. 872, 890 (1990).

50. *Id.* at 878-89.

51. *Id.* at 879 (citation omitted).

52. *Id.* at 886-87.

53. United States v. Lee, 455 U.S. 252, 263 n.2 (1982) (Stevens, J., concurring).

54. Fulton v. City of Phila., No. 19-123, 2021 U.S. LEXIS 3121 at 31 (June 17, 2021) (Alito, J., concurring).

55. Tandon v. Newsom, 141 S. Ct. 1294, 1298 (2021).

56. Masterpiece Cakeshop, Ltd. v. Colo. Civil Rights Comm'n, 138 S. Ct. 1719 (2019).

57. Bostock v. Clayton Cnty., 140 S. Ct. 1731 (2020).

58. *Id.* at 1754 (Alito, J., dissenting).

59. Newman v. Piggie Park Enters., Inc., 390 U.S. 400, 403 n.5 (1968).

60. SUNSTEIN, *supra* note 2, at Ch. 10.

61. *See* David A. Strauss, *Why Conservatives Shouldn't Be Originalists*, 31 HARV. J.L. & PUB. POL'Y 970, 970-71 (2008) ("[O]riginalism makes it too easy for people to find, in the law, the answers they are looking for; and originalism causes people to hide the ball, to avoid admitting, perhaps *even to themselves*, what is really affecting their decisions") (emphasis added).

ACKNOWLEDGMENTS

I am grateful to many people who made this book possible. First and foremost, I want to thank my editor at Yale University Press, Bill Frucht. He suggested that I write this book, helped me to conceptualize its approach, was persistent in his desire to publish it, and provided me a terrific edit of the manuscript. This is our third book together, and I look forward to many more.

I am very appreciative of my wonderful literary agent, Bonnie Nadell. We have worked together for a decade now on many projects, and I cannot begin to thank her enough for all of her assistance, including in making this book happen.

I was greatly aided by a very talented group of research assistants. My tremendous thanks to Haley Broughton, Daria Butler, Summer Elliot, Benji Martinez, Rachel Thompson, and Annabelle Wilmot.

My spectacular assistant, Whitney Mello, facilitates all I accomplish, including this book. I cannot imagine doing my job without her assistance.

And I owe huge thanks to my family and especially to my wife, Catherine Fisk. She encouraged me to do this book when I had doubts and talked through so much of it with me. I have a very blessed life thanks to Catherine and our wonderful children and

---

grandchildren: Jeff, Kim, Adam, Katherine, Alex, Mara, Andrew, Sarah, and Amy.

One of the great pleasures in writing a book is choosing its dedication. There are so many to whom I owe gratitude. I dedicate this book to my teachers, from whom I learned enormously and who encouraged and mentored me, and especially to Earl Bell and David Zarefsky. They were my high school and college debate coaches. Other than my parents, they were the individuals who had the greatest effect on my life. It is not hyperbole to say that whatever I have accomplished in my career would not have happened without them and all they did for me.

INDEX

INDEX

INDEX

INDEX

INDEX

INDEX